Mary Bell's
Complete
Dehydrator
Cookbook

Mary Bell's
Complete Dehydrator Cookbook

Mary Bell

wm

WILLIAM MORROW
An Imprint of HarperCollins*Publishers*

IMPORTANT NOTICE

Please make sure to follow all of the instructions that come with your electric dehydrator, especially with regard to recommended drying times for various foods, dried food storage instructions, and operating procedures for the machine.

Library of Congress Cataloging-in-Publication Data

Bell, Mary (Mary T.)
    Mary Bell's complete dehydrator cookbook / Mary Bell.
        p.   cm.
    Includes index.
    ISBN 0-688-13024-0
    1. Cookery (Dried foods)   2. Food—Drying.   I. Title.   II. Title:
Complete dehydrator cookbook.
TX826.5.B45   1994
641.4'4—dc20   93-38487
                                                  CIP

Printed in the United States of America

40 39 38 37 36 35 34

Book design by CIRCA 86, INC.

This book is dedicated to my parents,
Helen T. Bell and Harold C. Bell,
who have just celebrated their sixty-fifth
wedding anniversary. Over the years I have
learned from them the art of living well
and
how to have a memorable meal around
a simple table.

Contents

Acknowledgments   ix
Introduction   xi

PART ONE: Food Dehydration

CHAPTER 1   A Brief History of Food Drying   3

CHAPTER 2   Food Dehydrators:
             What They Are and How They Work   9

CHAPTER 3   Basic Facts About Food Dehydration   18

CHAPTER 4   Preparing Fruits and Vegetables for
             Drying   30

CHAPTER 5   Fruits and Vegetables:
             What You Need to Know Before
             Drying Them   52

CHAPTER 6   Drying Meats and Fish   82

CHAPTER 7   Drying Herbs   102

CHAPTER 8   Making Food Leathers   117

CHAPTER 9   Trail Food: Backpackers Take Note   139

PART TWO: The Recipes

CHAPTER 10   Cooking with Dehydrated Foods   169

CHAPTER 11   Soups and Starters   179

CHAPTER 12   Main Courses   195

CHAPTER 13   Salads, Side Dishes, and Sauces   208

CHAPTER 14   Cakes, Pies, and Puddings   221

CHAPTER 15   Quick Breads, Cookies, and Snacks   231

CHAPTER 16   Beverages and Syrups   242

CHAPTER 17   Beauty and the Beast   251

Index   265

Acknowledgments

THANK YOU . . .

I have heard it said that if you repeat something three times, then it really is true. I hope that all the people listed here and everyone who shared with me their ideas and concerns over the course of my writing this book will hear me saying over and over again thank you—for your time, energy, support, ideas, and love.

A very special thank you to Joe Deden, my loving husband, for his strong hands and warm heart. It is wonderful to be in a relationship where food preparation is central to both of our lives. I knew Joe was the man for me when—right after we first met—he proudly showed me his freeze drier!

To our children, Sally and Eric and Zack and Gabe, for being themselves and ultimately the best of all of our teachers. Included in the family circle are two very special people—Shayla Johnson and Bob Zank.

To my mother- and father-in-law, Adeline and Vince Deden. Adeline is a very good cook, and she deserves a lot of credit for helping me with the recipes in this book. It is a treat for me to be able to spend time with my family and friends who use food dehydrators and then enthusiastically share the results. This kind of food not only feeds the belly—it feeds the soul.

And to my niece, Diane Bell, with whom I share a curiosity about food.

I am grateful, too, to the women who worked on putting this manuscript together: Diane Cook, for her time and energy in amassing information; Pam Eyden, for organizing and asking good questions; Evie Righter, for strengthening the voice and helping me with the style.

To Caroline Krupp and Julian Bach at the Julian Bach Literary Agency, a thank you for taking me seriously and validating my efforts. And to Will Schwalbe, Director of Special Publishing Projects at William Morrow, for saying yes to the manuscript. To Zack Schisgal, my appreciation for his always friendly voice and helpful ways. And to Sonia Greenbaum for her expert copy-editing.

I am grateful to many people for the gift of friendship. Lee and Len Weiss provided support in so many ways, including sharing great meals together. Colleen and Dale Westerberg deserve lots of thanks for joining my team a long time ago. To those friends with special visionary spirit, like Jack and Genea Pichotta, from Wolf Ridge Environmental Learning Center, for their dedication in being environmental activists; and Paul and Barbara Stitt, from Natural Ovens in Manitowoc, for continuing to be clear-sighted in their goal to get good food to all people. To Margaret and Jim McHale for always being ready to help and for taking a look at the manuscript; and last but not least, to Gloria and Larry Martony, for being loving and loyal friends.

To Sue Miller and Marney Sheele and all the friendly folks in our aqua fitness class. And to Annie Beckmann, food writer, for her magnanimous spirit.

Over the months of writing this book, Gabrielle Laden helped me maintain my focus. And the Forest Resource Center staff—Pat Bahl, Sue Fisher, Doreen Bergo, Tom Hasvold, and Erik Ronneberg—deserve a round of applause for their willingness to participate in the recipe-testing process. Special thank yous to Mel Baughman for testing recipes, too, and for feedback on outdoor adventuring. Jerry Cleveland helped with the trail food cooking and baking. Thank you to Kathe Abrams, President, Twin Cities Herb Society, for all the help. And bless you Scott Bowe for keeping my Madison house together.

Deep appreciation is given to all the people I have met at home shows and at classes who asked questions, shared recipes and ideas, and provided information. My role in this project, I have come to understand, was as a vessel—in getting as much information to as many people as possible. To that end, I would also like to thank Betsy Oman and Barbara Sanders for their help at shows. And to all the helpful folks at American Harvest, especially Ed Coyour, Mike Gutzmer, and Harvey Little.

To end on a high note, I am very grateful to Michael Schuller, my minister, for spiritual nourishment.

Introduction

One evening, just as I was completing the manuscript of this book, my mother telephoned. "Be sure," she said, "to tell your readers that food drying is really nothing new. People have been drying peas, beans, and grains for centuries. And don't forget to remind them that we routinely buy dried foods like noodles, and tea, and soups at the grocery."

My mother is right, of course. Drying food at home is not new—it is just new to the generations of people who have grown up since the food-processing industry became so large and efficient. We may be sophisticated and knowledgeable about electronic scanning and bar codes and high-tech appliances, and we may even be aware of the importance of good food for good health, but we've forgotten, if we ever even knew, what our ancestors knew about drying food. That means until recently we had forgotten how wonderful a home-prepared sun-dried tomato or piece of beef jerky or candied apricot can taste. There are whole new—or should I say old?—worlds to explore when it comes to food drying. This book will be your guide.

When I first became really aware of food drying, more than twenty years ago, I was overjoyed. It would solve the problem of surplus vegetables and fruits from my garden. It would be a welcome alternative to the tediousness, at least for me, of canning and the worry of it, too. And it would be less expensive than preserving foods by freezing them. For all those reasons, food drying satisfied my interest in good nutrition for good health.

Over the years I grew to know the benefits and possibilities of food dehydration from many points of view. As a mother and homemaker, I liked being able to provide my family and friends with nutritious, healthful foods, including desserts and even snacks. As a gardener, I was able to put up my organically grown harvest in a fraction of the time it took my friends who canned or froze their bounty. As an outdoor enthusiast, I really appreciated the value of lightweight dried foods that were high in energy—and many of them high in protein, too—and that were much less expensive to make than to buy from outfitters. Using my own home-dried foods meant that I could avoid the many chemical additives and residues commonly found in processed food. And, last but not least, I felt I was doing my part for world hunger and sponsoring an environmental ethic in trying to live the adage: Waste not, want not.

My evolution as a dried-food advocate started simply. At first, I tried to dry food in the oven, which sometimes worked and sometimes did not. The food generally turned dark in color, something I could not control. So I tried something else: the old-fashioned method of sun-drying food. My first outdoor solar food-dehydrating contraption—and that may be an understatement!—consisted of two window screens tied together with a piece of rope. I placed the pieces of food in it and hung the screens from the branch of a tree to dry in the sun. Little did I realize then that the humidity in Wisconsin, where I live, on any given day in summer hovers somewhere around 90 percent plus! Needless to say, my vegetables did not dry: They grew a magnificent coat of mold! My attempt led me to an important discovery, though—hot, dry circulating air, as opposed to wet still air, would dry food. Granted, I had not successfully dried any food outdoors, but I had succeeded in grasping a basic principle of food dehydration.

After I had made a few more tries at drying herbs and vegetables outdoors, a friend, who had observed my interest in this process, gave me an electric food dehydrator that had been made in Switzerland. It was a very simple machine: a metal bowl with a popcorn popper–style heating element in the bottom; on top of it you stacked trays made of wire mesh screened material. From the moment I put that dehydrator on my kitchen counter, I could not stay away from it. Everything I dried in it became more and more fascinating. I realize that not everyone is turned on by beautiful dried tomatoes, which you can eat as chips, but to me it was really thrilling. Buoyed by the friendship of a struggling yet adventurous graphic artist, who actually liked to eat the dried tomatoes I was drying, I realized I was hooked!

Several months after being given my first electric dehydrator, I went on a ten-day canoe trip in the splendid Boundary Waters between the United States and Canada. Half of the food I carried was commercially dried; the other half I had dried myself. The food that I had prepared tasted more like what it was and more wholesome than the food I had bought at the outfitters store.

In those days there was very little information available about how to dry and use dried foods, so when I got back home I wrote down how I had prepared what I had taken with me. This led to my first book, *Dehydration Made Simple*. The success of that book gave me the courage and conviction to prepare a second edition, which was published in 1981. This book evolved as a consequence of what I had learned from many conversations with food scientists and researchers and food-drying enthusiasts. Since 1981 I have made a lot of new discoveries.

I have come to the realization that there is a connection between food drying, the wasting of food, and world hunger. In 1981, I traveled as a volunteer to Central America with the Wisconsin/Nicaragua Partners of the Americas and taught classes on appropriate food technology, which in this context meant food drying. My experience in Nicaragua was fascinating, and I believe I learned more than I taught. I will never forget the man who stood up one day in the back of a classroom in the jungle village of Pearl Lagoon and said, "Mary Bell, thank you for coming all this way. I never knew I could dry my tomatoes and onions. I thought all I could dry was corn and shrimp."

I suddenly understood that what I was sharing with my classes was much more important than information: It was permission, permission for others to try something new. "Yes, not only can you dry your tomatoes and onions, but you can dry bananas and mangoes, too!"

I returned to the United States from Nicaragua knowing two things: that I wanted to do more to promote home food drying and that I would start with my own culture first. I began traveling around the country, promoting the concept and selling food dehydrators at state fairs and home shows. I learned how to load and unload portable display booths; endure long-distance drives and then set up displays, hook up lights and microphones. I packed more dehydrators into small places than you could believe possible and talked for hours on end about how they work and what they produce. Believing in the importance of dried food was what kept me going. It still does.

Over the years, I have been asked many questions by people interested in food drying and I have done my best to answer them. Along the way I have learned new, improved ways of drying foods from folks as curious about the challenge as I am. All these discoveries have led me to write this book.

I am convinced that drying food is a great way for people to get back in touch with the earth and connect with their own food supply. In Thomas Moore's book, *Care of the Soul*, he speaks of embracing the ordinary. Drying food is one form of embracing the ordinary.

Writing a book like this one is somewhat like building a house. You have to make decisions about every little thing—and every big one, too. When a house is finished, you must live within its walls. You can remodel, change the decor, or make adjustments. I hope that this book and my experiences, or at least some of them, will compel you to look at food in a new way, to experiment with drying it, and to make both the practical and philosophical aspects of food drying, an ancient tradition worldwide, a way of life for you. As a simple food dehydrator changed my life one day in 1971, I hope the ideas in this book will affect yours.

I believe that you only need to learn 14 key techniques to master the art of food dehydration. I have placed these techniques throughout the book, each one in an appropriate chapter, so that you can learn them in context.

For quick reference, all the techniques are listed in the Index.

Part One

FOOD
DEHYDRATION

Chapter 1

A Brief History
of Food Drying

$\mathcal{F}$ood dehydration is the world's oldest method of food preservation. Think for a moment: Before refrigerators and freezers how did people preserve food? For the most part, they dried it. Today we are living in a time of canned this, frozen that, irradiated something else. Canning, which is another way to preserve and store food, is only about two hundred years old. Both the canning and freezing of food rose to popularity during the early 1900s, when electricity became more and more available to people, no matter where they lived. However, ignored until recently was the age-old process of drying food as a method of storing it.

Centuries past, people in the Near East preserved fruit by wrapping it in dried palm leaves and burying it in hot sand to dry. Only a century or so ago, people in the Arctic created caches of surplus "freeze dried" walrus meat by piling stones on top of their treasure to keep predators from devouring it. Native Americans in northern parts of the United States used smoke (dry circulating air) from a fire to dry meat, herbs, vegetables, or fish. Indians in Peru dried potatoes (and do to this day) by first freezing them overnight outdoors, then trampling them the next day while the potatoes thawed, thus squeezing out the water remaining in them. Then, they air-dried the potatoes until crisp enough to store. Almost everywhere in the world, people have utilized some food-drying method in order to save food from one season to the next, be it hay or corn or seal meat or apples.

Why did people dry food? Quite simply, because fresh food

was not always available. Without dried foods, a nomadic lifestyle would have been impossible. The sun and wind, or the smoke from a fire, provided the means to remove water from grains, meat, fruits, and herbs; thus were they preserved from one season to the next. However, success in drying food depended upon choosing the right days on which to dry it, luck, and more than a little ingenuity. The elements were unpredictable. Food that was left to dry in open fields, for example, could be gone in a flash: It could rain, insects might infest it, wild animals and birds might help themselves.

Over time, people in different cultures perfected drying wild and cultivated foods. The Greeks and Romans dried peas and grapes successfully. The Persians learned how to preserve dates, and apricots, and melons. The Chinese and Japanese, clever at the art of food preservation, cured fish and sea vegetables. Mongolian explorers, en route to Europe, packed bundles of dried milk products to sustain them on their long journey. In our own country, early settlers, observing the practice of sun-drying food by Native Americans in the northern regions, learned to dry many varieties of corn, squash, and herbs, plus buffalo meat and venison as they pioneered west.

In the United States, during the nineteenth century, many housewives preserved fruits in sugar, vegetables and nuts in salt, fruits and vegetables in brine. Dried food was a traditional alternative to fresh food, but before the age of glass canning jars and self-sealing zinc jar lids, which were not patented until 1858, food was likely to be stored in stone or earthenware crocks, tin cans, and glass containers. Sealing wax, beeswax, corks, and even putty were sometimes used to seal the lids.

Throughout history, dried meats and fish have provided life-sustaining protein for people around the world. Our ancestors dried meats and kept them year after year, without benefit of refrigeration. Meats and fish, in fact, were the foods most commonly dried. The irony of this is that fish is one of the most difficult types of food to dry because of the potential for bacterial growth in the raw product. Historically, meat, like fish, was pretreated in a dry salt cure or a brine solution, the salt serving to draw water out of the food. Lastly, meats and fish were also smoked.

Many foods today would not be part of the world's cuisines were it not for people having figured out how to dry and thus preserve them. How different Chinese, Japanese, Thai, and other

Asian cuisines would be without dried fish, shellfish, or sea vegetables, including seaweed. Over centuries of experimenting, Asian peoples found that many foods when dried had intriguing flavors and textures that they did not have when eaten fresh. For instance, the Chinese enjoy fresh sea scallops in cooking, but even their delicacy cannot be compared to the exquisite taste of a dried scallop. Flowers, too, like lily buds, are eaten fresh in the Orient but more commonly are dried, as are fungi, such as tree ears. Some items, such as shark's fin and sea slug, are more prized (and more expensive) in dried form than fresh.

The Chinese lay claim to being the first to cure pork products—ham, bacon, and sausage—calling ham *huo-fu*, or fire-dried meat. Actually, the word refers to any meat that is cured by having first been soaked in a soy sauce marinade, then dried over a slow fire. The Chinese treated bacon in the same way. To this day, strips of cured pork belly, dark golden in color, hang in Chinese meat markets.

MODERN TIMES

The twentieth century has transformed food drying into a science—food dehydration—and its success no longer rests upon luck or happenstance. Today, advanced technology can provide constant, thermostatically controlled heat and a consistent air flow to dry an extraordinary range of foodstuffs.

In 1943, in the United States, there were more than 139 vegetable-drying plants in operation, producing more than 115 million pounds of dried food per year. In 1944, during the war, more than 375 million pounds of dried potatoes and 76 million pounds of dried vegetables were produced. In 1970, there were 18 fruit-drying plants alone for raisins, 307 plants for prunes, and 11 for apples. In the 1980s, we witnessed the phenomenal popularity of fruit roll-ups, and in the 1990s, we watch dancing, singing raisins as an advertisement on television. We've come a long way in subconsciously, if not consciously, accepting dried foods into our diets.

Today, potatoes and powdered milk are the most popular dried foods, followed by onions, garlic, chili peppers, carrots, bell peppers, and tomatoes. One quarter of the grape crop is dried for raisins. The average person uses approximately twenty pounds of dried food per year, or about 1 percent of his or her total food consumption. This figure is based on a variety of food items, such as herbs, pasta, baked goods, fruits, milk, vegetables, coffee, and so on.

Along with the growth of commercial food-drying companies, there has been a resurgence of interest in drying foods at home. The counterculture movement of the 1960s and 1970s brought an awareness of food drying into the mainstream of society. In addition, outdoor enthusiasts quickly learned the advantages of carrying nutritious, lightweight foods along on their journeys. How better to ensure its healthfulness than to dry the food yourself? During the 1970s and 1980s, the United States military turned from canned C-rations to all-dried-food rations, MRE— Meals Ready to Eat. Several large baby food companies also developed complete lines of dehydrated baby foods. NASA, too, has experimented with dehydrating food in order to provide compact, healthful staples for our astronauts to take into outer space.

Food drying has been propelled even further into the consciousness of many people by the recent (at least in the last two years) appearance on television of infomercials about food dehydrators and food dehydration. Half-hour programs, in front of an audience, on the machines and their functions appear frequently in certain areas of the country. These infomercials have had a powerful impact and have definitely increased awareness about food drying in general. Many's the time at a state fair or home show that I have been asked a specific question by someone whose interest in food drying was either initially piqued or rendered deeper as a result of having seen an infomercial on this subject.

FOOD DRYING: OTHER OPTIONS

In addition to the most obvious and traditional ways of drying food and herbs and flowers—in the sun or by drying in the open air or in your stove oven over a protracted period of time— modern technology provides a handful of other opportunities. Here I am not addressing drying food in a food dehydrator, but in other small electrical appliances. These include the convection oven, in which foods can be successfully dried due to the ability the user has to control both temperature and air flow. In some convection ovens, the fan speed can be varied, a decided advantage. Should you attempt to use your convection oven for food drying, be sure to check with the manufacturer to ensure that it is recommended and to find out if specific directions are available.

Similarly, herbs and flowers can be dried in certain microwave ovens, but here, too, I urge you to check with the oven manufacturer to make sure that the brand of microwave you are working with can be used for this purpose. Within this text I have not mentioned drying food in a microwave: My attempts at doing this, as well as trying to make leathers in a microwave, have proven woefully unsuccessful. The end products have been more overcooked than dehydrated in appearance, texture, and flavor.

A discussion of the options available to dry food would be incomplete without mention of freeze drying, although for me and for all practical purposes, a freeze drier is not a real alternative for most people interested in home food drying. To begin with, the driers themselves are extremely expensive, and the process takes days to complete. What basically happens in freeze drying is that food is frozen very quickly. The pressure in the freeze drier is substantially lowered, which creates a vacuum, which in turn causes the ice crystals to change to water vapor without passing through the liquid stage. The ice crystals condense and collect in a chamber separate from the food. The moisture content of the dried product is usually 2 percent or lower. What is exceptional about freeze drying is that it leaves the finished product with basically the same cell structure it had when fresh. Therefore, the size of the food is the same as when fresh, but it weighs a fraction of what it did originally. As mentioned, though, for most people freeze drying food is not a realistic option.

Clearly, when it comes to food drying, there are quite a few alternatives. For me, the most viable way—and by that I mean successful, fun, interesting, and challenging—is to use an electric food dehydrator, something I have been experimenting with now for over twenty years.

Which brings me to yet another point, one on which I would like to close this chapter. Over the years that I have been selling food dehydrators at home shows and state fairs, I have observed an interesting fact: The buying of food dehydrators is done pretty much equally by women and men. Just as in ancient times, food was gathered by men and women, so too in the late twentieth century, food is dried in the home by both men and women. The more things change, the more they remain the same. Food drying, whether it is done by natural elements or by machine, by man or by woman, has stood the test of time. The chapters that follow will explain some of the reasons why.

Chapter 2

Food Dehydrators: What They Are and How They Work

*T*he more you know about food dehydrators in general, the more informed you will be when you buy one. Food dehydrators are basically simple machines: They create an environment in which water is removed from food. The machines vary in design, size, price, and effectiveness and, as a consequence of any or all of these factors, they can turn out very different qualities of dried-food products.

Over the years, home food dehydrators have become more sophisticated and the quality of the foods dried in them has improved. Updated features on the machines encourage the food-drying enthusiast to experiment with different varieties of foods because the results can be so gratifying. For example, years ago I experimented with drying carrots and orange juice together in an attempt to make a special breakfast leather to take on a camping trip. Unbeknownst to me, I had added too much sugar, I had not oiled the solid leather sheets, the dehydrator I was using had neither temperature control nor adequate air flow, and what I ended up with was dark-colored, sticky, sticky goo! Recently, I tried again, using a different dehydrator: I combined homemade fresh carrot juice with thawed orange juice concentrate, poured the mixture on lightly oiled solid leather sheets, and dried the puree at 135°F. Some hours later I had just the product I wanted. The leather was a little sticky, but it tasted great and had a good color; it peeled right off the drying surface, made a great snack, and when I rehydrated it into a breakfast drink, it put some commercially dried orange juice products to shame. Because the dehydrator I use works well, my ongoing experiments at food drying are very rewarding.

In selling dehydrators at home shows and state and county fairs, I have discovered that when people buy their first machine, a lot of the time what they are really buying is the concept. They like the idea of home food drying, they want a dehydrator, and their only question is "How much does it cost?" I can understand that cost is an important consideration—people can only afford to spend so much—but it is not necessarily the best place to start. Interestingly, I now sell more dehydrators to people who are buying their second or third one because they bought their first machine thinking of price alone.

Dehydrators can be purchased for as little as $30 to $40, with more sophisticated ones costing from $100 to $300. Instead of concentrating on the price, I encourage prospective buyers to ask, "How does it work?" When you understand how something works, you are more apt to use it, making however much money you spent on it well worth it.

With a food dehydrator, you need adequate heat and air flow, so it is very important that you find out before buying the unit how the air is heated and how the dry air is circulated (if it is), and whether or not you have any control over these facets of the machine. There are a lot of inexpensive food dehydrators on the market. Some of them do not have a fan, and because of their vertical air flow pattern, it is difficult to dry fruit purees into leathers. Other machines do not have a temperature control. Of course, you can manually rotate the trays, thus moving the food on the bottom to the top of the machine, making the food-drying process more even throughout and producing a product that dries faster and has a better color. Assuming that you are going to like dehydrated foods, one of those rudimentary models may not be up to the tasks you have in mind for it. (And you may become weary of having to move trays about all the time.) Also, as with many lower-end models of small electrical appliances, there is a certain built-in obsolescence. My experience, and it is over a twenty-year period now, says buy better for more satisfying and versatile results.

ELECTRIC FOOD DEHYDRATORS

Electric food dehydrators eliminate much of the guesswork in food drying and provide you with options of being able to dry food anytime, day or night, whatever the weather. As mentioned above, if the food dehydrator you have does not have a fan, you may not be able to dry foods overnight or while you are out of the house, due to the need to rotate the trays.

The major components of an electric food dehydrator include:

- a source of heat
- air flow to circulate the dry air
- trays to hold the food during the drying process
- accessory mesh and solid leather sheets to ensure the successful drying of certain types of foods

A Source of Heat

A food dehydrator heats air and it is the hot, dry air that absorbs the water from the food placed in the dehydrator. Over the years, various devices have been used to heat the air: electric light bulbs, coils, nycromium wire, as examples. In the most rudimentary form, a food dehydrator that does not have either a fan or any means of controlling temperature relies on the age-old principle of hot air rising, thereby drying the food contained in the drying chamber.

As the design of electric food dehydrators has become more sophisticated, control features for both temperature and air circulation have been introduced. One type of temperature control has a thermostat with mechanical contact points, which shuts off the electricity (and the heat) when they expand. When the machine cools down and the contact points "contact" again, the heating unit automatically switches back on. This on-and-off-again feature attempts to maintain a consistent temperature in the machine. The problem is that the contact points can wear down over time. As to the accuracy of the temperature with this type of thermostat, there is roughly a ten-degree variance, which means if you set your dial at 135°F, the temperature in the unit may vary from 130°F to 140°F.

An even more sophisticated design of food dehydrator includes solid-state circuitry, which means more reliable temperature control and no moving parts to break. With solid-state circuitry, you can expect the temperatures to be accurate within two or three degrees of the desired setting.

Some new models feature digital thermostats along with electric timers. Lastly, some food dehydrators on the market today have temperatures, preset at the factory, between 130°F and 140°F. Even though these temperatures are preset, actual temperature in the unit can vary as much as ten degrees, meaning that if it is preset to 135°, it can range between 130°F and 140°F.

As to the wattage of electrical food dehydrators, and this again depends upon the brand and type of unit, it can range from 115 to 1,000 watts. Of course, the higher the wattage, the faster the potential for drying food, which, naturally, impacts on the drying time.

A Source of Air Flow

In design, electric food dehydrators can be round, square, or rectangular in shape. Two styles predominate—the cabinet and the stackable unit.

The cabinet-style unit resembles a microwave oven, with a door and sliding, removable drying trays. The heating element is in the back or on the side, and a fan blows the heated, dry air through the drying chamber. In this type of unit, the number of drying trays can range from four to twelve. However, you can dry food on only one tray, if desired.

The stackable style of dehydrator, most of them round in shape, have a heat source at the base of the unit. Many, but not all, stackable units have fans at the base of the unit. With many of these units the number of trays that can be stacked on top can be increased or decreased depending upon the amount of food to be dried. Some dehydrators can utilize as many as thirty-five drying trays. Some stackable designs also have a cover or a lid.

Food dehydrators without fans are known as "passive" units and work on the principle of hot air rising. Air is heated at the base of the unit, then rises, absorbing the moisture in the food on the drying trays it passes through. However, by the time it reaches the top drying tray, the air may already be heavy with moisture and unable to absorb as much water from the top tray of food as it did from the bottom one. As noted earlier, for best results, you will most likely want to rotate the drying trays in a passive unit to compensate for a lack of control over air flow. Given that the best time to dry food is at night (or while you are out at work), this means you then have to set your alarm clock, get out of bed, make your way down the stairs in the middle of the night, turn on the kitchen light, rotate the trays, and then make your way back to bed and to the dream you were having before the alarm jarred you from your slumber! To my mind, this is baby-sitting a food dehydrator, and for obvious reasons most people do not want to use a machine that requires that amount of attention. And they don't.

A food dehydrator with a fan is called a "nonpassive" unit. Some dehydrators give you control of the fan and therefore of the amount of air flowing through the drying chamber. The more dry air that is created, the faster the drying process. And the higher the wattage of your machine, the faster the drying process. Many food-drying enthusiasts have told me that they value a fan-control feature enormously because they are not enslaved to their machines. In fact, a man in Fresno, California (the raisin capital of the world), told me that he likes to dry his grapes at 130°F, with minimal air circulation. In this way, he says, he is replicating the slow process of sun-drying, which, he also noted, increases the sugar content of the raisins by 30 percent.

Air flow patterns vary with different dehydrators. The pattern of how the air is distributed in the unit is very important. The more sophisticated electric food dehydrators give you control over the temperature and the speed of the fan. Needless to say, with that amount of control over the food you are drying, the results can be excellent. Units with both of these features are among the more expensive you can buy.

One final point about fans and air flow in some electric food dehydrators is that a fan can make a pulsating sound: This is normal.

Drying Trays

As already mentioned, the sizes of food dehydrators vary, as do the designs. As a consequence, the drying trays that fit in them vary in size and shape and number as well. All drying trays— no matter the shape or size—have holes in them to allow the air to pass through. Some dehydrators allow you to add on trays to adjust for the amount of food you have to dry. This can be a real advantage when you find yourself with a lot of extra food to dry in a short period of time.

Two important facts you will want to know about drying trays in general is how to clean them: One, do they fit in the dishwasher (some do not); and two, if they do fit in the dishwasher, are they dishwasher safe? This may sound insignificant now, but when you are staring at a stack of thirty-five used drying trays, you will want to know how best to wash them! After they are washed, I simply put them back in the food dehydrator and turn on the unit. The trays, as might be expected, dry beautifully and you have the added benefit of having already stored them.

Accessory Sheets

Two types of sheets—mesh and solid leather—will enable you to dry many food items that simply cannot be dried directly on the drying trays.

Mesh sheets are plastic sheets with small holes in them that are placed directly on top of the drying trays. The purpose of a mesh sheet is (1) to keep food that contains considerable sugar—bananas, tomatoes, and watermelon—from sticking to the drying trays; (2) to prevent small pieces of food—celery, corn, and herbs—from falling through the drying trays; (3) to hold the juice from a food, through a type of capillary action, next to the food that is being dried; (4) to help prevent moisture from the food on one drying tray from dripping onto lower trays in the drying chamber.

Solid leather sheets actually are liners placed in the drying trays and are used for foods—fruit and vegetable purees, spaghetti sauce, yogurt, and other items that are very high in liquid content—which cannot be dehydrated directly on the drying trays or mesh sheets because they would drip through. Solid leather sheets go by different names and, depending upon the make of dehydrator, may be made of different materials. If your unit does not come with solid leather sheets, check with other dehydrator manufacturers to see if you can adapt their sheets to your machine. An alternative is to stretch plastic wrap over the drying trays and up over the edges to act as a liner. It is helpful to remember that when using solid leather sheets, and mesh sheets as well, that by lightly oiling them you can prevent foods from sticking to them.

Mesh and solid leather sheets are often used together to dry foods that contain a great deal of fat—ground beef, bacon, salmon, commercially prepared luncheon meats, to name a few. In certain instances, you may have to use both types of sheets and also remove the food to blot up any fat that comes to the surface as the food dries. You may also insert both types of sheets (leather on the bottom and mesh on top) when drying foods that shrink to very small pieces, such as rice or dried garlic.

To clean mesh or solid leather sheets, rub them with warm, soapy water, let sit for a few minutes, and rinse them well. Rub really sticky places gently with a scrub brush. Solid leather sheets can become stained—from food coloring—and in those instances, I keep those sheets aside and use them exclusively for the food that has originally stained them, such as certain brands of commercial spaghetti sauce or tomato paste.

Now that you have a basic understanding of what a food dehydrator looks like and how it works, here is a list of questions you should be able to answer before you purchase a unit. Over the years I have repeatedly been asked these by prospective customers, and it is fascinating to observe the freedom that comes from knowing the answers. Find out:

How does the machine work? What is the heat source? Does the unit have a fan? Are there controls and are they easy to use? Does the unit have solid-state circuitry or a mechanical thermostat? Has the make been tested and approved by the Underwriters Laboratories?

What is the square footage of the drying trays? How much food can be dried at one time? Can more trays be added? How are additional trays and accessory items purchased after the initial sale?

Is the machine easy to load and unload? How much does it weigh?

What is the wattage of the unit? The range for electric food dehydrators is from 115 to 1,000. What is the cost to use?

What are the terms of the warranty? Is the machine repairable, or can you fix it yourself? Is it designed for continuous, long-lasting use? If you have to send it to a service center, what will it cost to repair? And how long will you be without your dehydrator? (These questions may seem a little alarmist in nature, but I assure you that the answers, even if you never need them, are important.)

Can food purees be dried in the dehydrator you are considering? Does it come with mesh sheets? Solid leather sheets? How many of each? How and where can you buy more?

Do you have to rotate the drying trays to get air to circulate evenly over all the surfaces of the food for a good-quality product?

What kind of sound, and how much of it, does the unit make?

Is the machine easy to clean? Is there any special treatment for cleaning that you need to know about? Are drying trays dishwasher safe? Are they durable? How often will you need to replace them, and where do you obtain them?

Does the machine you are considering have a built-in timer and automatic shutoff? These two features may prove to be very helpful. Realize, however, that when you start using this type of machine, you'll need to refer to the instruction manual for directions on what size piece the food you are intending to dry should be cut and how long it should be dried. Food can spoil if the dryer shuts off automatically and you do not remove the food before it reabsorbs moisture from the air.

If the model is a cabinet type, is the door removable for cleaning purposes and accessibility? Does it open, close, and seal easily? Can you see into the drying chamber? How do the trays in this design slide in and out?

Congratulations! With satisfactory answers to the above questions, you are now the owner of a brand-new food dehydrator. I know that what I am about to say may sound simpleminded, but I want you to be sure to take your new purchase out of the box when you get home! I cannot tell you the number of times I have heard people tell me that they never even took their dehydrator out of its original carton.

Yes, take it out of the box, put it on the kitchen counter, plug it in. Now, check out how it works. Using the directions, turn it on; put your hand over (but not on) the heat source; check out the air flow. Examine the drying trays and accessory sheets. Wash them.

Be sure that you have put your dehydrator in a convenient place in the kitchen, one that encourages use. You need easy access to it. Dehydrators that do not make it into the kitchen and end up stored in the garage or basement are dehydrators that are infrequently (if ever) used. If the unit sits in front of you on the kitchen counter, you are more likely to think of slicing and drying the bananas that are overripening in the fruit bowl instead of throwing them out. With your dehydrator handy and your using it an ongoing pleasure, see if you don't have energy-producing, nutritious, fat-free foods more and more often.

A final tip before we get down to how to use your food dehydrator now that you have it: Remember that after buying any small or large appliance, it is a good idea to keep the warranty, sales slip, and any other pertinent information regarding the purchase. Your receipt should also include an address for repairs. Should your machine at some later date stop working—the two most common problems are that it no longer heats or there is no air circulation—be sure to tell the repair service what appears to be the malfunction. If you do not identify the problem, you will be surprised at how long it can take to get service on it.

Chapter 3

Basic Facts About Food Dehydration

*T*his book is intended to be a user-friendly guide for people who are about to use a food dehydrator for the first time, as well as a book for devotees of food drying who are ready for new adventures and challenges. Food drying is part of our human heritage and, whether our grandmothers were German, Sioux, Chinese, or Hispanic, we all share this heritage.

This chapter will address some of the "first things" about food drying, then move on to discuss some of the more technical questions. Let's begin with the most basic question of all:

Q. What is food drying?
A. Food drying, also called food dehydration, is the process of removing water from food, thus inhibiting the growth of microorganisms (enzymes) and bacteria by the circulation of hot, dry air through the food. Removing water from food is the easiest, cheapest, and, in my opinion, the most appropriate method of food preservation.

Q. Will I have a lot to learn before I can start drying food?
A. No, food drying is not difficult. It means less work, not more. And the benefits are many. Your dehydrator heats the air inside the unit; it dries and circulates the air so that it absorbs the water in the food placed in the drying chamber. The temperature of the air is low enough to dry the food, not cook it. It is as simple as that.

Q. What are the benefits of food drying?

A. Many. Here are some:

You will save money. Keep in mind that food drying is a one-time cost. Canned foods, once opened, must be used promptly, but containers of dried foods can be repeatedly opened, ingredients removed or added, and closed again with no deleterious effects on the contents.

You will be able to reap the rewards of your own garden and of both locally grown and regionally grown produce, because you can keep up with abundant seasonal harvests. There is a movement now away from the importation of foodstuffs, not so much because of safety considerations but because of an increasing awareness of the importance of self-sufficiency when it comes to one's own food supply.

You will be able to feed family and friends safer, pesticide- and chemical-free foods because you control what you are drying.

You can create a food supply which, in a financial crisis or when a natural disaster strikes, can be like money in the bank.

You will be able to take advantage of supermarket specials and the savings they offer.

Food drying is a form of creative recycling. In drying your own foods, you are cutting down on packaging; wait until you see how little storage space you will need. You can store 20 to 25 dried bell peppers in a 1-quart jar; 16 to 20 dried tomatoes in a 1-quart jar.

What I like best about incorporating dried foods into my diet is that it allows me to control the quality of the food I eat whether I am at home or backpacking in the wilderness. Dried foods are tasty, nutritious, lightweight, easy to prepare, easy to carry, and easy to use.

Q. What does food that is dried look like?

A. Many foods are a little darker in color, more fragrant, and sweeter in taste. Do not expect food dried at home to look or taste like commercially dried food. In my opinion, home-dried is much better. Much industrial food drying uses additives and preservatives that the home food dryer does not need to and—more important—want to add.

Q. Does drying affect the nutritional value of foods?

A. Dehydration only minimally affects the nutritional value of foods, especially when the process takes place in your own home. Most research on the nutritional value of dried foods has been conducted on foods that are commercially dried. When you dry foods at home under gentle conditions (correct temperature and a reasonable amount of drying time), you produce a high-quality product. Compared with canning and freezing, both of which involve extreme temperatures, food drying is the least damaging form of food preservation.

Here are some specifics:

Vitamin A is retained during the drying process. Because vitamin A is light sensitive, foods that contain it—like carrots, bell peppers, mangoes—should be stored in a dark place.

Some vitamin C is lost during the drying process because vitamin C is an air-soluble nutrient and food drying is an air-based process. When a food is sliced and its cells are cut, the surfaces that are exposed to air lose some vitamin C content.

The caloric value of a fresh food stays the same when it is dried, although some dried foods, fruits for example, taste sweeter because the water has been removed and the sugar is concentrated.

Dried fruits and vegetables are high in fiber and carbo-hydrates, neither of which is affected by drying.

Dried fruits and vegetables are naturally low in fat. Minerals available in certain fresh fruits—such as potassium, sodium, magnesium, and so on—are also not altered when the fruit is dried.

Q. How safe to eat is dried food?

A. In comparison with foods preserved by other methods, like canning, it is quite safe. Botulism is feared in canning because the bacteria that cause it thrive in a liquid environment. Botulism could only occur with a dried food that had been rehydrated, then left unattended long enough for bacteria to grow.

Mold may form on dried food if it was not dehydrated long enough or if the container it was stored in had moisture in it. If you see or smell mold, all the food in that container must be discarded. Remember that the organisms that cause food spoilage—mold, yeast, bacteria—are always present in the air, water, and soil. It is important to observe sanitary precautions at all stages of the drying process.

As to the safety of drying meats, the latest word from food-science researchers at the University of Wisconsin in Madison is that microorganisms are effectively killed when the internal temperature of meat reaches 145°F for 45 minutes; or 167°F for 20 minutes; or 200°F for 15 minutes. This means that the internal temperature of the meat must remain steady for the designated amount of time, which is not the same as putting meat in a 200°F oven for 15 minutes.

If your food dehydrator does not reach a temperature of 145°F or if its temperature control is inaccurate, then transfer the food to a preheated 200°F oven for a minimum of 20 minutes to eliminate safety concerns.

You can also store dried food in the freezer, another form of ensuring its safety.

A Sampler

Here is a sampling of food items (pictured on the book's cover) that shows fresh versus dried poundage. I think you will agree that the differences between the two are remarkable. For more information on the water content of fruits and vegetables, see Chapter 5.

Weight, Fresh	Weight, Dried
4 pounds (10) bell peppers	= 4 ounces
3½ pounds onions	= 4 ounces
2 pounds Golden Delicious apples, peeled and cored	= 4 ounces (crisp)
1¾ pounds (3) zucchini	= 4 ounces
1 pound strawberries	= 2 ounces
One 30-oz. bag frozen vegetables	= 5 ounces

Q. What equipment is needed?

A. In addition to your dehydrator, of course, you will need:

a good sharp knife
a spatula or two
several heavy-bottomed saucepans
a blender for pureeing and chopping
a strainer
steamer trays

Nice to have on hand and very helpful, but not mandatory are:

a cherry pitter
an apple parer-slicer-corer
a corn kernel cutter
a pea and bean sheller
a bean Frencher
a mortar and pestle
a salad spinner (for predrying herbs and flowers and for washing greens)
a food processor with a shredding disk
a Salad Shooter for slicing potatoes

But what is *really* necessary? A good sharp knife.

Q. What foods can be dried?

A. You can dry fruits, vegetables, meats, fish, herbs, flowers, and much more, including frozen and canned foods. In fact, you can dry almost anything that contains water—items you may never have considered, such as tofu.

Here are some other ideas that will keep your dehydrator in constant use:

Use it to revive limp potato chips or soggy popcorn.

Dry leftover bread to make crumbs and croutons.

Instead of draping homemade noodles to dry all over the kitchen and dining room, dry them in your dehydrator.

Make your own bagel chips by seasoning thinly sliced bagels with garlic, onion powder, or cinnamon sugar, then drying them until crisp in your dehydrator.

Q. Is it necessary to pretreat foods before drying them?

A. Pretreatment is not necessary for successful drying, but it can enhance the color, flavor, and texture of certain foods. Pretreatment options include dipping, blanching, marinating, and sulfuring.

Pretreatment affects the enzymes, a group of special proteins that cause chemical reactions—ripening and eventual spoilage—and determine the color, texture, flavor, and aroma of certain foods. The microorganisms that cause spoilage need moisture to live and reproduce. Drying foods above 140°F halts enzyme activity.

Foods also contain simple yeasts, molds, and bacteria, all of which can cause deterioration. Again, reducing the moisture content of food inhibits their growth. When dried, vegetables contain only about 3 percent moisture, and fruits, depending upon sugar content, up to 15 percent water.

For an in-depth discussion of pretreatment methods for fruits and vegetables, see pages 33–37.

Q. What is sulfuring?

A. In the most simple definition, sulfuring helps to preserve the color of some dried foods, like apricots. Fumes from burning sulfur or gaseous sulfur dioxide penetrate the surfaces of foods before they are dried. I do not sulfur the foods I dry. I do not believe that it is necessary when drying foods in an electric food dehydrator. Sulfuring is mainly used as a pretreatment when foods are dried out-of-doors.

Q. How long does it take to dry food?

A. This is the question I am asked most frequently and it is the hardest one to answer because many factors affect drying time:

- the water content in the food
- the sugar content in the food
- the size of the piece of food
- the amount of air circulation when the food is dried
- the level of humidity in the air entering the dehydrator
- the air temperature inside the dehydrator
- last and most important, the type of dehydrator you are using will affect the time needed to dry food.

Let's examine each factor one by one:

Water Content

The higher the water content of a specific food, the longer it will take to dry. Generally, meat contains 60 to 70 percent water; fruit and vegetables, 80 to 95 percent. Therefore, a ½-inch thick piece of meat will dry faster than a ½-inch thick piece of fruit or vegetable.

Different varieties of a food contain different amounts of water, depending upon the growing season, the amount of rainfall, the type of soil, and numerous other environmental factors. Apples, for example, vary in natural moisture content. It follows that a naturally drier fresh apple will dehydrate faster than a naturally moister one.

Sugar Content

The more sugar a food contains, the longer it will take to dry. For example, homemade, unsweetened yogurt will dry in about six hours; commercial brands, which usually contain sweetener, can take as long as 24 hours to dry. Ripe bananas with brown spots on the peel will take longer to dry than green ones will because they contain more sugar.

Size and Surface Area

The thicker the piece of food, the longer it will take to dry; the thinner it is, the less time it will take. A ½-inch thick piece of food takes longer to dry than a ¼-inch thick piece. Cutting food into pieces exposes surface area; therefore, the more surface area is exposed, the faster the drying time will be. Here, again, there will be mitigating factors: Is your dehydrator passive or nonpassive? You must understand the features of the machine you are using.

Humidity

The higher the humidity in the air entering the dehydrator, the longer it will take to heat the air and, thus, the longer it will take to dry the food in the unit. The lower the relative humidity, the greater the capacity of the unit to absorb moisture in the food. If the air contains, say, 60 percent humidity rather than 90 percent, food will dry in less time.

Air Temperature Inside the Dehydrator

The lower the air temperature inside the dehydrator, the longer the drying time. Raising the temperature in the unit will increase the amount of water removed from the food and decrease the length of time it will take to dry. The temperature should be high enough to draw the moisture from the food but not high enough to cook it.

Temperatures that are too low may cause food to spoil; temperatures that are too high may cause the surface area of the food to harden and prevent moisture from escaping. The three food categories—meats and fish, fruits and vegetables, and herbs—require different drying temperatures:

Meats and Fish	145°F and above
Fruits and Vegetables	130°F to 140°F
Herbs and Flowers	100°F to 110°F

The wider the range of temperature and the amount of air flow inside your food dehydrator, the better the quality of the finished dried product. For more information on differences in the design of food dehydrators, see Chapter 2.

Q. Will flavors mingle if I dry different foods at the same time?
A. I am often asked this question. In my experience, the answer is no, although I do not recommend drying pears and onions at the same time! If you combine foods that are in the same category—fruits with other fruits, vegetables with other vegetables—each retains its own flavor.

Q. How can you know when foods are dry?
A. The best way of finding out if a food is dry is to touch it. It will feel sticky, moist, leathery, or hard. When touching foods for dryness, remember that they feel softer when they are warm. Therefore, always let the foods cool for a few moments—either turn off the dehydrator or remove the drying tray. If you are not sure if an item is sufficiently dry, it is better to overdry it somewhat than to underdry it. However, know that foods that are overdried in some dehydrators may turn brown and become brittle.

If you are concerned about the safety of a dried food, you

The Touch Test for Dryness

Fruits are dry when they are bendable and leathery, with no pockets of moisture. Of course, if you want a crisp, crunchy chip, you will dry the food longer. Fruits that contain a lot of sugar, like pineapple, do not need to be dried hard because their natural sugar acts as a preservative. (Dried fruits have a water content of 10 to 15 percent.)

Vegetables are dry when they are hard; they will rattle in a jar when you shake it. (Vegetables have a water content of 3 to 8 percent.)

Meats are dry when leathery in texture.

Fish are dry when leathery in texture.

Herbs are dry when crisp and crushable.

Leathers are dry when they peel off the solid leather sheet easily, with no tackiness. Most leathers are flexible when dry. Leathers that contain a lot of sugar may take longer to dry and may be stickier even when dried.

Tip: Foods, like pineapple or pears, that have been over-dried and are hard to chew, can be left out to absorb moisture gradually from the air. Or place them over boiling water or steam for a few moments.

To crisp up a dried food, put it in the freezer overnight. Dried tomatoes, for example, are much easier to break into pieces if they are frozen.

can freeze it. The freezer will keep frozen any water remaining in the food, thus preventing spoilage. You can freeze dried foods at any stage of the drying process. A woman I once met at a home show told me that she only half-dries her mushrooms because she likes how quickly they rehydrate.

Q. How do you store dried foods?

A. Moisture is the enemy of dried foods. Dried foods exposed to the air absorb the moisture in the air and become limp. Always store dried foods in airtight containers and label the contents. Store the containers in a dry, dark place with a moderate temperature. Your kitchen cupboard is an ideal spot. After all, dried foods take up so much less space than fresh or canned ones that it is easy to keep them in a handy place.

Remember to store any dried food containing vitamin A away from direct light.

Here is how I store certain items: I always keep some dried tomatoes in the refrigerator. When I want to make spaghetti sauce, I retrieve the tomatoes from the fridge, take my dried herbs from the cupboard, and collect my dried peppers and onions from the pantry. Economies of scale make all of this possible, and if you have a small kitchen, you will appreciate the extra space gained simply by using dried foods.

When storing dried foods, contamination from insects may occur. The only insect I have ever found to be a problem is the Indian meal moth, in both the worm and adult stages. A University of Wisconsin food researcher told me that the food may have been contaminated with the insect eggs already sealed in the jar. To destroy the insects, pasteurize the food right after it has been dried. There are two ways to do this:

Place the food in the freezer for 48 hours, or

Preheat your oven to 175°F, or the lowest possible setting, and heat the infested food on a cookie sheet in the oven for 15 to 30 minutes. Let cool before before rewrapping.

Q. How long can dried foods be stored?
A. Dried foods will last from one season to the next. Dry garden tomatoes this year and replace them next year when fresh ones are again dropping from the vines. When fresh tomatoes have gone, I immediately start using dried ones. (And if I run out of dried tomatoes—what an awful thought!—I just promise myself to grow and dry more of them next year.)

For optimum quality, dried fruits and vegetables should be replaced annually. Herbs and flowers, once dried, last a very long time. And although our ancestors may have kept dried meats for long periods of time without benefit of refrigeration, I recommend storing dried meats in the refrigerator or freezer after one month at room temperature. Remember, many jerkies, with the exception of poultry jerkies, have not been cooked.

I repeat, I think it is a good idea to use dried foods within one year of drying them, just as you would canned and fro-

What to Use as Storage Containers

Jars My first choice for storing dried foods is a wide-mouthed canning jar. Any clean, dry glass container—an empty mayonnaise or peanut butter jar—with a tight-fitting lid will do. They do not need to be sterilized but do need to be clean and dry. Glass jars let you easily check the contents and the condition of the food. You can use the same lids over and over again. Store the jars in a cool, dry, dark place away from high humidity.

If you are new to food drying, use smaller jars for storage, just in case some food pieces weren't dried long enough. It's much less painful to discard a quart of dried food than a full gallon because mold has developed.

Plastic Bags Plastic bags take up less space and adapt themselves to assorted shapes. They can be stored easily in the refrigerator, freezer, or elsewhere. Squeeze out any excess air before sealing the bag. Fill bags that will be heat-sealed as full as possible. Of course, plastic bags are ideal for storing foods to take backpacking or outdoor adventuring.

Paper, cloth, or lightweight grocery bags are unsatisfactory storage containers: They simply aren't secure enough. Store plastic bags in a critter-proof location; critters know that chewing through the plastic can be very rewarding.

Freezer Dried foods can be stored in the freezer for a very long time. You need not have completely dried foods before storing in the freezer.

Vacuum Packing There are small appliances that will vacuum-pack—remove the air from—the bag or jar in which you are storing dried foods. These appliances take storage one step further.

zen foods. First of all, you will enjoy their quality year round by using them at their peak and replacing them when fresh foods are in season again. Second, and no less important, dried foods that have been squirreled away for too long lose their taste and tend to darken in color. Follow the rule of first in/first out and be sure to rotate the containers on the shelf so that you use the oldest dried foods first.

Q. **Is it possible to dry food in a microwave oven?**
A. I have never attempted to dry food in a microwave oven. A food dehydrator is always my first choice. I have, however, heard of people who have dried herbs or flowers in a microwave. Before attempting either of those procedures, it is important to check the warranty of the microwave oven you own to see if the manufacturer recommends using it for these purposes. Some manufacturers do not and will not honor the warranty agreement if their machine breaks down when it has been used for this purpose.

Chapter 4

Preparing Fruits and Vegetables for Drying

*W*ith many of the basic questions about food dehydration now behind us, I would like to present the seven basic ways fruits and vegetables should be handled before being dried. I call each of the separate preparations a "key technique." As you will see, I begin with slicing the food, and while that may seem obvious to some home food-drying enthusiasts, it may not be so apparent to the beginner. Many's the time at county or state fairs or home shows I have been asked, "What do I do? How do I begin?"

Begin by reading the section on slicing, then continue to read about peeling, dipping, blanching, cooking or baking, seeding, and candying. By the time you reach the end of this chapter, you will not only be well acquainted with how to handle foods for home drying, but you will learn about options you can avail yourself of or leave behind.

I think you will agree after you have familiarized yourself with these key techniques that it becomes very easy to look at a certain type of fruit or vegetable and know how to dry it. Then, when someone whom you hope will share your interest in food drying asks you, "Will it be difficult to learn?" you can reply wholeheartedly, "No, it's fun. Just taste these tomato chips, or dried apple slices, or tomato leather." The list goes on and on.

Key Technique 1: Slicing
Cutting a fruit, vegetable, or piece of meat or fish allows dry air to get inside the food to remove the water in it. The size of the

piece of food, its surface area as well as its thickness, along with certain characteristics of your food dehydrator, will determine how long it takes to dry.

Generally, I cut most foods into ⅛- to ½-inch-thick pieces. On the average, I expect about 24 slices from one large Golden Delicious apple. I cut watermelon, however, into 1-inch-thick slices or chunks because watermelon's very high water content causes thinner-cut slices almost to disappear when dried.

Before you begin drying fruits and vegetables, refer to Chapter 5. There you will find in list form what you need to know about a fruit or vegetable's water content, plus other information. Knowing the amount of water in a fruit or vegetable will affect how you cut it and how long you can anticipate it might take to dry. The more you know about what you are drying, the more satisfying, and creative, the experience will be.

Example: To Slice and Dry a Tomato

Tomatoes are second only to zucchini as garden giveaways during harvest time. I will never forget the call-in radio show I was listening to some years ago: Someone asked for ways to get rid of excess zucchini. The answer: "Find an unlocked parked car!"—a silly, and not very practical, response. My response: Dry them! Dry everything!

Tomatoes, for me, are treasures. I grow them, I dry them, I pulverize them, I use them throughout this book to demonstrate important procedures and in many recipes in Part Two.

1. Select red tomatoes that are ripe but still firm. Softer tomatoes are more suitable for making puree, which, in turn, can be dried into Tomato Leathers (see pages 132–135). Plum tomatoes, being meatier, are generally used for making sauce or paste, or can be dried as sun-dried tomatoes (see page 38). If you want to dry cherry tomatoes, halve them and scoop out the seeds. There is not much flesh in a cherry tomato, and a lot of effort goes into seeding it. Lastly, even green tomatoes can be dried.
2. Core the tomato and cut off the stem and bottom ends. Slice the tomato crosswise into slices ⅓ to ¼ inch thick.
3. Arrange the slices in a single layer, touching but not overlapping, on a mesh sheet on a drying tray. Place the drying tray

in the dehydrator and dry anywhere from 8 to 12 hours, depending on the style of dehydrator, or until the slices are leathery and no pockets of moisture remain. The color of tomatoes when dried intensifies into a wonderful, not necessarily darker hue. If your tomatoes dry dark, it could be the result of their being overly ripe, having been dried at too hot a temperature, or the high acidity of the tomatoes.

4. Store in an airtight container.

Tip: To dry tomatoes without the skins, drop them into boiling water until the skins break. Remove the tomatoes with a slotted spoon and plunge into a bowl of cold water. You should be able to peel the skins off with your hands.

Key Technique 2: Peeling

Peeling certain fruits and vegetables, tomatoes among them, is optional. With other fruits or vegetables, peeling is anything but optional. Some obvious examples of fruits that need to be peeled include bananas, pineapples, mangoes, melons, and kiwifruit. Winter squash, cucumbers, onions, and pumpkins are only some of the vegetables that must be peeled.

I use a banana to demonstrate this simple procedure because banana, as you will soon taste, is much sweeter dried than when it is fresh—another dividend of the drying process.

Example: To Peel, Slice, and Dry a Banana

1. Remove and discard the peel of the banana.
2. Slice the banana into ¼-inch slices.
3. Arrange the slices in a single layer, touching but not overlapping, on a mesh sheet on a drying tray. Place the drying tray in the dehydrator and dry for 8 to 12 hours, depending on the make of dehydrator. To check the banana for doneness, first let it cool, then test it: When properly dried, a banana should be chewy and a little sticky and have a caramel-like color and texture. It does not need to be dried so long that it is hard to the touch, but should you want a crisper, dried product, that is always an option.

A Comparison

As anyone who has tried commercially dried bananas knows, they taste different from home-dried bananas: The commercial bananas are light in color and crisp in texture because they have been fried in either coconut or palm oil, then dipped in a blend of sugar and/or honey to which banana flavoring has been added. Home-dried bananas, if prepared as instructed above, are 100 percent natural.

If you want to dry bananas to taste more like the store-bought kind, select the less ripe ones for drying.

Slice them ¼ inch thick.

Dip them in ½ cup pineapple juice (or lime juice) with (or without) ¼ cup honey added.

Dry them as described on page 32. If you do add honey to the dipping solution, be prepared for a very sticky product that takes longer to dry. For more about dipping, see Key Technique 3.

Even though this version of dried bananas might taste sweeter, you have still not fried them.

Key Technique 3: Pretreatment by Dipping

The flesh of certain fruits (apples, peaches, pears, nectarines, and apricots, to mention just a few) and vegetables (potatoes, mushrooms, cucumbers, zucchini, parsnips, and turnips) darkens a little when exposed to the air. The change in color is caused by a chemical reaction called oxidation.

To preserve the original color of the fruit or vegetable, it is frequently advised to dip it into an antioxidant solution. (Please note the word "advised"; in only a few instances is dipping absolutely necessary. In almost all cases, it is an option on the part of the home dryer.) Such antioxidant liquids include fresh or bottled lemon juice or pineapple and orange juices. If you use undiluted lemon juice for dipping, a more lemony-tasting dried product will result. My favorite dipping solutions to impart flavor are natural fruit juices—pineapple and orange juices for fruits; lemon juice for vegetables.

Use:

¼ cup lemon juice to 2 cups water and dip the fruit or vegetable for only a couple of minutes. Apricots are one of the few fruits that benefit from being dipped for a longer time, about 20 to 30 minutes.

Or, in the canning sections of most supermarkets, purchase antioxidant products like Fruit-Fresh. Allow:

½ tablespoon Fruit-Fresh to 2 cups of water

Another antioxidant is made by dissolving vitamin C tablets in water and using the combination as a dipping solution. I use:

1 500-mg tablet to each cup of water

Salt, vinegar, and water can also be used to prevent foods from darkening. Allow:

1 tablespoon salt or vinegar to 8 cups of water

Lastly, you can also prevent a certain amount of oxidation by combining sodium bisulfite with water and using it as a soaking solution. Since sodium bisulfite is a chemical, I do not use it.

In addition to aesthetic considerations another good reason to dip foods before drying them is to impart flavor.

Try dipping apple slices in cranberry juice or 7Up. Or add Kool-Aid powder or Jell-O to pineapple juice. Or flavor the juice with spices. Or soak fresh fruits in liqueur before drying them. You can add herbs to a lemon-juice solution. For a very interesting flavor contrast dip one side of an apple slice in a juice solution and the other side in cinnamon sugar. Dry the apple on a mesh sheet placed in a drying tray.

Rainbow Bananas

One 3-ounce package each cherry, strawberry, lime, and orange Jell-O
Bananas

For each package of Jell-O, halve the amount of hot and cold water called for in the directions. Combine the reduced water measurement with each flavor of Jell-O and use the mixture as a dipping solution.

When you have finished dipping the fruit, put each Jell-O mix in a blender with a sliced banana and blend into a puree. Dry into fruit leather (for procedures, see pages 120–121).

Example: To Dry a Dipped Sliced Pear

1. Core the pear and slice it lengthwise into ¼-inch slices.
2. Pour a 6-ounce can of unsweetened pineapple juice or orange juice into a small bowl.
3. Add the unpeeled pear slices, submerging them completely for about 2 minutes.
4. Remove the slices to a mesh sheet on a drying tray and arrange them in one layer, touching but not overlapping. Put the drying tray in the dehydrator and dry for 8 to 12 hours, or until the slices are leathery.

Key Technique 4: Pretreatment by Blanching

As the key technique of dipping affects both the color and flavor of a fruit or vegetable, blanching—using either boiling water or steam to pretreat the food—affects the color, by helping to set it, and the texture, by breaking down the cell structure, which allows for faster drying and rehydration.

Blanching is recommended for asparagus, green beans, broccoli, Brussels sprouts, cauliflower, and peas, because they are enjoyed most frequently as side dishes or in soups or stews, where quick rehydration and good color are desirable.

Blanching is not recommended for tomatoes, celery, mushrooms, okra, bell peppers, radishes, greens, onions, and Swiss chard.

There are three main ways to blanch:

Water-boil blanching: Allow 4 cups of prepared fruit or vegetable for every gallon of water. Bring the water to a boil; as it is heating, put the food in a wire basket, like a spaghetti cooker, that you can lower into and lift out of the water. Place the basket in the boiling water for 3 to 6 minutes, depending upon the size and type of food.

Steam-blanching: Bring about 2 inches of water to a boil in a large pot. Place the sliced fruit or vegetable in a single layer in a wire colander or basket and place over the boiling water. Do not let the colander touch the water. Cover the pot and steam for 4 to 6 minutes, depending upon the size of the pieces. Steam-blanching requires about one third more time than water-boil blanching does, but may result in less nutrient loss.

Microwave-blanching: Place the prepared fruit or vegetable in one layer in a microwave-safe container. Place the container in the microwave and cook at high power for 4 to 6 minutes, depending upon the size of the pieces. Turn the pieces halfway through the cooking process.

Checking, a form of blanching, breaks down the tough outer skins of certain fruits and vegetables. You can break the skin in two ways. Pouring boiling water over the food or bring water to a boil, then turning off the heat under it. Immediately add the food to the water and let sit until the skin pops. Do not boil the food or the flesh will turn mushy.

(Checking is recommended for cranberries, citrus peels, grapes, rhubarb, and for blueberries.)

Example: To Dry Blanched (Checked) Cranberries

1. In a heatproof bowl, pour boiling water over the cranberries or submerge them in a pot of boiling water off the heat. Let sit until the skins pop. Do not let the berries boil. Drain.
2. If desired, coat the berries with either light corn syrup or granulated sugar.
3. Transfer berries to a baking sheet and place in the freezer for 2 hours. (Freezing also breaks down the cell structure, thus promoting faster drying.)
4. Arrange berries in a single layer on mesh sheets in drying

trays. Place drying trays in dehydrator and dry for 10 to 16 hours, depending on the make of dehydrator, until chewy and with no pockets of moisture.

Key Technique 5: Cooking or Baking

This technique is used to break down food tissue and to loosen the skins on certain vegetables, such as beets, squash, pumpkins, and yams, for easy removal.

Example: To Dry Cooked Sliced Beets

1. Cut off beet greens, reserving them for another use. Leave about 2 inches of stem at the top.
2. Bring a pan of water to a boil. Add the beets and cook until fork-tender, about 10 to 15 minutes. Drain off the hot water, and cover the beets with cold water. Let cool.
3. When cool, slip off the skins.
4. Slice the beets ⅛ to ¼ inch thick.
5. Arrange the slices on a drying tray. Place the tray in the dehydrator and dry for 8 to 10 hours, or until hard.

Key Technique 6: Seeding

Some vegetables must obviously be seeded, like pumpkins and squash, and some benefit by it, like large zucchini. Generally, I don't seed tomatoes other than some of my Roma tomatoes. I have never found the seeds in dried tomatoes to be bitter and acidy-tasting as some claim (especially in dried Romas). Nonetheless, here is how to seed a tomato. Actually, I have an ulterior motive: By seeding Roma tomatoes I can then follow with a procedure for making sun-dried tomatoes—one of my most favorite foods.

Example 1: Seeding Roma Tomatoes

1. Gently roll a semiripe tomato between your hands to detach the seeds inside.
2. With a sharp knife, cut the tomato in half lengthwise.
3. Remove the seeds by holding a tomato half in your hand and tapping it gently against the edge of the sink. Or squeeze the tomato over a paper towel, forcing out the seeds.

Example 2: Sun-Dried Tomatoes

After defending sun-dried tomatoes for years, I am delighted to see them now in major food stores and gourmet shops all over the country.

The Italians call sun-dried tomatoes *pumate*. Strangely enough, commercial "sun-dried" tomatoes are actually dried on grates that are not in direct contact with the sun. First, Roma tomatoes are split in half, seeded, salted lightly, ventilated, and sprayed occasionally with water. Once dry, they are marinated from 3 to 6 weeks in virgin olive oil. Before use, the oil is drained off and the tomatoes are rehydrated in either water or wine. They are then cooked and pureed in a blender.

These make great gifts. Just tie a ribbon around the jar and attach a recipe. As you use the tomatoes, add more oil to the jar to lessen the amount of air in the jar and minimize the potential for spoilage.

1. Follow the directions in *Example: To Slice and Dry a Tomato* on page 31. Dry tomatoes until they have no soft spots but are still bendable.
2. Pack the dried tomatoes in a sterilized 1-quart canning jar, pressing them down into the jar with a spoon or fork, forcing out any air pockets.
3. Pour the best-quality pure virgin olive oil to within 1 inch of the top of the jar. Make sure none of the tomatoes are peeking up over the surface, as it will invite spoilage.
   Option: Add to the jar dried basil leaves, oregano, bay leaf, parsley, or chili peppers.
4. Seal the jar with the lid and let sit 3 to 6 weeks.

Key Technique 7: Candying

Candying, which is also called glacéing, is a very popular cooking and drying technique. The principle is a straightforward one: Sugar and water are combined over heat into a syrup. The syrup is allowed to boil, which evaporates some of the water. As the water boils off, the temperature of the sugar gradually rises and caramelized sugar forms. Increasing the sugar content in a food

---

To Make Sugar Syrup

You can make sugar syrup in four different ways: Directions for cooking the syrup appear on page 40.

1. In a saucepan, combine 1½ cups water with 1 cup granulated sugar, 1 cup honey, and 1 tablespoon light corn syrup; or
2. In a saucepan, combine 1¾ cups water, ¾ cup light corn syrup, and one 3-ounce package fruit-flavored Jell-O; or
3. In a saucepan, combine 1 cup granulated sugar, 1 cup orange juice, 1 cup water, and ¼ cup light corn syrup; or
4. In a saucepan, combine 1½ cups water, 1 cup maple syrup, and 1 tablespoon light corn syrup.

Options: Flavor the boiling syrup with pieces of fresh or dried lemon or orange rind. Or let the syrup cool and stir in 1 teaspoon vanilla or rum extract or kirsch liqueur.

Different fruits can be candied in the same syrup and the syrup can be used over again.

---

prevents the growth of microorganisms and lengthens its shelf life.

Health-food stores, in particular, often have dried sugar-coated or glazed pineapple or papaya. In the commercial process of candying, the fresh food is cooked in syrup, drained, and dried until it is halfway between being fresh and being dried. Then it is soaked repeatedly in a sugar/honey solution and dried and soaked again until the desired product is obtained. The process can take from 4 to 7 days, with the syrup and food becoming increasingly high in sugar content.

Choose foods firm enough to hold their shape during the cooking process. Glacéed kiwifruit has become very popular. Other choices might include cherries, apricots, blueberries, pineapple, figs, watermelon rind, and, of course, citrus peel. Even vegetables—bell peppers, carrots, peas, and corn—can be glazed. Once a food has been candied, it can be dipped in melted chocolate, just like the fruits displayed in fancy candy shops.

Any size piece can be used, from halved kiwi slices to cubed citrus peel. As a result of the candying process, the pieces will shrink to about half their original size. Therefore, be sure to start off with big enough pieces. Foods being candied do not need to be dipped beforehand.

Example: To Candy Cut-up Fruits or Vegetables

DAY 1

1. In a saucepan, stir together the ingredients for the sugar syrup of choice (see page 39). Bring to a boil, stirring. Boil gently (and this applies to all four syrup combinations) for 20 minutes to thicken. Slowly bring the syrup to the soft-ball stage, 189°F on a candy thermometer. If the temperature gets too hot, the syrup will darken in color, burn, and be brittle when cool.
2. Remove the pan from the heat and carefully add 1 pound cut-up peeled (if necessary) food. Stir gently to make sure all surfaces are covered with syrup.
3. Return the pan to the heat and bring the mixture to 189°F on the candy thermometer.
4. Remove the pan from the heat. Cover and let the pan stand at room temperature for 24 hours.

DAY 2

1. With a slotted spoon, remove the candied food from the syrup and put into a strainer set over a container large enough to catch the drips.
2. Return any syrup to the pan.
3. Arrange the candied food in a single layer on mesh sheets on the drying trays. Place the trays in the dehydrator and dry halfway, about 2 to 4 hours. The length of this partial drying time will depend upon the size of the pieces of food and the make of dehydrator used.
4. When the food is half dry, reheat the syrup and add ½ cup sugar. Bring the syrup to a boil, skimming foam from the surface with a large spoon. Remove the pan from the heat.

5. Add the half-dried food to the syrup and heat until the syrup registers 189°F on the candy thermometer. Remove the pan from the heat. Cover the pan and let it stand at room temperature for 24 hours.

DAY 3

1. Repeat Steps 1, 2, 3, and 4 of Day 2, adding 1 cup sugar instead of ½ cup. Complete Steps 4 and 5 of Day 2.

DAY 4

1. Repeat Steps 1 and 2 of Day 2. If desired, at this point, rinse candied dried food in colander with cold water to minimize stickiness.
2. Arrange candied food in a single layer on mesh sheets on drying trays. Place the trays in the dehydrator and dry about 2 to 4 hours. Candied fruit should be leathery and chewy. The drying time for glacéed fruit is much shorter than it is for fresh fruit because much of the moisture has been replaced by sugar.
3. Optional: When dried, sprinkle or roll glacéed fruit in granulated or confectioners' sugar.
4. To store, pack candied food in separate layers separated by wax paper in an airtight container.

DAY 4 (Continued)

For a really elegant touch, dip candied dried fruits—apricot or pineapple pieces, strawberries, or cherries—in melted dark or white chocolate.

1. Melt chocolate chips or chunks carefully in the top of a double boiler.
2. Spear one end of a piece of candied fruit with a toothpick. Dip either the whole piece or half of it into the melted chocolate, then let the coating dry, using the toothpick to prop the fruit up on the countertop.
3. Store chocolate-dipped candied fruit on sheets of wax paper in an airtight container in the refrigerator or the freezer.

CANDIED TREATS

~~~

Candied Lemon or Orange Peel

The white membrane right beneath the outer skin of citrus fruit has a bitter taste and as much of it as possible should be removed from the peel before candying begins. While this recipe calls for lemon or orange peel, grapefruit and lime peels are also superb candied.

As a general rule, the peel from 1 thick-skinned orange or lemon measures about 1 cup.

1 cup orange peel slices or 1 cup lemon peel slices (from 1 large orange or lemon)
½ tablespoon salt
2 cups water, divided, plus 2 tablespoons
½ cup granulated sugar
2 tablespoons light corn syrup

Cut the peel into ¼- to ½-inch cubes.

In a small bowl, stir together the salt and 1 cup of the water; add the cubed peel. Cover and refrigerate for at least 12 hours.

Drain the peel and rinse it under cold water. In a saucepan, combine the peel and the remaining cup of water. Bring to a boil and boil for about 10 minutes until about half of the water evaporates. Drain in a colander and rinse.

Return the peel to the pan and add the granulated sugar. Stir in the remaining 2 tablespoons water and the corn syrup, and simmer slowly for about 10 minutes. Bring the mixture to a boil. Cover the pan, remove it from the heat, and let the peel stand at room temperature for 24 hours.

The following day, bring the syrup and peel to a boil and boil for 5 minutes. Remove the pan from the heat. With a slotted spoon, remove the peel from the syrup to a strainer. Drain, then rinse the peel with cold water. (The sugar syrup can be stored in the refrigerator and used again.)

Arrange the peel in a single layer on a mesh sheet over a solid leather sheet on a drying tray. Place the drying tray in the dehydrator and dry for about 4 hours until chewy when tested.

Optional: Sprinkle the dried peel with confectioners' sugar before storing it in layers separated by wax paper in an airtight container.

Makes about ¾ cup

Honeyed Orange Peel

For this recipe you can use thick-skinned oranges that have already been juiced. Or cut oranges in half and scoop out the pulp. Cut the halves crosswise into ¼-inch thick rounds and halve the rounds.

2 cups water
1 cup halved orange slices (1 large orange)
¼ cup honey
¼ teaspoon ground cinnamon
⅛ teaspoon ground cloves

In a saucepan, combine the 2 cups water and the orange peel, and bring to a boil. Boil until half of the water evaporates. Drain the peel in a colander and rinse under cold water. Return the peel to the pan.

In a small bowl, combine the honey, the cinnamon, and the cloves. Pour the mixture over the orange peel. Over very low heat, simmer the peel, stirring gently, until the honey has permeated the fruit, about 15 minutes.

Strain the peel in a colander set over a bowl and rinse quickly with warm water. Remove the peel from the colander and arrange it in a single layer on a solid leather sheet. Place the tray in the dehydrator and dry the peel for about 4 hours or until chewy.

Store in layers separated by wax paper in an airtight container.

Makes ¾ cup

Candied Watermelon Rind

An enthusiastic home food dryer from Wausau, Wisconsin, once told me she colors her candied watermelon rind with Jell-O. So

I tried it, and here it is. The colors—red for raspberry or straw-berry, green for lime, and so on—are beautiful, particularly when rolled in confectioners' sugar or granulated sugar.

1 small watermelon
3 cups water, plus 1½ cups water
½ cup light corn syrup
1¾ cups granulated sugar
One 3-ounce package fruit-flavored Jell-O
Confectioners' sugar for dredging

Slice the watermelon and remove the green outer peel from each slice. Discard the green peel. Then cut the pink flesh from the lighter-colored flesh. The lighter-colored flesh is the rind. You will need 4 cups rind, cut into strips 2 inches long and ¼ inch thick.

In a 4-quart saucepan, cover the watermelon strips with the 3 cups water and bring to a boil. Boil until the rind turns trans-parent, about 30 minutes. Drain.

In another saucepan, combine the corn syrup, the sugar, and the 1½ cups water, and bring to a boil. Boil until the sugar dis-solves. Gently stir in the watermelon rind, reduce the heat to medium low, and cook until most of the sugar syrup has been absorbed, about 40 minutes.

Remove the pan from the heat, and stir in the Jell-O until it is dissolved. Be sure all surfaces of the rind are coated. Let cool.

With a slotted spoon, remove the rind to drying trays lined with mesh sheets. Arrange the pieces in single layers. Place the drying trays in the dehydrator and dry the rind until it is leath-ery but not hard, about 4 hours.

Roll the rind in confectioners' sugar and store in layers sepa-rated by wax paper in an airtight container.

Makes 4 cups

~

Candied Ginger

Candied ginger is at once hot and sweet, and is marvelous chopped into bits for baking. Or pulverize it and use as a topping on ice cream or frozen yogurt. Candied ginger makes a great gift, too.

1 cup thinly sliced peeled gingerroot
¾ cup water
½ cup maple syrup

In a small saucepan, combine all the ingredients and bring to a boil. Reduce the heat to low and simmer until the syrup completely evaporates, about 20 to 30 minutes. During the last few minutes of cooking time, stir constantly to avoid any scorching.

With a slotted spoon, remove the ginger from the pan and place on a leather sheet on a drying tray. Separate the pieces of ginger with a fork into one layer. Place the tray in the dehydrator and dry the ginger for about 6 to 8 hours, or until the pieces snap when broken.

Store in an airtight container.

Makes 1 cup

~~~

Mock Figs

Mock figs, really candied Roma tomatoes, make wonderful snacks; you can eat them like candy they are so good! One caution: Don't try to make these with any other type of tomato; the thicker texture of the Roma is necessary to the success of the finished product.

1 pound (about 7 medium) Roma tomatoes
4–6 cups boiling water
1 tablespoon butter
¾ cup brown sugar
Confectioners' sugar for sprinkling

Peel the tomatoes: Drop the tomatoes into the boiling water to loosen the skins. Remove with a slotted spoon and plunge the tomatoes into a bowl of cold water. With a serrated knife, core the tomatoes, remove the skins, and cut off a slice from both the top and the bottom. Quarter the tomatoes lengthwise.

In a saucepan, melt the butter, add the brown sugar, and cook until the sugar melts. Add the tomatoes and cook them over low heat until the brown sugar permeates the tomatoes, about 10 to 15 minutes.

With the slotted spoon, remove the tomatoes to lightly oiled solid leather sheets on drying trays. Place the drying trays in the dehydrator and dry for about 8 hours, during which time the tomatoes will darken in color, resembling figs. When dried, sprinkle the tomatoes with confectioners' sugar.

Store in layers separated by wax paper in an airtight container.

Makes 28 pieces

COMBINING TECHNIQUES

Slicing, Cooking, and Dipping
Sometimes the foods you are drying benefit from combining certain key preparatory techniques. Here's how to handle potatoes so that they retain not only their texture but their color as well.

Example: Drying Cooked Dipped Potato Slices

1. Peel the potatoes and remove any green tinges on the flesh directly beneath the skin.
2. Slice the potatoes into ⅛- to ¼-inch slices.
3. Bring a pot of water to a boil and add the potatoes. Cook until the slices change color but remain firm, about 5 minutes. Drain and let cool.
4. Dip the slices into a solution of ¼ cup lemon juice mixed with 2 cups water.
5. Arrange the slices in single layers on mesh sheets on drying trays. Place the drying trays in the dehydrator and dry for about 8 hours until the slices are hard.
6. Store in an airtight container.

Slicing, Peeling, and Dipping
Here's another example of combining key techniques before drying. It is important to note that you do not have to dip apples. This is a cosmetic treatment used mainly to retain a lighter color. Depending upon your own individual tastes, both peeling and dipping are optional.

Example: Drying Peeled Dipped Apple Slices

1. Wash and core the apple.
2. Peel the apple, and remove any bruised or inedible parts.
3. Slice the apple ¼ inch thick.
4. Dip the slices into a bowl of pineapple juice and let soak for 2 minutes.
5. Remove the slices with a slotted spoon to a solid leather sheet on a drying tray. Arrange the pieces in one layer. Place the drying tray in the dehydrator and dry for about 6 to 8 hours, or until the slices still bend when tested but do not contain any pockets of moisture.
6. Store in an airtight container.

Tip: Sprinkle the slices with ground cinnamon on the drying tray, or drop the dipped slices into a bag of cinnamon sugar. Then arrange the slices on a mesh sheet on top of a solid leather sheet. Dry as directed above.

A friend of mine puts hardened chunks of brown sugar in the jar with plain dried apple slices. The apples take on the brown sugar flavor. How's that for simple?

Slicing and Peeling in Preparation for Candying

Candied pineapple is plain glorious, although candying is an optional technique. Simple, plain cut pineapple dries beautifully and is delicious. Before candying pineapple, you must slice and peel it correctly. Here's how to do it. You can simplify the process greatly by buying a peeled, cored whole pineapple, available in many large supermarkets. Or you can even leave the core in the pineapple, as it will become more tender during the candying process.

Example: Slicing, Coring, and Peeling Fresh Pineapple

1. With a sharp knife, cut off the top of the pineapple. Then cut the pineapple in half lengthwise and cut each half into 3 equal boat-shaped pieces.
2. Cut out the section of hard core on each piece.
3. Pare off the skin and remove any "eyes" in the flesh.
4. Slice the pineapple crosswise into pieces ½ inch thick.
5. Candy the pineapple, following the directions on page 40.

Making Vegetable Chips

Example: Soy-Dipped Zucchini Chips

This technique combines slicing and dipping in preparation for drying. In addition to zucchini, you can make vegetable chips with turnips, parsnips, cucumbers, and carrots. They are wonderful, high-energy snacks; a selection of dipped chips enliven Vegetable Gorp (page 241). The more you add, the better.

1. Cut off the top and bottom of the zucchini. If the zucchini is large, peel off the tough skin, halve the zucchini lengthwise, and scoop out the seeds. If small, leave whole and cut rounds that look like poker chips.
2. Lay the zucchini halves cut side down and slice crosswise ⅛ inch thick. If using small zucchini, simply cut into thin rounds using a sharp knife or a vegetable peeler.
3. Dip the rounds or slices into a mixture of ¼ cup soy sauce and ½ cup water, and let soak for 3 to 5 minutes.
4. Arrange the slices on a mesh sheet on a drying tray and sprinkle with salt and garlic powder. Place the drying tray in the dehydrator and dry for 4 to 8 hours, depending on the make of dehydrator.
5. Store in an airtight container.

Tip: Before drying, sprinkle the slices with cayenne pepper, or lemon juice, or dried herbs.

Barbecue-Soy Sauce Dip: Combine bottled barbecue sauce, soy sauce, chopped garlic, and salt to taste.
French Dressing Dip: Combine ½ cup French dressing, ½ cup water, and 1 teaspoon lemon juice and use as a dip.

EASY CHIPS

~~

Crisp Carrot Chips

You need only three ingredients to make these good chips. Other firm vegetables that can be substituted for the carrots include turnips and parsnips.

carrots
light vegetable oil
salt

Peel the carrots and slice them as thin as possible.

In a skillet, heat a thin layer of vegetable oil until hot and in it sauté the carrots, stirring them gently, until almost cooked but not fried crisp. (The edges of both turnips and parsnips will turn a little brown.) With a slotted spoon, remove the slices to paper towels to drain.

Sprinkle the rounds with salt, then arrange them in a single layer on a solid leather sheet in a drying tray. Place the drying tray in the dehydrator and dry for 4 to 8 hours, depending on the make of dehydrator, until crisp.

Tomato Chips

These chips make a delicious, healthful snack as is, or serve them with a vegetable dip.

Roma tomatoes
Garlic powder, or dried basil or oregano, and/or lemon pepper for seasoning

Core the tomatoes, then slice them crosswise into rounds ¼ inch thick. Sprinkle the slices with the seasoning of choice.

Arrange the slices on a lightly oiled solid leather sheet in a drying tray and place the tray in the dehydrator. Dry about 8 hours, depending on the make of dehydrator, until crisp.

Dried Pickled Mushroom Chips

These fancy chips make a good addition to Vegetable Gorp (page 241). Or add them to sandwich spreads or toss them in salads, like olives. Here is a shortcut to preparing them: Use bottled pickling spices.

2 cups sliced stemmed fresh mushrooms (¼ inch thick)
½ cup white wine vinegar

⅓ cup olive oil
1 tablespoon dried parsley
1 teaspoon chopped garlic
½ teaspoon salt
¼ teaspoon pepper

Combine all the ingredients in a 1-quart canning jar and stir. Cover with the lid. Let the mushrooms marinate in the refrigerator for 12 hours.

Drain the mushrooms in a strainer set over a bowl. Arrange the mushrooms on a solid leather sheet in a drying tray. Place the tray in the dehydrator and dry until the mushrooms are firm, about 10 to 12 hours.

Store the marinade in the refrigerator and use as the base for salad dressing.

Simple Dried Mushroom Chips: Marinate the sliced mushrooms for 1 hour in French Dressing Dip (page 48). Drain and dry them as directed above. Add to Vegetable Gorp (page 241).

~~~

Dried Pickles

Remove either homemade or commercial sweet or dill pickles from their liquid, and slice ½ inch thick. Arrange the slices on drying trays, place the drying trays in the dehydrator, and dry for 8 hours, depending on the make of dehydrator.

These are also good added to Vegetable Gorp (page 241).

~~~

Dried Toasted Vegetable Snack

Slice onions and dry them until they are two-thirds dry. Slice cabbage and dry it until two-thirds dry. Remove onions and cabbage from the dehydrator to a baking sheet, and bake in a preheated 300°F oven until light brown in color and crisp in texture.

This combination makes a tasty snack and can also be added to Vegetable Gorp (page 241).

Temperature Reminder

Meats and Fish 145°F and above
Fruits and Vegetables 130°F to 140°F
Herbs and Flowers 100°F to 110°F

Chapter 5

Fruits and Vegetables: What You Need to Know Before Drying Them

With the key techniques you have learned in Chapter 4 you are now ready to start drying fruits and vegetables. The alphabetical listings that follow will provide you with information on water content, nutritional values, and other pertinent data. Use this as a guide and inspiration for your own creative ideas.

FRUITS

APPLES
84% water
While apples were once native to the Mediterranean area, today there are nearly 7,500 varieties grown worldwide. Apples contain some potassium and vitamin A, but it is their fiber content, most of which is healthful pectin, that is their best asset.

> Recommended Techniques: Slicing
> Peeling (optional)
> Pretreatment: Dipping (optional)

> See *Example: Drying Peeled Dipped Apple Slices* (page 47).

APRICOTS
85% water
Apricots were originally cultivated in China about four thousand

years ago and were brought to the United States from Europe. Once picked, this delicate fruit has a relatively short life span, making it ideal for home drying. Apricots are a very good source of vitamin A, iron, and potassium.

Recommended Techniques:	Slicing
	Peeling (optional)—To loosen skin, steam pitted halved fruit for 5 minutes or dip into boiling water.
Pretreatment:	Dipping (optional)—Soak sliced or quartered pitted fruit in pineapple juice for 20 minutes to minimize discoloration.

Tip: To flatten apricot halves for dehydrating, push out at the back of the pit cavity with your thumb. Halves will take longer to dry than slices.

BANANAS
76% water
Native to both Asia and Africa, bananas are the top-selling fruit in the United States. They are the seedless fruit of a tropical plant of which there are more than one hundred cultivated varieties. A tough, inedible skin protects the fruit from both germs and dust. In addition to providing three valuable vitamins—A, B, and C—bananas are also a good source of potassium and dietary fiber. Banana flour can be used as a milk substitute by those allergic to dairy products.

Recommended Techniques:	Peeling
	Slicing
Pretreatment:	Dipping (optional)

See *Example: To Peel, Slice, and Dry a Banana* (page 32).

Tip: Choose bananas that have brown specks on the peel, indicating that the fruit is ripe and that the sugars have developed. All varieties of bananas, including plantains and finger bananas, can be dried.

BERRIES
Blueberries
83% water
The blueberry is one of the most recently domesticated fruits. In the 1920s, selected varieties of wild blueberries were crossbred to develop the first highbush berries for commercial production. Blueberries are high in fiber and therefore act as an excellent natural laxative. They contain vitamins A and C and a fair amount of potassium.

Recommended Technique: Blanching (optional)

Tip: Before blanching, pick over and discard all moldy, soft, or bruised berries.

Raspberries
81% water
You can home-dry either black or red raspberries. Pick the berries over to remove any moldy or mushy ones.

Recommended Technique: Dry berries, whole

Strawberries
90% water
Choose sweet-smelling, ripe, but still firm berries. Remove the stems and any white, unripened flesh around them.

Recommended Technique: Slicing

CHERRIES
Sour cherries, 84% water; *sweet cherries*, 80% water
Sour cherries contain a significant amount of vitamin A and potassium, as well as vitamin C, iron, and calcium.

Bing cherries are especially tasty when dried. A friend of mine pitted almost one hundred pounds of sweetened cherries, then froze them. Then she thawed and dried them, reserving the juice, which she later used in preserves or fruit leather purees.

One summer I sat out on my porch for two full days, pitting sweet cherries that I had purchased in Door County, Wisconsin. Dried, they filled four gallon jars. A friend of my son's came to our house for an extended stay and liked them so much he polished off all four gallons in a matter of a couple of weeks!

Recommended Technique: Slicing

Tip: Cherries have to be pitted before drying. If you do not have a cherry pitter, steam the cherries for two minutes, which makes it easier to pit them. (I learned this the hard way—after my two-day cherry-pitting marathon on the porch.)

CITRUS FRUITS
Lemons, 90% water; *limes,* 89% water; *tangerines,* 87% water
Citrus fruits, in general, are an excellent source of vitamin C and also contain vitamins A and B plus potassium. Because they have little starch, they do not sweeten after picking. Scrub the outer skins to remove any chemicals or dyes before drying.

Recommended Technique: Slicing

Valencia oranges, 87% water; *Florida oranges,* 73% water
Oranges were cultivated in China for nearly four thousand years before the seeds were brought to America by Christopher Columbus and planted circa 1493. Generally speaking, there are two kinds of oranges: juice oranges and eating oranges. Juice oranges have thin skins and seeds; eating oranges, such as navel oranges, are seedless, pulpy, and good-tasting.

Recommended Techniques: Slicing
                           Peeling (optional)

Citrus Peel
Candied citrus peel can be made with mandarin orange, lemon, lime, grapefruit, tangerine, or tangelo peel. Be sure to scrub all nonorganically grown citrus fruit well to remove as much of the chemical residue on the skin as possible before candying.

Recommended Techniques: Peeling
                           Candying (optional)

Tip: Historically, plain dried orange peel was used as a seasoning, like cinnamon or ginger. To this day, it is frequently used in Chinese cooking.

COCONUT
51% water
Even though you can easily buy shredded coconut in all supermarkets, you should try preparing it at least once yourself. Begin by selecting a coconut in which you can hear the milk sloshing around when you shake it. Poke the three eyes with an icepick and let the milk drain out. Then, cut the coconut into rough pieces, and remove the shell from the meat. Grate the meat on a box grater, or cut it into strips or chunks and dry. Then grate the coconut. It seems like a lot of work for dried shredded coconut, but I think you will like the results. A little dried coconut is very tasty mixed with granola or sprinkled over fruit salad.

Recommended Techniques: Peeling
Slicing

CRANBERRIES
88% water
Cranberries are high in dietary fiber and constitute a good source of vitamin A.

Recommended Techniques: Candying (optional)
Blanching (Checking)

See *Example: To Dry Blanched (Checked) Cranberries* (page 36).

DATES
86% water
Originating in Mesopotamia, the date palm has been cultivated for over five thousand years. Dates can be eaten fresh, although most people are more familiar with dried dates, which are used in baking or eaten out of hand as snacks. Dates are rich in potassium, iron, and other minerals.

Recommended Techniques: Slicing
Candying (optional)

Tip: Dates must be pitted before being dried.

FIGS
78% water

Native to the Mediterranean region, figs, when dried, contain large amounts of sugar, calcium, and iron, and are an excellent source of dietary fiber, potassium, and B vitamins. If allowed to ripen on the tree, figs also become partially dry. The two most available sweet varieties are the Mission fig, purplish-black in color; and the Calimyrna fig, amber in color.

Recommended Techniques:	Slicing
	Candying (optional)
Pretreatment:	Dipping (optional)—Bring 1½ cups pineapple juice to a boil, add 2 cups halved figs, and simmer for 10 minutes.

GRAPES
82% water

Botanically, the grape is a berry. Grapes have been cultivated for at least six thousand years, making them one of the oldest foods. The Romans have taken claim for being the first to grow different varieties of grapes for different purposes, such as winemaking and eating.

Grapes were sun-dried into raisins more than three thousand years ago in the Middle East, but it wasn't until 1873, following a severe heat wave that struck the San Joaquin Valley, that raisins were "discovered" in California. Due to soaring temperatures in the valley, most of the grapes shriveled on the vines. An enterprising farmer nonetheless took his ruined crop to San Francisco, where the dried grapes were sold as "Peruvian Delicacies" and became a popular snack food.

Choose seedless varieties, including the Black Corinth or Champagne grape and the Thompson grape, for home-drying. Wild grapes can also be dehydrated. Red Malaga grapes dry on the vine and are considered the aristocrat of dried fruit. Dried grapes, commonly known as raisins, contain significant amounts of iron, potassium, phosphorus, and calcium.

Recommended Technique:	Dry grapes whole
Pretreatment:	Blanching

KIWIFRUIT
84% water

Native to New Zealand, with small edible black seeds in translucent lime-green flesh, kiwis are high in vitamin A and have twice the potassium of bananas. A 3-ounce kiwi provides twice the recommended daily requirement of vitamin C for an adult. High in fiber and low in calories (about 45 per fruit), kiwis also contain no cholesterol or sodium. It is the high acidity in kiwis that allows them to retain their magnificent color when sliced. Lastly, kiwi contains an enzyme that prevents gelatin from setting and makes it a good meat tenderizer. There is a lot to recommend kiwifruit!

Recommended Techniques: Slicing
Candying (optional)

Tip: To remove the brown peel on a kiwi, use a sharp paring knife. Pare off the peel carefully, removing as little of the flesh as possible.

MANGOES
82% water

Nearly 80 percent of the world's crop of mangoes still comes from India, where the fruit has been grown for thousands of years. In the nineteenth century, mangoes, the fruit of an evergreen tree, began to be cultivated in southern Florida. Mangoes contain potassium, calcium, and magnesium as well as significant amounts of vitamins A and C.

Underripe, ripe, and overripe mangoes can be home-dried; overripe mangoes are best turned into puree for drying into leather. Ideally, select mangoes that give slightly to the touch, but are not soft or mushy.

The challenge of dehydrating mangoes comes in peeling and pitting them. I recommend two methods:

Method Number 1: Quarter the mango to the pit, leaving the flesh still attached. Peel off the skin on one quarter. With a potato peeler, cut the flesh off the pit in thin strips. Skin and cut the remaining quarters in the same manner until you work your way to the pit. **Method Number 2:** Stand the mango upright on end. With a sharp knife, starting at the top, cut the peel and flesh off the pit in 4 sections—front, back, and both sides. Remove the peel from all mango pieces and scrape remaining flesh off the

Dried Fruit Powders and Sugars

Put dried fruits, such as papaya, apricot, fig, prune, apple, and date pieces, in the freezer and then pulverize the frozen pieces in a blender. Use the powder, as is, in the ways suggested below. Or, for a sweeter treat, add an equal part of raw, white, or brown sugar to the powder in the blender and combine.

Single fruits or dried fruit combinations make splendid powder and/or sugar; just be sure that the fruit you pulverize is dried as hard as possible. Know, too, that the fruit sugars you make from home-dried fruits will not dissolve as fast as commercially made fruit sugars.

How to Use Fruit Powders and Sugars:

- Sprinkle over ice cream or frozen or fresh yogurt.
- Blend with yogurt to make fruit roll-ups.
- Add to fruit salads as a sweetener instead of raisins and/or coconut.
- Use to flavor jellies and jams; in puddings; in breads, cakes, and cookies.
- Enliven cream cheese frosting: Combine 3 ounces softened cream cheese with 1 cup confectioners' sugar, 1 tablespoon milk, 1 tablespoon dried fruit powder, and ½ teaspoon vanilla, and beat until fluffy.

pit with the knife. The flesh that turns to mush should be dried as a leather on a lightly oiled solid leather sheet.

Recommended Techniques: Slicing
                                           Candying (optional)

MELONS
Honeydew, casaba, and *muskmelon,* 92% water; *Crenshaw* and *cantaloupe,* 91% water; for information on *watermelon,* see page 63.

If you grow your own melons, harvest them when the stem ends separate easily from the fruit. When purchasing melons in the market, look for ones that are heavy and smell fragrant. Cantaloupes are high in vitamin A in addition to vitamin C and potassium.

Recommended Techniques: Peeling
                                           Slicing

NECTARINES
82% water
These beautifully colored orbs are high in vitamin A and potassium. A properly ripened nectarine should not be too soft to the touch.

Recommended Techniques: Slicing
                                           Peeling (optional)
Pretreatment: Dipping

PAPAYAS
89% water
Originating in the Caribbean region, papayas are now grown in several tropical countries, including Costa Rica, Nicaragua, and Mexico. Papayas are very rich in vitamins A and C and also contain potassium. A ripe papaya should give slightly to the touch; if you intend to candy papaya, select firm ones only.

Recommended Techniques: Peeling
                                           Slicing
                                           Candying (optional)
Pretreatment: Dipping

Tip: Be sure to remove all the black seeds and any stringy flesh before slicing.

PEACHES
89% water
It has been said that the first peach was cultivated in China, where it is the symbol of immortality. In the United States, peaches are grown in many states, including Georgia.

Peaches contain niacin, potassium, and a fair amount of vitamin A. All varieties dry well. Select peaches that give slightly to the touch for home drying, and if they are bruised, simply cut out the affected areas.

Recommended Techniques: Slicing
                                           Peeling (optional)
Pretreatment: Dipping

PEARS
83% water
The origin of the pear remains a mystery, but its supply of vitamins A and C is well documented. Pears also contain fiber and potassium. Bartlett (including the Red), Anjou, and Bosc pears are popular varieties that dry well. Harvest pears when they are still green in color and firm. The fruit does not ripen properly on the tree. When ripe, a pear should give slightly to gentle pressure. To ripen store-brought pears, place in a plastic bag and leave at room temperature for 2 or 3 days.

Recommended Techniques: Peeling (optional)
                                             Slicing
                                           Candying (optional)
Pretreatment: Dipping

Tip: To core a pear, cut off the bottom and top of the fruit. Stand the pear upright and cut into quarters. Cut out the core section on each quarter with a small knife.

See *Example: To Dry a Dipped Sliced Pear* (page 35).

PINEAPPLES
85% water
The only difficult part of drying a pineapple is finding one that is sufficiently ripe in the market! To select a good-for-drying

pineapple, seek out one with a yellow-golden color, especially around the bottom of the base. Pull a leaf from inside the top cluster: If it pulls out easily and feels moist, the chances are high that you have chosen a ripe fruit. It should also smell sweet. You want a juicy pineapple, but beware of very soft places in the flesh, which indicate that the fruit is overripe. You can also sometimes smell a musty, fermenting odor. Overripe pineapples, I hasten to add, can still be used to make delicious leather.

Recommended Techniques: Slicing
                                    Peeling
                                    Candying (optional)

Tip: See page 47 for ideas on peeling and coring.

PLUMS
80% water
There are over one hundred varieties of plum, ranging in size from a cherry to a nectarine, and they come in beautiful shades of red, green, and purple. All are good for drying. When dried, the prune plum—and that really is its name—is called a prune. Dried plums are a good source of fiber and vitamin A.

Recommended Technique: Slicing

Tip: Like peaches and nectarines, plums must be pitted before being dried.

RHUBARB
95% water
A vegetable, rhubarb nonetheless is generally thought of and used as a fruit. The pretreatment of blanching helps to eliminate some of the acidity in the stalks, which, in turn, means that the dried product will need less sweetener.

Select young tender stalks for drying; the older ones have lost much of their flavor. To prepare rhubarb for pretreating, remove all leaves—they are toxic—and woody ends of the stalks, and cut the stalks into ½-inch pieces. I love rhubarb, and when I've dried as much of it as I can, I pulverize it into powder to use in fruit punches and leathers.

Recommended Technique: Slicing
Pretreatment: Blanching

WATERMELON
92% water
Because watermelon has essentially no starch reserves before ripening, it cannot get sweeter after picking. Therefore, leave watermelon on the vine as long as possible. A reliable indication of ripeness is a clean break between the melon and the stem end; another one is a hollow rather than sharp sound when you rap or thump the melon on the side with your hand.

Don't forget that melon seeds can also be dried, then toasted.

Recommended Techniques: Slicing
                          Peeling
                          Candying the rind (optional;
                          page 43)

Tip: Because of its high water content, watermelon that is cut into thin slices will be paper-thin when dried. To avoid this, I often cut watermelon into chunks and put it on mesh-sheet–lined dehydrator trays. This results in pieces that will come off the drying trays more easily.

VEGETABLES

ASPARAGUS
92% water
While asparagus was grown by the Greeks and Romans, it wasn't until the late 1700s that this vegetable was cultivated in American gardens. A substantial source of vitamin A and potassium, asparagus has a fair amount of vitamins B and C and iron as well. Select either wild or domesticated edible shoots and spears from the rootstock. Wash, cut off the woody stems, and scrape off any tough skin on the stalks, if necessary. I like to cut the tips off the stalks and dry them separately; the stalks should also be cut into 1-inch pieces. When drying asparagus to pulverize into powder, you can use more of the tough ends of the stalks.

Recommended Techniques: Slicing
                                     Peeling (optional)
Pretreatment: Blanching (optional)

Tip: For water-boil blanching, allow 3 to 5 minutes; for steam-blanching, allow 5 minutes.

BEANS

90% water

There are many varieties of fresh beans, including green, string, snap, and purple beans, and many of them are high in protein, vitamin A, and potassium, with smaller amounts of calcium and vitamin C. Beans are easy to grow, easy to store, and easy to dry. Fresh beans should snap when you bend them. Harvest beans when the seeds in the pods are immature and still succulent. In some instances, both the seeds and the pods are edible. When buying beans in the market, avoid any that have rust marks or are limp, bulging, or blemished. To prepare beans for drying, snip off the stem ends, string if necessary, and cut into ½- to 1-inch pieces.

Navy, kidney, pinto, red, butter, and Great Northern beans dry on the vine. (The water content in each of these beans is naturally lower; lima beans, for example, contain only 68 percent water.) When the plants and the pods are dry and shriveled, pluck off the pods, open them, and shell the dried beans. To ensure that the beans are completely dry, you may need to put them in the dehydrator.

Recommended Technique: Slicing (fresh beans)
Pretreatment: Blanching

Tip: Steam-blanch cut fresh beans for 3 to 5 minutes.

BEETS

87% water

Beets are high in iron, contain more sugar than any other vegetable, and are a rich source of potassium. They are noted more for their laxative value than for the nutrients they provide.

Dried beet powder can be used as a natural food coloring. Another use for the powder: Add it to a mixture of water and sugar, and use it in hummingbird feeders.

Recommended Techniques: Cooking or Baking
Slicing

Tip: Depending upon the size of the beets, cooking time may range from 15 minutes to 1 hour. The beets are done when they are fork-tender.

BEET GREENS
See Greens, page 71.

BROCCOLI
89% water
Broccoli, as we know it, was first cultivated in Italy and was not grown in the United States until the early 1900s. Broccoli, a relative of cauliflower, is high in vitamins A and C and is a good source of potassium, niacin, iron, calcium, and dietary fiber. It contains about 5 grams of protein per cup. Broccoli is also noted for its anticarcinogenic properties.

Because homegrown broccoli (and cauliflower) can have worms, soak the head for 30 minutes in a solution of 1 part salt to 4 parts water, which will force any worms in the vegetable to float to the surface.

To prepare for drying, trim the broccoli head, remove any yellow bud clusters, and cut the florets from the stems. If desired, peel the tough outer skin from the stems with a vegetable peeler and cut the stems crosswise into ½-inch pieces. Blanch the stems before drying (see Tip). Dry the florets and the stems separately. Broccoli leaves can also be dried, then pulverized and used as a flavoring agent, much like celery powder.

Recommended Techniques: Slicing
Peeling (optional)
Pretreatment: Blanching

Tip: Water-boil blanch broccoli stems for 2 to 3 minutes; or steam-blanch for 3 to 5 minutes.

BRUSSELS SPROUTS
85% water
This member of the cabbage family originated in Brussels, Belgium, in the thirteenth century. Brussels sprouts are a rich source of vitamins A and C and provide significant amounts of potas-

sium, protein, and iron. If you are harvesting your own crop, remove solid, firm heads from the base of the plant first, then work your way up the stalk. To prepare for drying, remove any outer yellow or brown leaves and tough stems.

Recommended Technique: Slicing
Pretreatment: Blanching

Tip: Water-boil blanch sliced sprouts for 2 to 4 minutes; or steam-blanch for 4 to 6 minutes.

CABBAGES
92% water
Cabbage, green or red or Savoy, is one of the oldest known cultivated vegetables, with present varieties believed to have originated in Italy. Cabbage in general, and Chinese cabbage in particular, are very high in vitamin A and also contain vitamin C and potassium.

Select firm, heavy heads for home drying. Trim off any tough outer leaves and cut away the thick core and ribs.

Recommended Techniques: Dipping
                          Slicing
Pretreatment: Blanching

Tips: Dip sliced cabbage in lemon juice for 5 to 10 minutes to retain a light color for drying.

Shred leaves instead of slicing them and steam-blanch for 2 minutes. Or trim heads, cut them into chunks, and steam-blanch for 3 minutes.

CARROTS
88% water
Native to Afghanistan, carrots were used by the Greeks and Romans for medicinal purposes, which should not be surprising in that they are extremely nourishing, rich in vitamin A, and have a good supply of minerals and potassium.

Do not use old or woody carrots for drying. To prepare, cut off the ends. Depending upon how you intend to use the carrots when dried, peel, dip, or cut them into slices or even shred them. Shredded dried carrots are good for baking (see Carrot Cake with Cream Cheese Frosting, page 222) and are a suitable substitute for shredded dried coconut. Use a food processor fitted with a shredding blade to make quick, clean work of shredding them.

Recommended Techniques: Peeling (optional)
                                   Slicing
Pretreatments: Dipping (optional)
                                   Blanching (optional)

Tip: Steam-blanch small pieces of carrots for 3 minutes; larger pieces for 5 to 7 minutes.

CAULIFLOWER
91% water

Related to broccoli, cauliflower is noted for its anticancer properties. Cultivated in the United States since the seventeenth century, cauliflower contains significant amounts of vitamin C and potassium.

As with broccoli, check homegrown cauliflower for worms and, if necessary, soak the head to force them out as described on page 65.

The cluster of buds on a cauliflower is called the curd. Remove any discolored parts from the curd, and on the leaves and stems. Trim the florets from the stems and cut them into ½-inch slices.

Recommended Technique: Slicing
Pretreatments: Blanching
                                   Dipping (optional)

Tips: Water-boil blanch florets for 3 to 4 minutes; or steam-blanch for 4 to 5 minutes. Then dip florets in lemon juice for 5 to 10 minutes to set the color.

Dry the stems and pulverize them into powder; use for flavoring.

CELERY
94% water

Celery did not become a table vegetable until the Middle Ages. Because celery has a very high sodium content, when it is dried and pulverized into powder, it can be a natural substitute for salt. As dieters know, celery is extremely low in calories.

Both the stalks and leaves can be dried. Cut off any limp,

yellowing, or damaged parts on the stalks in preparation for drying. Then rinse and cut into pieces. When drying celery to be used in soups or main courses, choose stalks that snap when they are bent. If celery is beginning to go limp but is still edible, trim it and dry it to pulverize into powder.

Recommended Technique: Slicing
Pretreatment: Blanching

Tip: Water-boil blanch small pieces for 1 to 2 minutes, or until the color changes.

COLLARD GREENS
See Greens, page 71.

CORN
73% water
Corn is one of the most commonly dried foods. Over the years I have met many people who can remember their grandmother, aunt, or mother drying corn on a woodstove drier. My own Grandmother Bell dried corn in the attic, along with apples and pumpkin, and my father remembers stirring the corn as it dried.

As for the way old-timers used to dry corn, here is how *Cooking on the Frontier*, an 1877 Buckeye cookery book, recommended doing it: "Cut it from the cob and dry without preliminary treatment." The corn was then spread in a large pan lined with "flour-sack paper," put into a moderate oven for 15 to 20 minutes, and stirred frequently. Then it was dried some more on a cloth-covered table in the sunshine, brought in before sunset, and the next day, the process was repeated all over again. The corn, the book reads, "will be thoroughly dried on the evening of the second day, and when shaken will rattle." As lovely as this recounting is, I have to think of how easy it is to dry corn with the modern-day convenience of an electric food dehydrator.

Another nineteenth-century source advocates first boiling the ears for two minutes "to harden the milk," then cutting the kernels from the cob, setting the kernels on a cloth spread over a "baking board," and putting the board in the oven or the sun to dry. To reconstitute the corn, it was "soaked overnight in a bowl of water." The more things change, the more they remain the same.

The yellow variety that many Americans call "sweet corn" is

an excellent source of vitamin A, potassium, and other minerals. In addition to dietary fiber, corn contains some vitamin C and protein. It is one of the most cultivated plants in the world. All types of corn can be dried; sweet and field corn can be dried until hard, then pulverized into cornmeal. Degerminated cornmeal means that the kernels have been processed for the removal of the germ, corn oil, and protein casing. Home-ground dried corn has significantly more taste than commercially processed cornmeal.

Different names are given to the degrees dried corn is ground: "Corn flour" is a fine grind; "grits" are kernels, with the bran and germ removed, ground to a granular size bigger than cornmeal.

To dry corn, harvest it when the silk at the tip of the husks is brown. Remove the husks and silk, reserving it, if desired, as it too can be dried, then pulverize and use as a flavoring in soups or pasta dough. Cut any damaged kernels off the cobs. It is easier to cut cooked corn off the cob than uncooked; however, if you stand an uncooked cob on end and cut straight down on the kernels with a sharp knife or a corn cutter, the kernels do come off.

Begin the drying process as soon as possible after the corn has been picked, before the sugar in the kernels converts to starch.

Recommended Technique: Peeling (husking)
Pretreatment: Blanching (optional)

Tip: Steam-blanch kernels for 3 to 5 minutes; or water-boil blanch whole small ears for 7 minutes, medium-sized ears for 9 minutes, and large ears for 11 minutes.

What Is Hominy?

When people at home shows see my home-dried corn kernels and cornmeal, they invariably ask me about hominy. Hominy is the hulled kernel of corn with the germ removed. Hominy can be served whole, or can be ground into—what else?—grits.

CUCUMBERS

95% water

Strictly speaking, cucumbers are fruit. An ancient plant that originated in southwestern Asia, where cultivated seeds nearly twelve thousand years old have been found, the cucumber is low in calories but also quite low in nutrients. Cucumbers do contain some vitamin A, iron, potassium, and fiber.

When dried, cucumber skin becomes tough and bitter; therefore, peeling is recommended. Seed cucumbers to produce a better, more tender dried product.

Recommended Techniques: Peeling
                                  Slicing
                                  Seeding
Pretreatment: Dipping

Tips: Dip in lemon juice to prevent cucumber from darkening. Pickles, both sweet and dill, make interesting and delicious snacks. To dry pickles, cut them into long, thin strips or slices. Add to Vegetable Gorp (page 241).

EGGPLANT

92% water

Botanically, eggplant is a berry native to India, but it is Thomas Jefferson who is credited with bringing this unique plant to this country. The eggplant's best feature is its high protein content, although it also contains some potassium, iron, and protein.

Select firm eggplants for drying. Seedy, fleshy ones are less desirable than meatier ones. Trim off both ends, peel—reserving peel, if desired, for drying—and remove any bruised or dark brown spots on the flesh. Once cut, eggplant turns dark very quickly. To prevent discoloration, dip the slices (see Tips below).

Recommended Techniques: Peeling (optional)
                                    Slicing
Pretreatment: Dipping

Tips: Dip sliced eggplant into lemon juice or steam slices for 3 to 5 minutes.

If desired, dry eggplant peel separately from the slices, pulverize the dried peel and use the powder to flavor and color fresh pasta or noodle dough.

ENDIVE
See Greens.

GREENS
In general, greens, including different lettuces, spinach, Swiss chard, beet greens, and so on, contain about 92% water; some lettuce, 95%; spinach and Swiss chard, 91%.

Lettuce is America's most popular uncooked vegetable. All varieties are high in dietary fiber. Romaine and loose-leaf lettuces offer more vitamin A and calcium than does the ubiquitous iceberg lettuce. Butterhead lettuce also contains more iron than iceberg lettuce.

Beet greens are high in vitamins A and C and calcium; collard greens are a superior source of vitamins A and B, with large amounts of calcium, phosphorus, and other minerals.

Select young and tender greens, be they turnip greens, mustard greens, or kale. Wash them thoroughly to remove all dirt and insects and discard any wilted areas. Remove tough, fibrous leaves and stems, and remove the midrib by folding each leaf in half lengthwise and cutting it out. If desired, stems and veins can be dried and pulverized.

When dried greens, spinach in particular, are rehydrated and cooked, they are indistinguishable from fresh cooked greens.

Pretreatment: Blanching

Tip: Blanch bitter-tasting greens in either water or beef bouillon for 2 minutes to tone down their sharp flavor. Blanching renders leaves limp, making it harder to spread them evenly on drying trays.

JERUSALEM ARTICHOKES
80% water

The Jerusalem artichoke, a member of the sunflower family, is an edible tuber that resembles a small potato and is native to American Indian cultures.

To prepare them for drying, rinse the artichokes, then cut them in half. Once cut, Jerusalem artichokes discolor.

Recommended Technique: Slicing
Pretreatments: Blanching (optional)
                                        Dipping

Tip: Blanch halved Jerusalem artichokes for 10 minutes. If you plan to pulverize the dried artichoke, no blanching is needed.

KALE
See Greens, page 71.

KOHLRABI
90% water
Kohlrabi, which is German for "cabbage turnip," is high in potassium and vitamin C. This globe-shaped green or purple vegetable, a member of the cabbage family, is formed as a swelling at the base of the plant.

To prepare for drying, remove leaves and stem. No peeling is required.

Recommended Techniques: Slicing
                                        Cooking or Baking
Pretreatments: Dipping (optional)
                                        Blanching

Tip: To blanch, either water-boil blanch cubed kohlrabi for 3 to 5 minutes, or steam-blanch for 5 to 8 minutes.

MUSHROOMS
90% water
Botanically, mushrooms are one of the simplest plants, with no roots and no leaves; they produce no flowers or seeds and rely on spores to reproduce.

If you are gathering wild mushrooms for drying, it goes without saying that you should pick only those you are able to identify or know as edible. Mushrooms, in general, are easy to dry, have a long shelf life once dried, and rehydrate very well.

You can dry store-bought white button mushrooms, morels, puffballs, and, my favorite of all, shiitakes. Clean all mushrooms, especially morels, which tend to harbor sand, debris, and insects. Remove the stems. Slice the caps, and dry the sliced caps and stems separately.

Recommended Technique: Slicing

Growing Shiitake Mushrooms at the Forest Resource Center

I credit my interest and love for shiitake mushrooms to my husband. After he studied forestry in Germany, he returned to this country to devote his time and energy to creating an organization called the Forest Resource Center in Lanesboro, Minnesota. The FRC, as we refer to it, manages the surrounding forest, and provides demonstration areas, like living classrooms, that offer information on land management, management options, alternative agricultural crops, and environmental education. One such demonstration is growing shiitake mushrooms.

Established in 1983, the shiitake demonstration project is designed to encourage woodland owners to make profitable use of previously unused trees by using them for shiitake cultivation. Hardwood logs, in particular oak, ironwood, birch, and hard maple—all abundant in the area's forests—provide the host medium for growing shiitakes. The way it works is this: Logs are cut into approximately 40-inch lengths, and holes are then drilled in the logs. The holes are filled with shiitake spawn and covered with hot wax. The logs are then stacked for several months, during which time the mushrooms colonize within the logs. To encourage the fruiting of the mushrooms, the logs are soaked in water for one to two days, restacked, and then the mushrooms emerge from the host logs. Logs oftentimes produce up to seven separate mushroom crops.

Over the last ten years, the FRC has researched, collected, and published information on shiitake production and management techniques. As a result, the FRC has become one of the few U.S. research centers for the cultivation of shiitake mushrooms on hardwood logs.

OKRA
89% water
These tapered edible seed pods came to the United States from Africa, and became renowned the world over as an intrinsic ingredient in gumbo—one of the great regional dishes of the American South. Okra contains fiber and substantial amounts of vitamin A, potassium, and calcium.

Select small, young, tender pods. Trim off stem ends and tips, then slice.

Recommended Technique: Slicing
Pretreatment: Blanching

Tip: Water-boil blanch for 2 to 3 minutes, or steam-blanch for 4 to 5 minutes.

ONIONS
88% water
There are many types of onions—yellow, red, and white—and all vary in shape, size, weight, and aroma. Other members of the onion family are scallions (also called green or spring onions), shallots, and leeks. Both bunching and bulb onions can be dried.

To prepare for drying, trim off top and bottom ends. Remove outer papery skin by hand or drop onions in boiling water for 1 minute to loosen skin. If the onions you are drying have a strong smell, put the dehydrator in an out-of-the-way place.

Recommended Techniques: Peeling
Slicing

Tip: For a great snack combination, see Dried Toasted Vegetable Snack (page 50).

PARSNIPS
79% water
This edible root, so good in soups and stews, resembles a carrot in appearance. Parsnips contain a good deal of potassium and smaller amounts of protein, iron, and calcium. Nutritional aspects aside, during medieval times the parsnip was believed to be an aphrodisiac.

If you are growing parsnips yourself, harvest them in the fall, after the first freeze. It is the effect of the cold temperature that helps convert the starch in the root to sugar. If buying parsnips, avoid soft and woody ones. Should the core be woody, cut it away.

Recommended Techniques: Peeling (optional)
                                     Slicing
Pretreatment: Dipping

Tip: Use lemon juice for dipping the slices.

PEAS

78% water

Peas are a fair source of vitamin A. One pound of fresh peas in the pod generally equals 1 cup shelled peas.

While both seeds (the peas) and certain edible pods can be dried, the pods, such as sugar snaps, will lose some of their crispness once dehydrated.

Recommended Technique: Peeling (shelling)
Pretreatment: Blanching

Tip: Steam-blanch shelled peas for 3 minutes.

PEPPERS

Generally, peppers contain about 93% water.

Peppers—including bell peppers, hot or chili peppers, and banana peppers—contain vitamins A and C. The above-mentioned varieties and more can be very successfully dried.

Select peppers that have bright skins for drying. If you are drying peppers whole, puncture the skin to allow dry air to get inside. If you are cutting peppers, remove the cores and seeds. When preparing hot peppers you can moderate some of their "heat" by removing the white membranes and veins, seeds, and stems. When handling hot peppers, it is a good idea to wear gloves to protect your hands and avoid touching your face, especially your eyes and lips. If you do burn your hands when working with hot peppers, you can neutralize the sting by washing your hands with milk.

The world over, peppers are commonly air-dried. Whole peppers are simply strung together without touching and left to hang in a well-ventilated place. It is important that the string go through the stem and not penetrate the flesh.

Recommended Technique: Slicing

Tip: If you bite into a hot pepper, eat some bread or yogurt or rice. Don't drink water; it only fuels the heat.

POTATOES
80% water
This edible tuber has a high carbohydrate content. Low-starch potatoes yield the best dried product. To determine starch content, rub two potato halves together. If they stick, the starch content is high. Remember that old potatoes have more starch and absorb flavors more easily; new potatoes, therefore, dry better because they are lower in starch.

Mealy potatoes, in which the cells separate from each other when baked or mashed, contain more starch than waxy potatoes, which have moist, cohesive tissues. To tell them apart, put one potato type in a brine of 1 part salt to 11 parts water. The waxy potato will float, the mealy, more dense potato will sink.

To prepare potatoes for drying, it is important after washing and peeling them to remove any green-tinged flesh, as it will turn dark when dried. Potatoes can be sliced, cubed, or cut into shoestring strips for drying. Water-boil blanch cut potatoes only until the color changes, 3 to 5 minutes; the pieces should still be firm and hold together. Cool, then dip blanched potatoes in a solution of ¼ cup lemon juice and ¾ cup water.

Recommended Techniques: Peeling
                            Slicing
Pretreatments: Blanching
                            Dipping (optional)

Tip: You can also steam-blanch sliced potatoes for 5 to 7 minutes; or bake them with the skins on, slice, and then dip before drying. Mashed potatoes can also be dried on leather sheets.

PUMPKINS
92% water
Botanically, pumpkins are berries and a good source of vitamin A. Dry all varieties, no matter the size or shape. Cut the pumpkin in half, peel, remove the seeds and strings, and bake the flesh, cut into 1-inch strips, in a preheated 300°F oven until soft.

Recommended Techniques: Peeling
                                          Slicing
                                          Cooking or Baking
Pretreatment: Blanching (optional)

Tips: To dry pumpkin seeds, wash, then dry them in the dehydrator on mesh sheets until hard. When dried, sauté 1 cup seeds in 1 tablespoon vegetable oil over low heat until slightly colored. Sprinkle with ½ teaspoon salt.

Seeds to be used for sprouting must be dried at temperatures below 90°F.

RADISHES
95% water
Radishes, including daikon (white Oriental radish) and black and red radishes, can all be dried. There is no need to peel them. Trim off tops and bottoms, and cut radishes into slices before drying.

Recommended Technique: Slicing

RUTABAGAS
87% water
A large root, a rutabaga is sometimes called a Swedish turnip. Store-bought rutabagas are often coated in an edible vegetable wax to prevent loss of moisture.

To dry, first peel, then cut rutabagas into slices or cubes.

Recommended Techniques: Peeling
                                          Slicing
Pretreatment: Dipping (optional)
                                          Blanching

Tip: Water-boil blanch for 2 to 3 minutes; or steam-blanch for 5 minutes.

You can also bake rutabagas to soften the flesh, then mash and dry on oiled solid leather sheets.

SPINACH
See Greens, page 71.

SQUASH

81% water

Any hard-rind squash can be dried, including Hubbard, acorn, butternut, and buttercup.

To dry, peel the squash, halve it, then remove the stringy pulp and large seeds. Cut, chop, or grate the flesh.

Recommended Techniques: Peeling
                         Slicing
                         Cooking or Baking
Pretreatment: Blanching

Tip: Steam-blanch pieces for 5 to 8 minutes. Or bake in a pre-heated 300°F oven until just tender and/or dip in lemon juice to prevent darkening.

SWEET POTATOES

74% water

Because sweet potatoes and yams are both tubers, they are frequently grouped together, although technically they are not of the same family. The sweet potato, in fact, is a member of the morning glory family and is native to Central America. A good source of vitamins A and C, sweet potatoes contain less protein than white potatoes.

Christopher Columbus took the sweet potato back to Europe after his first voyage to the New World. By the end of the fifteenth century, the sweet potato was established in China and the Philippines. Now it is cultivated in most subtropical areas of the world.

To ready for drying, wash the sweet potatoes, then bake until softened but still firm to the touch in a 300°F oven. Let cool, peel, and slice.

Recommended Techniques: Baking
                         Peeling
                         Slicing
Pretreatment: Dipping (optional)

Tip: Steam-blanch peeled, uncooked slices for 8 to 10 minutes, then dip the slices in lemon juice to retain color.

SWISS CHARD
See Greens, page 71.

TOMATOES
90% water

Given the amount of information about tomatoes in this book and the frequent use I make of them in recipes, suffice it to say that they are superb dried. For specific information on tomatoes, see pages 31, 37, 45, 49, 132–135.

Recommended Techniques: Peeling (optional)
Slicing
Seeding (optional)

TURNIPS
88% water

Turnips should be topped, washed, and peeled before being dried. Then cut them into slices or cubes and dip to prevent discoloration.

Recommended Techniques: Peeling
Slicing
Pretreatment: Dipping (optional)
Blanching

Tips: Use lemon juice for dipping.

Steam-blanch small pieces of turnip for 2 to 3 minutes; larger pieces for 5 to 7 minutes.

Don't throw out the greens; they are wonderful dried and used in soups.

ZUCCHINI
94% water

While the word "zucchini" means "little squash" in Italian, it is considered an American plant and can grow to sizes that are anything but little!

Before drying, peel and remove the seeds of zucchini that are larger than 1 foot long. For smaller zucchini, simply wash the outer skin well before slicing.

Recommended Techniques: Peeling (optional)
Slicing
Pretreatment: Dipping (optional)

Tip: Use lemon juice for dipping to retain a lightness in color.

Vegetable Powders

If you are on a reduced-sodium or salt-free diet, you are undoubtedly aware of ways of adding flavor to foods without using salt. Let pulverized dried vegetables, or powder, provide another wonderful taste-enchancing possibility. Celery powder, for one, is super on a baked potato, and will perk up an omelet or a sauce very nicely, too. It is nothing short of heavenly sprinkled over sliced garden-fresh tomatoes.

Key Technique 8: To Pulverize Dried Vegetables to Powder

Example: Dried Celery Powder

1. Cut and discard the root end of celery stalks, then cut them, including the leafy sections, into ½-inch pieces.
2. Arrange the pieces in a single layer on a drying tray lined with a mesh sheet. Dry until hard. (Celery contains about 94 percent water, so don't be surprised at how small the pieces of celery are—how much they have shrunk—when dried.)
3. Pulverize the dried celery in a blender to the desired consistency—powder, flakes, or chunks. When grinding it, do not forget to inhale its delicious aroma!
4. Store the powder in an airtight container and label and date the jar.
5. Make your own celery salt by combining equal parts celery powder and table or low-sodium salt.

A Versatile Broth

~~~

Powerful Vegetable Powder Broth

Now that you have an array of dried vegetable powders on hand, here is a recipe that combines no less than seven of them. Use a tablespoon of this to enhance a soup base or to flavor a sauce.

1 teaspoon dried onion powder
1 teaspoon dried celery powder
1 teaspoon dried tomato powder
1 teaspoon dried spinach powder
1 teaspoon dried cornmeal
1 teaspoon dried bell pepper powder
1 teaspoon dried carrot powder
½ teaspoon dried parsley
½ teaspoon cayenne pepper
½ teaspoon all-purpose flour
½ teaspoon chopped dried garlic
Boiling water as needed

Combine all the ingredients. For each cup of boiling water, allow 1 tablespoon vegetable powder.

Makes 3 tablespoons, rendering 3 cups broth

Nutritional Variation: To each cup of vegetable broth, stir in 1 tablespoon nutritional yeast, 1 teaspoon wheat germ, and 1 teaspoon ground nuts or seeds.

Chapter 6

Drying Meats and Fish

Over many years of demonstrating food dehydrators at home shows and county and state fairs, I have noticed that the men in the crowd invariably begin to drift away when I start talking about drying fruits and vegetables, but when I mention the word "jerky," their eyes light up and they stay right where they are. They are the first takers when a tray of samples appears. Jerky—by definition, raw meat that has been seasoned with spices or marinated, then dried—seems to be a favorite with not only the men but the whole family. You can make *great* jerky in a food dehydrator.

Drying meats is a long-standing tradition for many peoples the world over, including Native Americans who dried meat by suspending it above a fire so that the smoke (dry air) rising from the fire could penetrate it, thus removing the water. The smoke not only provided flavor, but kept animals away from the raw meat. For the Indians, smoke was an environmental drying tool. Today, interestingly, people add liquid smoke to marinades for its flavor.

According to the book *Buffalo Bird Woman's Garden*, Native Americans also used the ashes from burned corn cobs to flavor meat that was being dried as well as for corn and bean dishes. Evidence that these ashes were used a very long time ago has been found in several archeological digs of the Oneota Indian culture in La Crosse, Wisconsin.

There are great differences, however, between making your own flavored dried meat, better known as jerky, and buying the commercially made kind. To begin with, check the label on the packaged jerky and note the number of added chemicals and preservatives. Your homemade version will have none of these. Nor will your homemade jerky cost the same per ounce as the commercial kind. To make jerky at home, figure 3 pounds of meat for a total of $9, plus 1 bottle of teriyaki marinade and sauce for about $1, plus a few cents' worth of electricity to run your food dehydrator. That comes to about twenty-one cents an ounce. Commercially made jerky generally costs $1 to $2 per 1-ounce package.

Dried meat is not only economical, it is also rich in protein and light in weight, making it an important staple for campers, backpackers, hunters, and travelers to take in their food packs. Most fresh meat contains 60 to 70 percent water; when dried, it contains 5 to 10 percent water. Figure, therefore, that meat reduces to about one third its original weight and volume when dried.

Once you make jerky, whether with meat—ground or in strips—or poultry, or dry fish, I am certain that it will become a staple in your house as it has in mine. In fact, I have to hide jerky if I want it to last to our next backpacking trip!

WHAT CAN BE DRIED INTO JERKY?

In considering what you want to dry into jerky, the most important factor is leanness: As a general rule, the leaner the meat, poultry, or fish, the better. You can use the fresh, frozen, or canned version of any of the categories that follow, remembering that if you go with a frozen item, it must be thawed before you season and/or dry it.

Beef: Any lean cut of beef—round steak, sirloin tip, rump roast, and even ground beef—can be dried into jerky. The beef can even be marbled, but all fat, gristle, and connective tissue must be removed before drying, thereby minimizing any rancidity arising from fat remaining on the dried meat.

Poultry: All poultry—including chicken, turkey, or Cornish game hens—can be dried into jerky. Be sure that the poultry is fully skinned and boned and that all filmy membrane tissue is removed. Because of the risk of salmonella, all poultry must be precooked before being dried into jerky.

Game: Lean meats, such as deer, elk, and moose, make great jerky, and even though venison is commonly used for making sausages, it too makes wonderful jerky. Fatty wild game, like bear, must be precooked to an internal temperature of 170°F before being dehydrated into jerky. The risk of drying wild game into jerky is that of trichinosis, a disease caused by eating undercooked parasite-infested meat.

Fish: Freshwater fish that are lean—sunfish, crappies, perch, walleyes, and bass—dry easily. Similarly, low-fat saltwater fish, such as sole, flounder, halibut, pollock, and rock cod, are ideal for making into jerky. Even smoked salmon can be dried.

Canned tuna, preferably packed in water, is also eminently dryable. See page 141 for the procedure. Canned salmon, too, although naturally higher in fat than tuna, can be dried.

Shellfish: Shrimp, lobsters, crabs are low in fat and can be dried. Each, however, must be precooked before drying.

Packaged luncheon meats: Pepperoni, hard Italian salami, and plain salami can all be dried. When drying other luncheon meats, remember that some of them, like packaged ham or pastrami, are high in fat content.

BEFORE MAKING JERKY: PREPARATION AND PRETREATMENTS

If you are making meat, poultry, or game jerky, begin by trimming the meat very well. Then cut it into strips or slices as directed in the recipe you are using. As a rule, semifrozen meat, poultry, or game is easier to slice than fully thawed meat.

If you are drying fish, clean it properly, remove all skin and bones and rinse thoroughly to wash off all blood. Cut fillets into 1-inch wide strips. If the fillet is thicker than ½ inch, make slashes across the flesh to allow the salt or marinade to penetrate.

Pretreat meat, poultry, or game for jerky by marinating and/or cooking it. The reason to marinate meat before drying it into jerky is twofold: to impart flavor and to tenderize it. Most marinades include some type of salt; it is the salt that helps extract water from meat and fish, thereby helping to preserve it. Marinades made with certain acids—wine, vinegar, or lemon juice—actually break down the tissues in the meat. Marinades also help to eliminate some of the "gaminess" in the taste of certain meats.

The reason to cook meats and fish before drying them into jerky is to ensure safety. Poultry *must* be pretreated before being dried into jerky, but any meat can be pretreated. The best cooking methods are steaming or roasting, because neither requires the addition of oil, and both help reduce the fat content in the meat.

According to food-science researchers at the University of Wisconsin, microorganisms are effectively killed when meat reaches 145°F for 45 minutes, or 167°F for 20 minutes, or 200°F for 15 minutes.

Pretreat fish by soaking it in a salt solution or marinating it, and pretreat shellfish by soaking it in a salt solution, then cooking it. If you choose to pretreat fish by cooking it, steam or bake it in a 200°F oven until flaky. Add flavorings during the cooking. If you chill the fish after cooking and before drying, it will be easy to remove any remaining traces of fat, pieces of bone, or skin.

Temperature Reminder

Meats and Fish 145°F and above
Fruits and Vegetables 130°F to 140°F
Herbs and Flowers 100°F to 110°F

Key Technique 9: To Make Jerky

The actual drying process and the word "jerky" came from the Native American culture. In Africa, where meat is also dried, jerky is called *biltong;* both the French and the Spanish refer to jerky as *char qui.* Today, jerky is the common term for all dried meat, regardless of the type used.

It is very important to trim the meat well; remember that fat does not dry and can later turn rancid if not removed before dehydration. During drying, it may be helpful to line the drying tray with a leather sheet on top of which is laid a mesh sheet.

Marinating

- The longer you marinate a meat, the stronger the taste of the marinade in the dried product.
- The thicker the cut or piece of meat, poultry, or fish, the longer it will take the marinade to penetrate it.
- Always use an acid-resistant nonreactive container— glass, porcelain, or stainless steel—when marinating meat, poultry, or fish.

  When marinating beef, you can heat the marinade to allow the flavors to penetrate the meat more effectively.
- Use milk as a soak to help reduce the gamy or fishy taste of certain wild meats and strong-flavored fish, and as a tenderizer as well.
- When making a salt marinade, choose canning salt because it does not cake.

Ingredients for good marinades:

Soy sauce; teriyaki marinade and sauce; barbecue sauce; chili sauce; sweet and sour sauce; Worcestershire sauce; Tabasco sauce; liquid smoke; ketchup; olive oil; sherry, wine, whiskey, brandy, beer; lemon juice; garlic; dried herbs, such as basil, rosemary, thyme, marjoram, dill, oregano; and spices, such as mustard, ginger, curry powder, whole peppercorns, cayenne pepper, paprika

Shortcuts to good marinades:

Begin with prepackaged jerky spice mix, or dried onion soup mix, or taco seasoning mix, or Sloppy Joe mix, or dried Italian salad dressing mix, or packaged meat marinade.
Then add liquid and a selection of spices.

During the drying process, remove the oily drying item from the sheet and blot up as much of the fat as possible. Then return the item to the drying tray. Lastly, contrary to recipes for jerky that tell you to cut the meat with the grain, I have found that cutting it across the grain results in pieces that are easier to break and chew.

If your dehydrator has a temperature control, I suggest drying jerky at 145°F and above. If your machine does not have a temperature control and you are unsure at the end of drying time if the jerky is sufficiently dried, transfer the jerky to a conventional oven, preheated to 200°F, and dry the meat for 20 minutes—at which point it will be dried.

No matter the cut of meat being dried, figure that when it is done its weight will diminish to about one third its original weight. If you start off, therefore, with 3 pounds of raw meat, you will end up with about 1 pound of jerky.

Example 1: Basic Beef Jerky

3 pounds lean beef, such as a 1-inch thick steak, preferably semifrozen
One 10-ounce bottle teriyaki marinade and sauce
1 teaspoon minced garlic
½ teaspoon pepper

1. With a sharp knife, remove all the fat, gristle, and connective tissue from the meat. Then slice it across the grain into ¼-inch thick pieces.
2. In a bowl, combine the sliced beef with the remaining ingredients, stirring to make sure the meat is covered with the marinade. Let sit for 1 hour or more; if marinating longer than 1 hour, refrigerate the meat. Drain.
3. Arrange the meat in one layer on mesh sheets in the drying trays. (You can also put a leather sheet under the mesh sheets to catch the drips. If you do this, turn the meat over halfway through the drying time to ensure that the meat is dried on both sides.)

4. Place the drying trays in the dehydrator. Jerky is dried when the strips are hard but still bendable and contain no pockets of moisture. Allow anywhere from 4 to 12 hours drying time at 145° or above, depending on the style of dehydrator. The color of the meat will darken when dried.
5. For long-term storage, keep jerky in airtight plastic bags in the refrigerator or freezer. Jerky can be kept, well sealed, at room temperature for about 1 month.

Makes about 1 pound

—~~

Example 2: To Oven-dry Beef Jerky

1. Trim, slice, marinate, and drain the beef as on pages 84–86 and above.
2. Line the floor of the oven with aluminum foil or cover it with a cookie sheet to catch the drips. Place the beef strips cross-wise over the racks in the oven. Or spear the strips of beef with drapery hooks, shish-kebab skewers, or metal shower hooks, and hang the hooks from the oven racks.

   Set the oven at 145°F to 180°F. Allow anywhere from 6 to 24 hours for the strips to dry.

Makes about 1 pound

—~~

Example 3: Basic Turkey Jerky

As a result of the infomercials on television about food dehydrators, many people have become aware of turkey jerky. This simple recipe provides a good way to use up all the leftover cooked Thanksgiving turkey. Cooked chicken may also be turned into jerky in the same manner.

¼ cup soy sauce
¼ cup water
2 tablespoons honey
1 pound cooked turkey, cut into 1-inch strips or in cubes

1. In a bowl, combine the soy sauce, the water, and the honey. Add the turkey and stir gently. Let marinate for 30 minutes.
2. Remove the turkey from the marinade and arrange in a single layer on a mesh sheet on a drying tray. Place the drying tray in the dehydrator. Dry at 145° or above for about 3 hours. Drying time will depend upon the size of the pieces and the make of dehydrator used.

Makes 3 to 4 ounces

~~

Example 4: Basic Chicken Jerky

Several years ago a health-conscious friend asked me to make this chicken jerky recipe for a long trek she was planning to take in the Alps. The same recipe can be used to make turkey jerky. A reminder—all poultry must be cooked before it can be dried into jerky.

1 pound skinless, boneless chicken breasts, sinew and transparent tissue removed
¼ cup olive oil
Juice of 1 lemon
1 teaspoon crushed garlic

1. Cut the chicken into strips 5 inches long, 1 inch wide, and ¼ inch thick.
2. In a plastic bag, combine the oil, lemon juice, and garlic, and add the chicken. Squeeze out the air in the plastic bag, making sure all the chicken surfaces are covered with marinade, and seal the bag. Refrigerate for 24 hours.
3. Preheat the oven to 300°F. Remove the chicken from the bag, place in a glass baking dish, and bake for 30 minutes. Remove the chicken from the baking dish, reserving the cooking juice, which can be used as a sauce. Let the chicken cool.

4. Place the baked chicken strips on mesh sheets in the drying trays. Dry for about 6 to 8 hours, depending on the style of dehydrator, until the strips are leathery.

Makes 4 to 5 ounces

~~

Example 5: Simple Fish Jerky Snacks

The marinade used in this recipe is very good with freshwater fish such as perch or bluegill. It can also be used successfully with lean beef.

¾ cup brown sugar
¾ cup soy sauce
1 teaspoon dried garlic powder
2 teaspoons grated fresh gingerroot
2 pounds skinned, boned, and cleaned freshwater fish, cut into strips ¼ inch thick
Sesame seeds for sprinkling

1. In a bowl, combine all the marinade ingredients and add the fish, making sure the pieces are fully submerged. Cover and marinate for 8 to 12 hours in the refrigerator.
2. Spread a thick layer of newspapers on your work surface and cover with a layer of white, noninked paper towels. Remove the fish strips from the marinade and let them drain on the paper towels.
3. Arrange the fish strips on mesh sheets in the drying trays and sprinkle them with sesame seeds. Place the trays in the dehydrator and dry at 145°F or above for 8 to 12 hours, depending on the make of dehydrator.
   Break into pieces and stir into soups, chowders, or stews. Or enjoy as hors d'oeuvres.

Makes 8 ounces

To Dry Bacon

1 pound sliced bacon

Cut the sliced bacon into strips that are 1 inch long and ¼ inch wide. In a skillet, sauté the bacon until crisp, then drain the pieces on paper towels.

Line each drying tray with a solid leather sheet. Top it with a mesh sheet.

Arrange the bacon pieces in one layer on the mesh sheet. Put the drying trays in the dehydrator. Twice during the drying process, remove the drying bacon and wipe it with paper toweling to remove as much of the fat as possible. Return the bacon to the drying trays. Dry the bacon until it crumbles easily, about 6 to 8 hours, depending on the make of dehydrator.

One pound bacon weighs 2 to 3 ounces dried.

FLAVORFUL JERKIES

All-American Marinated Beef Jerky

Remember, the longer the meat marinates, the more seasoned the jerky will be.

½ cup soy sauce
1 teaspoon liquid smoke
1 teaspoon onion juice (best made in a juicer)
1 teaspoon chopped garlic
1 teaspoon salt
1 pound trimmed lean beef, cut into strips ¼ inch thick

In a bowl, combine all the ingredients and let the beef marinate for at least 2 hours.

Drain and dry into jerky as described on pages 87–88.

Makes about 4 ounces

~~~

Elegantly Marinated Beef Jerky

1 cup sweet red wine
1 tablespoon liquid smoke
1 tablespoon onion juice (best made in a juicer)
1 tablespoon soy sauce
1 teaspoon chopped garlic
1 teaspoon minced fresh ginger
1 teaspoon salt
½ teaspoon pepper
1 pound trimmed lean beef, cut into strips ¼ inch thick

In a bowl, combine all the ingredients and let the beef marinate for at least 2 hours.

Drain and dry into jerky as described on pages 87–88.

Makes about 4 ounces

~~~

Beer-Marinated Beef Jerky

1½ cups beer
¼ cup ketchup
¼ cup brown sugar
1 tablespoon liquid smoke
1 tablespoon Worcestershire sauce
1 teaspoon onion juice (best made in a juicer)
1 teaspoon chopped garlic
1 teaspoon dried or prepared mustard
1 teaspoon salt
½ teaspoon pepper
2 pounds trimmed lean beef, cut into strips ¼ inch thick

In a bowl, combine all the ingredients and stir well. Marinate the beef in the refrigerator for 8 to 12 hours, or overnight.

Drain and dry into jerky as described on pages 87–88.

Makes about 10 ounces

———

Betsy and Jim Oman's Favorite Beef Jerky

One 15-ounce can tomato sauce
3 cups soy sauce
1 tablespoon garlic powder
1 tablespoon liquid smoke
10–15 pounds thinly sliced, trimmed lean beef, cut into strips ¼ inch thick

In a large bowl, combine all the ingredients. Marinate for at least 1 hour.

Drain and dry into jerky as described on pages 87–88.

Makes about 4 pounds

———

Soy-Marinated Turkey Jerky

¼ cup soy sauce
1 teaspoon fresh lemon juice
¼ teaspoon chopped garlic
⅛ teaspoon minced fresh gingerroot
1½ pounds skinless, boneless turkey, all sinew removed, cut into strips or slices ¼ inch thick

In a plastic bag, combine the soy sauce, the lemon juice, the garlic, and the ginger, and add the turkey pieces. Squeeze out all the air in the bag, making sure the turkey is covered with the marinade, and seal the bag. Refrigerate for 24 hours.

Remove the turkey from the marinade and arrange the pieces on a steaming rack. In a large saucepan, bring about 2 inches of water to a boil, add the steaming rack, and cover the pan. Steam the turkey for 15 to 20 minutes.

Let the steamed turkey pieces cool and arrange them on mesh

sheets in the drying trays. Place the trays in the dehydrator and dry the turkey for about 6 to 10 hours, depending on the make of dehydrator, until leathery.

Makes about 6 ounces

Teriyaki-Marinated Turkey Jerky

¼ cup teriyaki marinade and sauce
¼ cup soy sauce
¼ teaspoon pepper
Spices such as bay leaves or whole peppercorns
Pinch dried herbs such as oregano or basil
1½ pounds skinless, boneless turkey, all sinew removed, cut into strips or slices ¼ inch thick

Combine the marinade ingredients with the spices and herbs of choice, then steam and dry turkey jerky as directed in Soy-Marinated Turkey Jerky (page 93).

Makes about 6 ounces

Onion Ground Beef Jerky

If you can dry lean ground beef—see page 95—it should come as no surprise that you can also dry seasoned lean ground beef. If you are pressed for time, use already prepared jerky spices, which are frequently available from manufacturers. It is also fun to spice up your own ground meat jerky. This combination is one of my favorites.

One 2-ounce package dried onion soup mix
¼ cup water
¼ cup soy sauce
1 teaspoon chopped garlic
1 teaspoon salt
Dried herbs or flavorings of choice
1 pound lean ground beef

In a bowl, combine the dried onion soup mix and the water.

To Dry Lean Ground Beef

Lean ground beef is a high-protein food that is especially popular with backpackers and hikers, who rehydrate it and add it to Backpacker Spaghetti Sauce (page 161).

1 pound lean ground beef

In a skillet, sauté the lean ground beef until no traces of pink remain. Drain off the fat. If desired, drain the cooked meat in a colander and rinse it under hot water to remove as much of the fat as possible. You can also drain the cooked meat on layers of white, noninked paper toweling. Top the meat with a layer of toweling and press down with a rolling pin to eliminate remaining fat.

Sprinkle with dried herbs or flavorings of your choice.

Line drying trays with leather sheets, then top with mesh sheets as described in To Dry Bacon (page 91). Twice during the drying process, remove the trays and blot the beef with paper toweling to remove as much of the fat as possible. Return the trays to the dehydrator. Dry the cooked beef at 145°F or above for about 6 to 8 hours, depending on the make of dehydrator, until hard.

One pound beef weighs 4 ounces dried

Let sit for 10 minutes. Add the remaining ingredients, including the beef, and combine well. Let marinate for at least 2 hours. For a more pronounced flavor, cover and refrigerate for 8 to 12 hours.

Shape the meat into 1- to 2-inch balls. (If you wet your hands with water, the meat mixture is easier to handle.) Place the balls between sheets of wax paper and with a rolling pin roll them into 5-inch evenly thick rounds. Or use a jerky press, also available through food dehydrator manufacturers.

Line each drying tray with a solid leather sheet. Top it with a mesh sheet. Make sure that the paper towel does not extend over the edge of the drying tray. Arrange the meat rounds on the mesh sheets. Place the drying trays in the dehydrator and dry at 145°F or above until hard, about 6 to 10 hours, depending on the make of dehydrator. With some dehydrators, you will need to turn the rounds to ensure uniform drying. If beads of oil form on the rounds as they are drying, blot them up with a clean uninked paper towel.

Store in an airtight bag in the refrigerator.

Makes about 4 ounces

Spicy Ground Beef Jerky

You can also prepare the ground meat mixture for drying by rolling it out directly on the leather sheet. Then score it lightly into pieces or wedges, using a pizza cutter or a knife. If you like this jerky, see Backpacker Jerkied Tomato Rice (page 160), where it stars in a hearty one-pot dish that hits the spot when you have been outdoor adventuring and want a good, warm meal.

One 8-ounce package Adolph's meat marinade
½ cup teriyaki marinade and sauce
1 tablespoon grated fresh horseradish
1 tablespoon onion juice (best made in a juicer)
1 tablespoon sugar
1 tablespoon chopped garlic
½ teaspoon pepper
2 pounds lean ground beef

In a bowl, combine the meat marinade with the teriyaki marinade and add the remaining ingredients except the beef. Let sit for 10 minutes.

Add the lean ground beef. Combine well, cover, and let marinate for at least 2 hours.

Shape the meat and dry it as directed for Onion Ground Beef Jerky (page 94).

Makes about 10 ounces

～

Taco Ground Beef Jerky

One 1¼-ounce package taco seasoning mix
2 tablespoons water
2 tablespoons soy sauce
1 teaspoon Tabasco sauce
1 teaspoon chopped garlic
1 teaspoon onion juice (best made in a juicer)
1 teaspoon dried bell pepper powder
2 pounds lean ground beef

In a bowl, combine the taco seasoning mix in the water and the soy sauce. Stir in the remaining ingredients, except the beef, and let sit for 10 minutes.

Add the lean ground beef. Combine well, cover, and let marinate for at least 2 hours.

Shape the mix and dry it as directed for Onion Ground Beef Jerky (page 94).

Makes about 10 ounces

～

Pemmican

Pemmican is a Cree Indian version of dried meat that contains many calories and much protein. Years ago I came across a recipe for pemmican that began with, "Cut up one elk." I won't ask you to do that! In fact, note that, unlike the other recipes in this chapter thus far, you begin this one with *already dried meat*.

Exact measurements for perfect pemmican are difficult to arrive at. Experiment until you find the one most appealing to you in both texture and taste. Some people, in fact, consider pemmican something of an acquired taste.

1 cup dried meat in pieces, such as lean beef, deer, antelope, or
    buffalo
¾ cup peanut butter (a substitute for the more traditional suet
    or fat)

¼–½ cup cut-up dried fruit, such as prunes, apples, grapes, or berries

In a blender, chop the dried meat into small pieces.

In a bowl, combine the chopped meat, fat of choice, and dried fruit, and shape the mixture into logs or patties. Wrap each individually in plastic wrap.

Use pemmican on journeys, or on camping or backpacking trips. For long-term storage, refrigerate, wrapped in plastic, where it should keep for 1 year.

Makes 1 cup

~~~

DRIED FISH

Salt has long been used as a preservative, and one has only to read accounts of ocean voyages or peruse facsimiles of early ships' logs to understand the importance of salted dried fish as a source of protein and nourishment to sailors and explorers the world over.

A brine concentration of at least 10 percent salt—one part salt to nine parts water—will inhibit the growth of pathogenic microorganisms that cause spoilage. Indeed, the amount of salt can vary from 10 to 25 percent, depending upon the size of the pieces of fish (or meat) and the desired concentration of salt in the finished product. Large pieces need a higher concentration of salt.

What you should remember about dried fish is that it can taste very salty. To mitigate some of its saltiness once dried, soak it in water, being sure to change the water several times to remove as much of the salt as possible.

~~~

Old-Fashioned Salt-Marinated Dried Fish

Historically, not only fish but also wild game, such as venison, was treated with this solution before being either smoked and/or dried.

4 cups water
½ cup noniodized canning salt (available in canning section of most supermarkets)

½ cup sugar
1 teaspoon chopped garlic
1 teaspoon onion juice (best made in a juicer)
¼ teaspoon pepper
3–4 pounds skinned and boned, cleaned fish, rinsed in cold water, cut into strips 2–4 inches long by ¼ inch thick
½ cup brown sugar for glazing

In a large, nonreactive bowl, combine the ingredients for the salt marinade. Add the fish and be sure all the pieces are fully submerged. Cover and let soak for at least 8 to 12 hours in the refrigerator.

Remove the fish from the marinade and arrange them in a single layer on mesh sheets in the drying trays. Sprinkle the fish with the brown sugar. Place the drying trays in the dehydrator. Dry at 145°F or above until the fish is hard, about 10 hours, depending upon the make of dehydrator.

Makes about 1 pound

Tom's Spice-Marinated Dried Fish

4 cups water
½ cup noniodized canning salt (available in canning section of most supermarkets)
¼ cup granulated sugar
⅛ cup brown sugar
1 tablespoon onion juice (best made in a juicer)
1 tablespoon chopped garlic
1 tablespoon white wine
1 teaspoon paprika
1 teaspoon white pepper
1 teaspoon pulverized bell pepper
½ teaspoon ground allspice
2–4 pounds skinned and boned, cleaned freshwater fish, cut into strips 2–4 inches long by ¼ inch thick

In a large, nonreactive bowl, combine all the marinade ingredients and add the fish, making sure it is fully submerged. Cover and marinate for 8 to 12 hours in the refrigerator.

Dried Shellfish

In 1981, when I was in Pearl Lagoon, Nicaragua, I learned from the people how they dried shrimp. First, they cook them, then they spread the shrimp out on concrete slabs and let them dry in the sunlight. Every few hours, they stir the shrimp around. At night the shrimp are gathered up and taken inside to protect them from the moisture in the night air. The next day the shrimp are again spread out in the sunlight on the concrete slabs to dry.

When the shrimp are completely dried, however long that might take, a group of people remove the heads on the shrimp and put the bodies in sacks. They then beat the sacks against a hard, flat surface: The dried shells shatter off the shellfish, like rice winnowed in a stiff breeze. Then, by hand, all traces of shell are removed before the shrimp are stored in airtight containers.

My recipe for drying shrimp is not nearly as exotic. And more unsettling than that, you will need 5 pounds of fresh shrimp to get ½ pound of dried! There is a golden lining, though. Dried shrimp are very powerful in flavor. You will need only ½ cup to make 20 egg rolls.

5 pounds fresh shrimp
2 cups water
¼ cup salt
Shrimp boil (available in packages in the ethnic food section of many supermarkets) for flavoring

Rinse the shrimp well in cool water.

In a large, nonreactive saucepan, combine the remaining ingredients and add the shrimp. Bring the water to a boil and boil small shrimp for 2 to 3 minutes, large shrimp for 4 to 6 minutes, until the shrimp are pink and the meat separates from the shell. Drain and let cool. Shell the shrimp.

Spread the shrimp in a single layer on the drying trays. Place the trays in the dehydrator and dry until hard, about 6 hours, depending on the make of dehydrator.

Store in an airtight container.
Makes ½ pound

Drain and dry the fish and arrange in a single layer on mesh sheets on drying trays in the dehydrator. Allow anywhere from 6 to 10 hours to dry at 145°F or above, depending on the make of dehydrator, or until it feels totally dry.

Makes 8 to 16 ounces

~~~

Tom's Red Wine–Marinated Dried Fish

3 cups water or apple juice
1 cup dry red wine
½ cup noniodized canning salt (available in canning section of most supermarkets)
½ cup granulated sugar
¼ cup brown sugar
¼ cup soy sauce
1 teaspoon chopped garlic
1 teaspoon onion juice (best made in a juicer)
¼ teaspoon ground allspice
¼ teaspoon ground cloves
2–4 pounds skinned and boned, cleaned freshwater fish, cut into strips ¼ inch thick

In a large, nonreactive bowl, combine all the marinade ingredients and add the fish, making sure it is fully submerged. Cover and let marinate for 8 to 12 hours in the refrigerator.

Drain and dry the fish in a single layer on mesh sheets on drying trays in the dehydrator. Allow anywhere from 6 to 10 hours to dry at 145°F or above, depending on the make of dehydrator.

Makes 8 to 16 ounces

$\mathcal{C}hapter\ 7$

Drying Herbs

$\mathcal{A}$s I mentioned in Chapter 6, men seem to be inordinately attracted to making meat jerkies, while women are drawn to drying herbs and flowers, especially those from their own gardens. I can see the expressions on women's faces change when at a food-drying demonstration I talk about preparing dried herbal combinations or flowers to make potpourri (see Chapter 12). The women's countenances become less guarded at the anticipated pleasure of working with herbs or flowers. There is a mystery, a lore, a magic about it. There is color and fragrance and texture and, ultimately, art.

It should come as no surprise that your food dehydrator will enable you to dry both herbs and flowers, the treasures of your garden, and the results will be lasting and beautiful. With dried herbs or flowers on hand, you will be able to create your own blends of *fines herbs* or even make herb wreaths; with dried flowers you will be on your way to blending potpourri or sachets, or both. Like the dried fruits and vegetables in your pantry, dried herbs and flowers know no season.

DRYING HERBS IN A FOOD DEHYDRATOR

Herbs dried in a food dehydrator are not only better-tasting than store-bought dried herbs, which, by the way, are likely to have been irradiated, but they are also far less expensive. Think how few ounces of dried herbs there are in those jars bought in the grocery store in comparison with all the branches, sprigs, leaves, and seeds on your homegrown plants. Even if you buy herbs for drying at your local farmstand or greengrocer, you are still ahead of the game economically.

The traditional, and for some people the most charming, way to dry herbs—air-drying them by suspending them in paper bags—tends to make the subtle oils and flavors in the herbs evaporate and the herbs themselves shrivel and turn brown. A food dehydrator that is equipped with separate controls for temperature and air circulation offers the best conditions for drying herbs. Here are some of the reasons why:

Certain makes of food dehydrators operate at substantially lower temperatures (90°F to 110°F) than standard ovens do. Lower temperatures help preserve the delicate oils in the herbs as they dry. Drying herbs at high temperatures not only causes them to lose color but also flavor.

Food dehydrators offer more air circulation than other drying environments. The more dry air that can be produced in the dehydrator, the quicker the herbs will dry. A protracted drying period will diminish flavor.

The indirect light inside a food dehydrator—unlike strong light, especially sunlight—will not break down the chlorophyll in the herbs, thus preserving more of their color (and flavor) when they are dried.

WHAT CAN BE DRIED?

The leaves, seeds, and roots of edible herbs can all be dried. Many herbs, parsley for one, can be cut continually throughout the growing season, and in some cases, such regular cuttings actually help stop the plant from flowering.

Leaves

You will find the greatest amount of oil in the leaves of an herb plant just before the plant blossoms.

Pick the tender leaves at the top of the plant (those around the bottom are usually tougher). Large leaves, such as basil, bay, or sage, should be removed from the growing stems, cleaned, and placed in single layers on drying trays. Herbs with small leaves or with small stems, such as thyme or rosemary, can be dried while still attached to the stems. Try to strip away as much of the stem as possible to get the smallest floweret. Some, like chamomile flowers and leaves, are easier to separate after drying is completed. Any tough thick veins on the leaves should be removed before drying. With large-leafed herbs, like basil, you can cut the leaves into ¼- to ½-inch strips to facilitate faster drying.

As to the time to pick leaves, do it in the morning after the night dew has evaporated and before the sun is hot. Before beginning the drying process, clean the herb, removing all dirt and insects, as suggested on page 105.

Seeds and Berries

Harvest seed pods for home drying when the color changes from green to brown or gray, but before the pods burst open and the seeds fall out. By monitoring the growth of your herbs, you will actually be able to dry some of the seeds naturally, that is, while they are still on the plant. Pick the seed pods or flower heads. Clean them, then arrange them on mesh sheets on drying trays. Remember that as the seeds dry they may separate from the pods or stalks. That is the reason why a mesh sheet is used to line the drying trays; it prevents the seeds from dropping through the trays. Place the trays in the dehydrator and dry until the pods are brittle and the seeds release easily, about 4 to 8 hours, depending on the make of dehydrator.

To remove the outer covering from the dried seeds, simply rub the seeds between the palms of your hands. Store seeds in airtight containers, label them, and write down the date.

Roots

The ideal time to dig up the roots of herbs for drying is at the very beginning of the plant's dormant season. Because the food supply of the plant is in the roots, it is at this time that the roots are most flavorful and nutritious. Should a plant have many root clusters, remove only a few to ensure the continued growth of the plant. If you are foraging and digging up wild herbs, be sure that what you are extracting is not threatened.

To prepare roots for drying: Scrub the roots to remove all dirt, then peel them. Cut the roots into ½- to ¼-inch slices or cubes. Arrange the pieces on the drying tray and place the tray in the dehydrator. Dry until hard, 6 to 10 hours, depending on the make of dehydrator.

Some roots, like horseradish, have such a pungent aroma when being dried that you may want to put the dehydrator in the garage or, at the very least, away from the living quarters of the house. Another tip about horseradish: Harvest it in any month that does not have an "r" in it (May, June, July, August).

Dried roots make great teas. Simmer dried pieces of root in water for 10 minutes—do not let the mixture boil. Then pour the infusion into a teacup and enjoy!

You can even make delicious candy from roots: Soak peeled, fresh root pieces, such as angelica, in honey before drying them. Then dry them on mesh sheets on the drying trays to prevent the pieces from sticking. Allow 6 to 10 hours, depending on the make of dehydrator.

Some herb roots, like caraway and chervil, can be dried, then rehydrated and used as a flavoring for other vegetables, such as steamed green beans.

Three Ways to Clean Herbs Before Drying

1. Wash the leaves or leafy stalks in cool water and pat gently dry with paper towels, or shake to remove all excess water. (Herbs that are still wet when put into the dehydrator may darken more than those that have been shaken or patted dry with towels.)
2. Swish each leafy stalk in a solution of 2 tablespoons salt mixed with 1 gallon water. Rinse in cool water, then shake or pat off excess water, or spin gently in a salad spinner.
3. Wipe clean with a damp towel each separate leaf or the leaves on stalks.

Key Technique 10: To Dry Herbs

Example 1: To Dry Fresh Parsley Sprigs

1. Pick parsley sprigs in the morning after the dew has evaporated. Remove any tough or damaged parts and large stems.
2. Wash and dry as suggested on page 105.
3. Arrange the sprigs in a single layer on a drying tray and put the drying tray in the dehydrator. Use low temperatures— 90°F to 110°F. If possible, increase the amount of air flow through the dehydrator. Allow from 4 to 6 hours, depending on the make of dehydrator, until the sprigs are crushable.
4. Store the sprigs in an airtight container as suggested on page 109. Be sure to label the container and note the date of drying.

Example 2: To Air-dry Herbs (and Flowers)

1. To air-dry herbs that have long stems—sage, basil, mint, for example—tie the root ends of 10 to 20 stems together tightly with string, a wire tie, or a rubber band. All parts of the herb will shrink when drying, including the stem, so be sure to tie the stems tightly.
2. Put the bunch upside down in a cheesecloth bag or paper bag, and label and date it. Tie the bag closed with string. If desired, you can poke very small holes in the paper bag for air flow.
3. Suspend the bag in a well-ventilated warm place, such as an attic or a closet, or on the mantel, or high above a fireplace. The theory behind hanging the herbs upside down is to encourage the oils in the stems to flow into the leaves. The bag simply protects the herbs from dust or dirt.
4. Natural drying like this can take days or weeks. Check every 2 or 3 days to see how quickly the herbs are drying. (Should you be using this method to dry herbs outdoors, bring the bag in the house each night to avoid dew remoistening the herbs.)

FLOWERS, HERBS, AND ROOTS GOOD FOR DRYING

I have annotated the list below with initials that follow the name of the herb:

$$L = \text{leaves} \quad SE = \text{seeds} \quad R = \text{roots}$$
$$F = \text{flowers}$$

Where multiple initials are indicated, this means you can dry as few or as many of the suggested parts as possible. The more the merrier. For me, growing and drying herbs is much like growing and drying tomatoes—there is no end to the fascination and enjoyment that comes with simply doing it.

Note: You will see on the list that follows that most of the entries, but not all, can be used for culinary purposes.

Angelica: *L, R, SE*

Anise: *L, SE, F*

Basil: *L, F*

Bay: *L*

Bergamot: *L, F*

Borage: *L, F*

Burdock: *R*

Burnet: *L*

Calendula: *F, SE*

Caraway: *L, R, SE*

Catnip: *L*

Chamomile: *L, F*

Chervil: *L, R, F*

Chives: *L, F*

Comfrey: *R*

Coriander: *L, SE*

Cumin: *SE*

Dandelion: *L, R, F*

Dill: *L, SE, F*

Fennel: *L, SE, F*

Garlic: *R* (It is well known that garlic is, in fact, a bulb, but for our purposes here we are using it as a root.)

Geranium: *L, F*

Ginseng: *R*

Horehound: *L*

Horseradish: *R*

Lavender: *L, F*

Lemon Verbena: *L, F*

Lovage: *L, R, SE*

Marjoram: *L, F*

Mint: *L, F*

Mustard: *SE, F*

Nasturtium: *L, SE, F*

Oregano: *L, F*

Parsley: *L, R*

Poppy: *SE*

Rose: *L, SE, F*

Rosemary: *L, F*

Sage: *L, F*

Sassafras: *L, R, F*

Savory: *L, F*

Sesame: *SE*

Sorrel: *L*

Tansy: *L, F*

Tarragon: *L*

Thyme: *L, F*

Woodruff: *L, F*

How to Store Dried Herbs and Flowers

Dark glass jars with tight-fitting lids are the best storage containers for herbs. The tinted glass reduces exposure to light and thus helps retard color fading in the dried product. I like to use what some might now consider collector's items: blue-glass canning jars and brown-glass Ovaltine jars.

It is wise to store dried herbs in the form in which they were dried rather than crushing them for storage. In so doing and then crushing them when you are ready to use them, you will be releasing the finest, fullest flavor and aroma into the dish you are preparing instead of into the storage jar!

To crush dried herbs, use your hands, or a mortar and pestle, or grind them to a fine powder in the blender. All parts—leaves, roots, seeds—can be pulverized.

Place jars of dried herbs in a cool, dry, dark place. Sealed airtight, they will last for years. Always remember to label the jar with the name of the herb and the date of drying.

WAYS TO USE DRIED HERBS

Dried herbs are two to four times stronger in flavor than fresh herbs. While rehydrating dried herbs is not necessary, it is a good idea to add them to warm liquid to bring out their fullness.

Generally ¼ teaspoon dried = 1 teaspoon fresh

Herbs are also calorie-free. Some reports claim that herbs contain nutritional value; other sources, and there are many of them, avow that herbs are medicinal in nature. For people who want to limit their intake of salt, herbs offer many a welcome option.
Here are some ways to enjoy them:

Add dried herbs to soups and stews during the last half hour of cooking time.

Add dried herbs, generously, to turkey or chicken stuffings.

Remember that tarragon combines beautifully with chicken during roasting. Either sprinkle the top of the bird with crushed, dried leaves or insert sprigs of dried tarragon in the cavity.

Flavor dairy products—cream cheese, cottage cheese, and yogurt—with dried herbs and flowers. One particularly good, easy dip combines sour cream, chopped garlic and onion, and crushed dried dill.

Dress up deviled eggs or omelets with a sprinkling of dried herbs.

Flavor jellies, jams, preserves, conserves, and marmalades with dried herbs and flowers. Try adding dried mint to pineapple jam; dried thyme to grapefruit jelly; oregano to orange jelly; thyme to citrus marmalade.

Add dried herbs—oregano, thyme, or chives, for example—to bread dough. Simply knead the herb of choice into the dough before placing the loaf in the oven.

Even the smallest addition of a dried herb to a salad dressing, to a sauce, to a soufflé makes a considerable and marvelous difference. I leave the combinations to you, but hope that you grow fresh herbs and dry them and use them with all the foods you have dried in your dehydrator on an ongoing basis, no matter the season, no matter the reason. And, of course, use herbs as suggested in the recipes that follow.

The Pleasure of Herbs

Making culinary dried herb blends is almost as gratifying as growing the herbs themselves. You soon learn which ones are compatible and which are more preferable used solo. Be wary of the stronger-flavored herbs overpowering the ones that are more delicate in flavor. A harmonious blend is the goal.

As I learned from Kathe Abrams, president of the Twin Cities Herb Society, the tasting of herbs, however, is a very subjective and not easily quantifiable matter. The amount of flavor in the herb will depend upon when it was picked, the amount of oil in the leaves, and, of course, how much of the herb you used in whatever you are preparing. What one person may find strong in flavor, another may find less strong. Suffice it to say, and I think many herb lovers, including Kathe, would agree, that rosemary and sage are strongly flavored; lemon thyme is mild; and summer savory is delicate. Parsley, interestingly, can be used to balance the whole. I leave all other herbal taste evaluations to you.

With that said, here is:

The Pleasure of Herbs/My Favorite Herb Blend

1 tablespoon dried oregano
1 tablespoon dried marjoram
1 tablespoon dried basil
2 teaspoons dried summer savory
1 teaspoon dried rosemary
1 teaspoon dried sage

In a glass jar, combine all the herbs together thoroughly. Close the jar with a tight-fitting lid and label the contents. Use to flavor soups, stews, or vegetable dishes.

Makes 4⅓ tablespoons

HERB RECIPES

~~~

My Version of Fines Herbes

Fines herbes, a standby of classic French cooking, is a blend of culinary herbs, either finely chopped or crushed, that is added to foods—fine sauces, cream soups, egg dishes, and vegetables, among them—during the last few minutes of cooking time or just before serving.

The rule of thumb when it comes to composing *fines herbes* is to use equal parts of dried herbs, with parsley and chives almost always included. (I am fully aware that celery powder and garlic are not herbs or traditional additions; they are, however, tasty personal touches.)

1 teaspoon dried tarragon
1 teaspoon dried parsley
1 teaspoon dried chives
½ teaspoon dried garlic powder

In a glass jar with a tight-fitting lid, combine all the ingredients. Seal, label the jar, and store in a cool, dark place.

Makes 1 tablespoon

~~~

Bouquet Garni

We have the French to thank for the culinary term *bouquet garni*—a small bundle of herbs tied together with string (or contained in a cheesecloth bag)—that is added during cooking to soups, stews, or other savory dishes, then removed before serving. The bundle usually includes parsley, bay leaf, and thyme.

2 tablespoons dried parsley
2 bay leaves
1 teaspoon dried rosemary
1 teaspoon dried thyme
1 teaspoon dried tarragon

Cut a piece of cheesecloth into a 4-inch square and place the dried herbs in the middle of it. Gather up the corners of the square and twist them to close. Tie with a piece of kitchen string, leaving enough at the end to retrieve the bag from the cooking pot. Be sure to remove the *bouquet garni* before serving.

Makes 1 *bouquet garni*

Herb Butters

Herb butters are very easy to make and lend quite an elegant note to whatever they accompany. Use herb butter to flavor sauces and soups, to melt over grilled or roasted meats, on sautéed foods, or as a spread on a delicious piece of homemade bread. Herb butter freezes beautifully.

2 sticks (1 cup) butter, softened
1 tablespoon crushed basil, cilantro, mint, dill, or a combination
   of herbs

In a small bowl, blend the softened butter with the herbs of choice, combining them completely. Spread the butter evenly in the bowl, making swirls in the top, if desired, or transfer it to a butter mold. Cover, and let it chill until hard.

You can also shape the softened butter into a log, wrap it in plastic wrap, and freeze it. When frozen, cut the log into pieces for individual serving.

Makes 1 cup

Herb-Flavored Oil

The popularity of herb-flavored oils is completely understandable. They add marvelous flavor to salad dressings and can be used in sautéing foods, adding a subtle touch to even the most everyday dishes. Like herb butter, an herb-flavored oil is remarkably simple to prepare and makes a grand gift during the holidays or any time of the year. One word of caution: Be sure to use good-quality olive oil.

Long-stemmed dried herb sprigs, such as basil, oregano, or rosemary
Pure olive oil

Put the dried herbs in a glass bottle or jar—the more sprigs you add, the stronger the eventual flavor—and then pour in the oil to cover the herbs. Put the top or lid on the container. Let sit in the cupboard for at least 1 week. Strain before using.

Once opened, keep the oil in the refrigerator.

~~~

Herb Vinegar

If herb-flavored oil is currently popular, I suspect some of its impact came from the acceptance of herb vinegar, which preceded it onto the shelves of fine food stores and gourmet markets. To farmers' wives and home gardening enthusiasts, though, the pleasures of herb vinegar have been known for many years. It is important to use a good-quality white or red wine vinegar; cider vinegar, with its strong taste, should only be used with other strong-flavored ingredients. Besides dried herbs, you can also use dried fruits or vegetables or edible flowers to flavor vinegar. No matter what dried foods you use, they do not need to be rehydrated before being added to the vinegar. Another plus: Vinegar acts as a preservative. A 5 percent solution is recommended.

In flavoring vinegar, remember the stronger the herb, the less you need.

Use herb vinegar, with oil, on your favorite salad combination. Nothing else is required by way of dressing.

½ cup dried herb, such as purple basil, tarragon, oregano, rosemary, sage, or woodruff
2 cups good-quality white or red wine vinegar, warmed

In a glass container with a nonmetal lid, put the dried herb of choice and pour the vinegar over it. (Vinegar, when warmed, helps extract the oils in the herb.) Cover the container and let it sit in a warm place for 1 week.

Strain the vinegar through cheesecloth into a clean glass jar or porcelain container and to it add a sprig or two of the flavoring herb. Cover and store in the cupboard.

Makes ½ cup

Flower Vinegar: Use the above method but with dried flowers, such as roses, lavender, or nasturtium, for an equally wonderful, haunting flavor.

Herb Sugars

Just like dried fruits and vegetables, herbs can be pulverized, then blended with sugar to make unique combinations. I would wager that our great-grandmothers knew about herb sugars and prepared them. Like other similar Old World touches of refinement, though, herb sugars seemed to have been passed over in favor of amenities more modern. Interestingly, your food dehydrator will enable you make these simple, exquisite pleasures, which also make good gifts. You can also sweeten the pot by combining dried herbs with dried flowers, such as rose petals or violets.

1 teaspoon crushed dried herbs
3 tablespoons white or brown sugar

In a jar, combine the crushed herbs and the sugar. Sprinkle on pancakes, French toast, ice cream, cereal, or use to sweeten beverages. A flavored sugar does not dissolve as quickly as simple granulated sugar.

~~~

Herb Mustard

Crush your own dried herbs, or dried flowers, and add them to any commercially prepared or homemade mustard for an intriguing taste treat.

1 teaspoon dried herb, such as basil, oregano, cilantro, or parsley, finely crushed
½ cup mustard

In a jar with a tight-fitting lid, combine the herb of choice and the mustard. Cover and store in the refrigerator until ready to use.

Makes ½ cup

Chapter 8

Making Food Leathers

$\mathcal{W}$hen you dry food in sheets instead of in pieces, you are making "leather." You may have purchased fruit leathers at the grocery store, where they are called "fruit roll-ups," "fruit paper," or "fruit rolls," and come in flavors like cherry, apple, apricot, strawberry, watermelon, and grape. With your own food dehydrator, not only can you make fruit leathers, but also dry vegetable leathers—tomato being a superb example. And the same drying technique can be employed for dehydrating yogurt, spaghetti sauce, canned soup, and much more.

First, some thoughts on the word "leather." In 1981, when I went to Nicaragua to teach classes on food drying, I noticed that the people seemed to find the idea of eating "leather" unappealing. When I handed out samples of fruit leather to about two hundred participants, they looked at me with great suspicion, took the leather nonetheless, but refused to eat it. Quickly, my translator and I came up with another word for "leather"—*tortilla*—*tortilla de fruta, tortilla de vegetal*. The fact that the newly adopted term represented an important and identifiable foodstuff for these Nicaraguans made a great difference in their interest in learning about it when made with fruit.

Call it what you will, the concept of fruit leather is nothing new. Pureed dried apricots, for example, have long been a traditional treat in Turkey, Afghanistan, and the Middle East, where the puree is used in main courses and desserts and eaten as a snack.

The appeal of fruit leather, as a snack food, can be easily observed. Walk down the aisle of any supermarket and count the number of brands of commercial fruit leather. It is usually made from an apple concentrate with other fruit purees, chemical additives, and sweeteners added. You can make your own leather at a fraction of the cost, without additives and extra sugars. Besides making great snacks, leathers can be a very convenient base for sauces and drinks. To say leathers make for easy carrying when you are outdoor adventuring is an understatement. Last but not least, children can make their own leathers, and they love doing it. Before bedtime, open up a jar of applesauce, have your child spread it evenly over a lightly oiled solid leather sheet, and put the drying tray in the dehydrator to dry overnight. In the morning, your child can peel the apple leather off the leather sheet. It's as easy as that!

Because tomatoes contain little or no pectin, a thickening agent must be added to a tomato puree, for example, before it can be dried into leather. (See Tomato Leathers, pages 132–135, for several choices for thickeners.) I've spent years experimenting with tomato leathers and hope you agree after you've tried them that they are a boon for making sauces or soups or drinks.

WHAT FOODS CAN BE DRIED TO MAKE FOOD LEATHERS?

You can make food leathers from many fruits and vegetables. Instead of throwing out those bananas on your counter that are darkening or the peaches that are turning soft, puree them to make leather. In fact, the riper the fruit, the sweeter the leather. (Banana puree is so sweet by itself that you will need to tone it down with a little applesauce for a really great leather.) Or you can make leathers with fresh, frozen, or canned foods; from leftovers; or from plain or sweetened yogurt, to mention only a few of the other possibilities.

WHAT EQUIPMENT IS NEEDED?

To make food leathers, you will need solid leather sheets made of plastic that fit inside and line the drying trays in your dehydrator. The sheets may be round or square and, depending upon the make, your dehydrator may have one sheet or as many as thirty. Most dehydrators sold today come with solid leather

118

sheets; if yours did not, call another manufacturer to learn if its solid leather sheets will work in your unit. Some electric food dehydrator manufacturers suggest improvising your own leather sheets: Stretch plastic wrap over each drying tray and make a lip by rolling the wrap up and over the edge of the tray to prevent the puree from spilling. Secure the plastic wrap with tape. With a spatula, spread the puree on the leather sheets; the back of a large spoon works very well, too. If you do improvise making your own solid leather sheet, be sure that the plastic wrap is nowhere near the heat source.

Whether you use the leather sheets that came with your unit or line the drying trays with plastic wrap, you will need to lightly oil the sheets—wiping them lightly with vegetable oil or spraying them with Pam or vegetable cooking oil—to prevent the puree from sticking to the sheets. Wipe off any excess oil with paper towels. Always make sure that the leather sheet is on a drying tray before you pour the puree onto the leather sheet.

TO MAKE SUCCESSFUL LEATHERS

Making successful leathers depends upon two important factors: the **sugar content** and the **pectin content** of the puree with which you are making the leather. The amount of pectin in a pureed fruit determines how well it will bond in a solid sheet as it dries. Certain fruits are naturally high in sugar and in pectin; others are low in sugar and pectin. It is important to note that practically all vegetables are low in pectin.

Sugar Content

A lot of sugar or sweetener in the puree will lengthen the drying time and cause the leather to stick to the drying surface. Pure orange juice concentrate and canned cranberry sauce are both so high in sugar that they remain sticky after many hours of drying! When sweetening a fruit puree to be dried into leather, therefore, know that the more honey, corn syrup, artificial sweetener, sugar, or maple syrup you add, the longer the drying time. Taste the puree as you prepare it, remembering that it will become sweeter when it is dried.

119

Pectin Content

Pectin is a carbohydrate present in pulpy fruits, more in under-ripe ones than in fully ripe fruits. A sufficient amount of pectin in applesauce is the reason the leather peels off the leather sheet in one piece. An insufficient amount of pectin is the reason plain tomato puree, with no thickening agent added, flakes when dried into leather. However, while flakes are not visually appealing, they are just as edible as tomato leather in one piece.

Fruits naturally low in pectin include cherries, citrus fruits, melons, pomegranates, raspberries, and strawberries.

Fruits naturally high in pectin include apples, apricots, black-berries, blueberries, cranberries, currants, figs, gooseberries, grapes, guavas, peaches, pears, pineapples, plums, and rhubarb.

Reminder: Most vegetables are naturally low in pectin.

To increase the amount of pectin in low-pectin fruit purees or in vegetable purees:

- Add a high-pectin food, such as applesauce, to a low-pectin ingredient, such as tomato puree. Combine in equal parts. See Easy Tomato Leather, page 132.
- Add powdered pectin to the puree to thicken it. In general, I use 2 tablespoons pectin per 3 cups puree. See 3-Ingredient Tomato Leather, page 133.

- Add unflavored gelatin to the puree to thicken it. See Fancy Tomato Leather Chips, page 134.
- Add 1 heaping teaspoon cornstarch for each cup of puree to thicken it. See Tomato Leather (made with Cornstarch), page 132.

Key Technique 11: To Make Fruit or Vegetable Leather

1. Wash the fruit or vegetable. Certain fruits like bananas or pineapple must be peeled; with others, like pears, apples, and peaches, peeling is optional. There are nutrients in the skins of certain fruits that you might want to retain.
2. Halve, core, pit, or seed the respective fruit or vegetable. Cut off any bruised or damaged areas in the flesh. Chop coarsely.
3. Puree the fruit or vegetable pieces, 1 cup at a time, in a

blender, food processor, or juicer, or press through a sieve until smooth. With some ingredients you may have to add juice or water to thin the puree to enable the blender to keep working. Remember, however, the more liquid you add to the puree, the longer it will take to dry. **The desired consistency of puree that is most suitable for drying into leather is that of applesauce.**

4. Taste the puree. Sweeten it, if necessary, recalling that it will taste sweeter when dried. Season to taste with ground spices or with herbs, extracts, or liqueurs.

5. With a spatula, spread the puree ¼ inch thick on lightly oiled solid leather sheets on the drying trays. (Depending upon the design of your food dehydrator, you may need only 1 solid leather sheet and 1 drying tray to dry the purees called for in the recipes that appear in this chapter.) You may also dry the puree into rounds. See Chocolate Pudding Leather Cookies (page 129) for instructions on measuring and spacing the rounds on the drying trays.

6. Place the drying trays in the dehydrator. Allow anywhere from 8 to 20 hours to dry the puree into leather. A leather is dried when it peels easily off the sheet. Drying time depends upon several factors: the make of dehydrator, the thickness of the puree on the leather sheets, the sugar content of the puree, and so on. Should the leather stick, dry it a little longer or loosen it with the spatula.

   To promote faster drying, once a piece of leather holds its shape, turn it over. Or transfer the leather to a mesh sheet.

7. *To store leathers:* Stack sheets of fruit or vegetable leathers on top of each other. If desired, and this is optional, you can sprinkle the finished sheets with cornstarch or arrowroot to prevent them from sticking together. Roll up, wrap securely in plastic wrap, and put in an airtight container.

   Kept at room temperature, leathers will keep for 1 year (or as long as you can keep them hidden from the children!). Refrigerated or frozen, leathers will keep indefinitely.

Sticky, Sticky, Sticky

If any food you are drying is really stuck to either the mesh sheet or the solid leather sheet (or the drying tray, for that matter) and will not come off, put the tray in the freezer, just until the food is frozen. Then try again to remove the food from the tray. I can't tell you the number of times people have told me how well this works. You can also spray the mesh sheets with oil as a way of preventing sticking.

Example 1: The Easiest-of-All Apple Leather

I call this the easiest-of-all apple leather because you need only your dehydrator and a jar of unsweetened applesauce in order to proceed. Now, that's easy! Make it as described here, then the next time add fresh, frozen, or drained canned strawberries, cherries, or pears (in an equal amount to the applesauce), and a pinch of cinnamon. If you like your leather to be more similar to commercial fruit roll-ups, add 1 tablespoon fruit-flavored Jell-O per cup of applesauce.

One 24-ounce jar natural (unsweetened) applesauce

Rub a solid leather sheet of the dehydrator lightly with vegetable oil or spray with Pam. Wipe off any excess with paper towels.

Spread a ¼-inch layer of applesauce evenly over the oiled sheet, then place in the dehydrator. The drying time will depend upon the dehydrator you are using and the thickness of the applesauce: Allow anywhere from 8 to 20 hours to dry. When finished, the applesauce will have dried into a paper-thin sheet that can be easily peeled off. If there are sticky or tacky areas, dry the leather a little longer.

Store as directed on page 121.

Makes one 12-inch square sheet, weighing 3 ounces

Easy Cherry or Raspberry Apple Leather: Fruit-flavored jarred applesauces can also be dried into leather. Because these contain more sugar than natural applesauce, they may take a little longer to dry. However, it's well worth it: Children absolutely love them! If you want, you can add flavorings to them, like vanilla or almond extract, or ground cinnamon or nutmeg.

Example 2: Spaghetti Sauce Leather

Spaghetti sauce, either homemade or storebought, with meat or without, dries into a splendid leather and is a wonderful lightweight food to take along when you go backpacking or camping.

To make spaghetti sauce leather, simply follow the directions for making The Easiest-of-All Apple Leather—but use spagetti sauce instead. That's how easy it is!

Yogurt Leathers

Not only do I make my own yogurt culture, but I also like to dry different-flavored yogurts. The leather makes terrific snacks and when sweetened is a really good source of quick energy when you are backpacking and need something to get you going again.

Here are a few of the combinations I particularly like. Dry flavored yogurt into leather, following the example of The Easiest-of-All Apple Leather, page 122.

Combine 1 cup plain nonfat yogurt with 1 tablespoon thawed frozen orange juice concentrate; or

1 cup cooked peaches or pears; or
1 cup applesauce; or
1 cup fresh carrot juice; or
1 cup fresh carrot juice and 1 cup applesauce

JUICE TO LEATHER AND BACK AGAIN:
THE EVOLUTION OF AN IDEA

The kitchen appliance I like second to my food dehydrator is my juicer. After that comes the blender. Here's a recipe that uses all three! In fact, if you experiment with drying food the way I do, you'll be using all these appliances frequently.

In my juicer, I made fresh carrot juice, poured it into lightly oiled solid leather trays, and dried it. It flaked off and was intensely sweet.

In my dehydrator on lightly oiled solid leather sheets on drying trays, I dried thawed orange juice concentrate, which turned out to be very sticky and also intensely sweet.

Then I combined ½ cup each fresh orange juice and carrot juice, and dried that on lightly oiled solid leather sheets. It, too, was very sticky and absolutely delicious.

Lastly, I combined ¼ cup thawed frozen orange juice concentrate, 1 cup fresh carrot juice, and ½ cup carrot pulp left over from making the juice, and dried the mixture on lightly oiled solid leather sheets.

Months later, I rehydrated 5 ounces of the orange-carrot leather in 2 cups water to make a marvelous breakfast drink!

OTHER IDEAS FOR USING FOOD LEATHERS

- Break tomato leather into pieces to use as chips with dips.
- Include a piece of vegetable leather in a sandwich, the way you would a lettuce leaf.
- Make cutouts by pressing cookie cutters into the leather when it is half-dried or just dry enough to hold its shape. Continue to dry the sheets. When finished, push out the shapes. Eat the cutouts as is or use them to decorate baked goods.
- It can never be mentioned frequently enough that fruit and/ or vegetable leathers make superb lightweight and nutritious snacks that fit easily into a backpack. You can actually have a "pocket" lunch—one that fits in your pocket, I mean!

FRUIT LEATHERS

~~~

Apple Leather from Homemade Applesauce

When the apple harvest is on and the fruit is literally dropping off the trees, you might want to make fresh applesauce for drying into leather. It's a good way to use up less-than-perfect apples, and who doesn't like homemade applesauce? We have it for dessert and for breakfast on pancakes. And we dry it.

1 pound apples, washed, unpeeled, but cored and cut into 1- to 2-inch pieces
1 cup water or apple cider
Ground cinnamon to taste

In a saucepan, combine the apples and the water or apple cider. Bring to a boil and simmer the apples about 20 minutes, or until soft. Let the apples cool, then puree them in a blender until smooth. Add the cinnamon to taste. (Makes about 3 cups.)

Spread the homemade applesauce evenly on a lightly oiled solid leather sheet, then place the drying tray in the dehydrator. The drying time will depend upon the make of dehydrator you are using and the thickness of the applesauce layer: Allow anywhere from 8 to 20 hours to dry, depending on the make of dehydrator. Peel the leather off the sheet and store it as directed on page 121.

3 cups applesauce makes one 12-inch square leather sheet, weighing 3 ounces

Minted Apple Leather: Instead of cooking the apples in water or cider, make 2 cups peppermint or spearmint tea. Cook the cut-up apples in the tea until soft. Let cool and puree in the blender. Add 1 teaspoon crushed dried mint leaves. Spread the puree and make leather as directed above.

Apple Leather from Uncooked Apples: If you are not in the mood to make your own applesauce and you don't have store-bought applesauce, you can *still* make your own leather, provided you have a pound of apples on hand. Simply wash, core, and peel the apples (or don't peel them if you are so inclined). Then puree them in the blender. During this process you may have to add a little liquid—water or juice—to smooth out the thick puree. Dry the puree into leather as described above; re-

125

member that when dried, uncooked applesauce is darker in color than cooked applesauce. To retain a lighter color in the leather, add 1 teaspoon lemon juice, orange juice, or pineapple juice for each cup of pureed apples.

Basic Fruit Leather

Once you become accustomed to making fruit leathers, you will always know to have a pound of apples or jars of applesauce in the pantry. And the fact that you can use cooked fresh, cooked frozen, or canned fruit to make this leather means that, with applesauce and a little orange juice concentrate on hand, the essentially nonsugared puree can be combined before you go to bed and dried into leather by the time you arise. Now, that's convenience!

1 pound cut-up fresh, thawed frozen, or drained canned fruit, such as pears, berries, or apricots
3 tablespoons frozen orange juice concentrate, thawed
Water as needed
One 24-ounce jar applesauce (natural or sweetened)

If using either fresh or frozen fruit, combine it in a saucepan with the orange juice concentrate and enough water to cover the fruit. Cook over medium heat until the fruit is soft. Let the mixture cool.

In a blender, puree the fruit until it is smooth. Add the applesauce and blend until combined. (If using canned fruit, combine all the ingredients in the blender.) Taste and add flavoring, if desired.

Spread the fruit puree evenly in a ¼-inch thick layer on a lightly oiled solid leather sheet. Place the drying tray in the dehydrator. The drying time will depend upon the make of dehydrator you are using and the thickness of the puree layer: allow anywhere from 8 to 20 hours to dry. Peel the leather off the sheet and store it as directed on page 121.

Makes one 10 × 20-inch sheet, weighing about 6 ounces

Rhubarb Leather

Here's a recipe that evolved over time, through experimentation. When I first started drying fresh rhubarb, I cut it up, dried it, and stored it only to discover a year later I had a lot of it still on hand. The next season, I decided to dry rhubard as puree into leather. To my surprise, I had to hide the leather to keep my family from completely depleting the supply! The very first time I ever made this leather, my son walked into the kitchen, looked inside the dehydrator, abruptly replaced the cover, and said, "What's that? It looks terrible." Appearance notwithstanding, this leather is first-rate.

Note that almost any other flavoring added to rhubarb will overpower it; see Cherry Rhubarb Leather below.

4 cups chopped fresh rhubarb (1-inch pieces)
4 cups boiling water
½ cup brown sugar
1 teaspoon ground cinnamon

In a heatproof bowl, combine the rhubarb and the 4 cups boiling water, and let sit for 10 minutes. This soaking softens the texture of the rhubarb and removes some of the acidity so that less sweetener is needed to offset the natural tartness of the fruit. You can also cook the rhubarb in boiling water until it changes from pink or red to light green in color. Drain.

In the blender, puree the softened rhubarb, in batches if necessary, to avoid overtaxing the blender and having to add liquid. Add the brown sugar and the cinnamon, and taste. Adjust the flavorings as needed and continue to puree the mixture until smooth.

Spread the rhubarb puree evenly on a lightly oiled solid leather sheet, then place the drying tray in the dehydrator. The drying time will depend upon the make of dehydrator you are using and the thickness of the puree layer: Allow anywhere from 8 to 20 hours to dry. Peel the leather off the sheet and store it as directed on page 121.

Makes one 12-inch square sheet, weighing 3 ounces

Cherry Rhubarb Leather: For a special treat, puree a 16-ounce can of cherry pie filling and add it to the rhubarb puree. Dry as directed above. Despite the rhubarb base, this will taste like cherry leather.

～～

Pumpkin Leather

This is an extremely simple recipe that also happens to be good for anyone on a diet, because it supplies all the flavor of pumpkin pie but not the crust. Besides the coconut, you can add chopped nuts. Note that you can also dry this into "cookies." Pumpkin pie filling can be used in place of plain pumpkin, if you like, the only difference being that the spiciness in the leather will be intensified.

2 cups (one 16-ounce can) pumpkin
1 cup canned evaporated milk
2 cups sweetened applesauce
¼ cup honey
¼ cup dried shredded coconut
1 teaspoon ground cinnamon
½ teaspoon ground nutmeg
½ teaspoon ground allspice
2 tablespoons finely chopped dried grapes (raisins)

In a large bowl, combine the pumpkin and the evaporated milk. Stir in the applesauce, add the honey, the coconut, the cinnamon, the nutmeg, and the allspice, and combine the mixture well. Taste and adjust the spices. Stir in the chopped raisins.

Spread the pumpkin-applesauce mixture evenly on a lightly oiled solid leather sheet or spoon it by the tablespoon on oiled sheets to make "cookies." Leave about ½ to 1 inch between the rounds. Place the drying trays in the dehydrator. The drying time will depend upon the make of dehydrator you are using and the thickness of the puree layer: Allow anywhere from 8 to 20 hours to dry. Peel the leather off the sheet and store it as directed on page 121.

For a quick treat, cut the leather into graham cracker–sized squares and top with whipped cream.

Makes one 10 × 20-inch sheet, or 65 cookies

Pumpkin Leather Made from Fresh Pumpkin: Cut a medium pumpkin in half and scoop out the seeds and stringy flesh. Place pumpkin halves, skin side up, in ½ inch of water in a large baking pan. Cover and bake in a preheated 325°F oven for 30 minutes to 1 hour, or until the pumpkin is soft. Let cool and scoop out the cooked flesh into a large bowl. Mash; use 2 cups for the pumpkin in the above recipe.

Cottage Cheese and Fruit Leather

Here's another combination that requires only one step of preparation before it can be dried. The cottage cheese acts as a very good source of protein; should you want to increase the nutritiousness of this leather, you can add wheat germ or brewer's yeast. This makes a great snack for dieters; it's healthful and sweet, but not loaded with refined sugar. My favorite fruits to use are applesauce, apricots, peaches, and nectarines. And don't forget plums.

1½ cups low-fat cottage cheese
1½ cups pureed fruit of choice
½ cup honey

In a blender, puree all the ingredients until smooth.

Spread the puree evenly on a lightly oiled solid leather sheet. Place the drying tray in the dehydrator. The drying time will depend upon the make of dehydrator you are using and the thickness of the puree layer: Allow anywhere from 8 to 20 hours to dry. Peel the leather off the sheet and store it as directed on page 121.

Makes one 10-inch sheet, weighing 3 ounces

Chocolate Pudding Leather Cookies

Several years ago, pudding roll-ups were popular snacks that you could buy at the supermarket. People used to ask me if they could make them in the dehydrator. Because roll-ups and leathers are really the same thing, I began experimenting. I started by making my own puddings from scratch and taking it from there, but that didn't work very well. Recently I bought lots of packaged puddings—both instant and noninstant—and tried again. Eventually, I got it right, and here's the result.

Using packaged pudding mix renders making this recipe as easy as pie—easier, in fact! These "cookies" are great for lunch boxes or snack packs, and are ideal to take along backpacking. Close your eyes when you eat one and see if it doesn't taste like a Tootsie Roll!

One 3.5-ounce package chocolate fudge instant pudding
1 cup milk
1 cup applesauce (natural or sweetened)
1 teaspoon vanilla

In a bowl, combine all the ingredients well. Drop the pudding mixture by the teaspoon onto lightly oiled solid leather sheets and with the back of a tablespoon spread it into rounds, each 1 to 2 inches in diameter. Leave ½ to 1 inch between the rounds. Place the drying trays in the dehydrator. The drying time will depend upon the make of dehydrator you are using and the thickness of the rounds: Allow about 5 hours, or until you can peel the rounds off the sheets. Turn the rounds over and dry for another 5 hours. Store as directed on page 121.

Makes 30 cookies

〜〜

Butterscotch Pudding Leather Cookies

The preceding cookie leather was made with milk and applesauce; this one is made with yogurt. Caramel-like and chewy in texture, these are hard to resist. They remind me of a candy I used to enjoy that went by the name of Slow Poke Sucker.

Of course, you can also dry this into one thin sheet. Allow the same amount of time for drying.

One 3.5-ounce package butterscotch instant pudding
1 cup milk
1 cup vanilla yogurt (regular or nonfat)

In a bowl, mix together all the ingredients. Drop the pudding mixture by the teaspoon onto lightly oiled solid leather sheets and with the back of a tablespoon, spread it into rounds, each about 1 to 2 inches in diameter. Leave about 1 inch between the rounds. Place the drying trays in the dehydrator. The drying time will depend upon the make of dehydrator you are using and the thickness of the rounds: Allow about 5 hours, or until you can peel the rounds off the sheets. Turn the rounds over and dry for 5 more hours. Store as directed on page 121.

Makes 30 cookies

~~~

Fruit Leather Breakfast Cookies

Breakfast? Juice, milk, cereal, and, with any luck, a piece of fruit. Realistically, how often do most of us have the time for more than one of these? Here, all of those healthful breakfast components are combined into a leather to make a first-rate way to start the day. Note that no baking is involved. Your dehydrator does the work. These may be called "cookies," but nutritionally they are better than even the most streamlined pastry or doughnut. *And* they don't get stale.

1 cup cut-up fresh fruit, such as bananas, peaches, or pears

½ cup frozen orange juice concentrate, thawed
½ cup powdered milk
1 teaspoon vanilla
Wheat germ, shredded coconut, sesame or sunflower seeds, or
   finely chopped nuts or dried fruits for the topping

In a blender, puree the fruit, the orange juice concentrate, the milk powder, and the vanilla, and taste. Add more flavoring, if needed.

Spoon the puree in 2-inch rounds onto lightly oiled solid leather sheets, leaving 1 inch between the cookies. Sprinkle with the topping of choice, then place the drying trays in the dehydrator. The drying time will depend upon the make of dehydrator you are using and the thickness of the rounds: Allow about 5 hours, or until you can peel the rounds off the sheets. Turn the rounds over and dry for 5 more hours. Store as directed on page 121.

Makes 12 cookies

Tip: You can also use drained canned fruit or frozen fruit, thawed.

TOMATO LEATHERS

The growing, eating, cooking, and home drying of tomatoes fascinated me for over twenty years. What follows are several of the ways to make tomato leather. The challenge, of course, was how to thicken the tomato puree, which on its own is low in pectin.

In each tomato leather recipe that follows, I have used a different thickening agent. The simplest recipe needs only two ingredients, tomato puree and applesauce. It's the pectin in the applesauce that makes the mixture thicken. As you have already noticed, applesauce comes in very handy in making fruit or vegetable leathers.

Easy Tomato Leather (Made with Applesauce)

½ cup tomato puree
½ cup applesauce

In a bowl, combine the tomato puree and the applesauce. Spread the puree evenly in a ¼-inch thick layer on a lightly oiled solid leather sheet. Place the drying tray in the dehydrator. The drying time will depend upon the make of dehydrator you are using and the thickness of the puree: Allow anywhere from 8 to 20 hours to dry. Peel the leather off the sheet and store as directed on page 121.

Makes one 4-inch sheet, weighing 1 ounce

Tomato Leather (Made with Cornstarch)

If you run out of apples or applesauce, you can still make tomato leather—with cornstarch.

3 cups pureed tomatoes with skins (about 4 large)
3 heaping teaspoons cornstarch

In a blender, combine the pureed tomatoes and the cornstarch until smooth. Transfer the puree to a saucepan and over medium heat cook it, stirring often, until it is the consistency of applesauce. Remove the pan from the heat and let it cool.

Spread the puree evenly on a lightly oiled solid leather sheet and place the drying tray in the dehydrator. The drying time will depend upon the make of dehydrator you are using and the thickness of the puree: Allow anywhere from 8 to 20 hours to dry. Peel the leather off the sheet and store as directed on page 121.

Makes one 10-inch sheet, weighing 3 ounces

~~~

3-Ingredient Tomato Leather (Made with Pectin)

I use powdered pectin here as a thickener, and opt for Sure-Jell light powdered pectin, which is nationally available.

3 cups pureed tomatoes with skins (about 4 large)
2 tablespoons powdered pectin
1 teaspoon sugar

In a saucepan, bring the pureed tomatoes, the pectin, and the sugar to a full rolling boil over high heat, stirring to avoid scorching, for 5 minutes. Reduce the heat to low, and simmer mixture, stirring often, for about 20 minutes. Let cool.

Spread the puree evenly on a lightly oiled solid leather sheet and place the drying tray in the dehydrator. The drying time will depend upon the make of dehydrator you are using and the thickness of the puree: Allow anywhere from 8 to 20 hours to dry. Peel the leather off the sheet and store as directed on page 121.

Makes one 10-inch sheet, weighing 3 ounces

Clear Tomato Leather: For tomato leather that is almost translucent, use 3 cups pure tomato juice, obtained by pressing pureed tomatoes through a sieve or strainer, or by putting tomatoes through a juicer. Follow the directions for making leather with the juice, pectin, and sugar.

VEGETABLE LEATHERS AND CHIPS

~~~

Fancy Tomato Leather Chips
(Made with Unflavored Gelatin)

This dressed-up rendition of tomato leather uses both fresh and dried ingredients. The fresh vegetables are best ground in a juicer. Failing that, you can use your blender.

These chips are positively delicious as snacks or with a dip. Or rehydrate the chips into soup or sauce. You can dry this mixture into sheets and top the sheets with a whipped cream cheese filling flecked with minced scallions. Rolled and then cut into pinwheels, they are delicious.

1 cup peeled fresh carrot chunks
½ cup onion pieces
½ cup celery pieces
1 tablespoon fresh lemon juice
1 tablespoon sugar
1 teaspoon chopped garlic
½ teaspoon dried basil
½ teaspoon dried oregano
½ teaspoon salt
4 cups pureed tomatoes (about 8 medium)
Three ¼-ounce packets powdered unflavored gelatin
¾ cup cold water

In a juicer, combine the carrots, the onion, and the celery, and juice. Remove the juice to a bowl and stir in the vegetable pulp from the juicer, the lemon juice, the sugar, the garlic, the basil, the oregano, and the salt. Place the vegetable mixture in a large saucepan and add the pureed tomatoes.

In a cup, combine the gelatin and the ¾ cup cold water, and let stand for 5 minutes to allow the gelatin to soften. Add the gelatin to the pan and bring the mixture to a rolling boil, stirring often to prevent scorching. Cook for 5 minutes over medium-high heat, stirring often. Remove the pan from the heat and let the mixture cool.

Onto lightly oiled solid leather sheets, spoon the puree in 1- or 3-inch rounds, leaving about ½ inch between the rounds. (Alternatively, you can spread the puree evenly over the prepared sheets.) Place the drying trays in the dehydrator and dry for about 5 hours. The drying time will depend upon the make of dehydrator you are using and the thickness of the puree. Salt the chips when they are dry enough to hold their shape. Turn the chips and salt them again. Dry for another 5 hours, or until the chips peel off the sheets. Store as directed on page 121.

Makes 108 rounds, or 9 dozen

～

Beet Leather

I love beets, and I am always looking for ways to use them. And should you happen to be anemic and don't like or can't take iron pills, you probably know that beets are a superb source of iron. Short of eating cooked beets frequently, I came up with this idea. Enjoy this leather as a quick natural source of iron, whether you are at home or out kayaking or backpacking.

This is a deep red, beautifully colored leather, sweet in taste. Top with softened cream cheese, roll, and cut into pinwheels for a pretty, nourishing snack. Try this recipe before you sign off on beets forever: I'll bet you'll like it.

2 cups canned beets, undrained
2 cups applesauce (natural or sweetened)

In a blender, puree the canned beets with their liquid. Add the applesauce and puree the mixture until smooth.

Spread the puree evenly on a lightly oiled solid leather sheet. Place the drying tray in the dehydrator. The drying time will depend upon the make of dehydrator you are using and the thickness of the puree layer: Allow 12 or more hours to dry. Peel the leather off the sheet and store it as directed on page 121.

Makes one 12-inch square sheet, weighing about 6 ounces

～

Mushroom Leather Chips

I'm a devoted lover of mushrooms, and have been challenged as to how to dehydrate them beyond simply slicing them up and putting them on drying trays. Here's a solution: Mushroom leather chips—to be used not as a snack but as a flavoring agent in sauces, to add to cream soups, or as the basis of bouillon. Vegetarians will like using shiitake mushroom chips as a source of protein. If you have mushrooms that are no longer at their peak of freshness, this is a super way to preserve them. The flavor of the rehydrated leather is magnificent. Add a mushroom leather chip or two to the Thanksgiving turkey gravy or to spruce up turkey leftovers.

2 cups fresh mushrooms, such as shiitake, or cultivated mushrooms, cut into 1-inch pieces
2 cups water, divided
⅔ cup chopped onions
1 teaspoon chopped garlic
1 teaspoon soy sauce
¼ teaspoon sugar
⅛ teaspoon salt
2 tablespoons cornstarch

In a skillet, combine 1 cup of the water with the remaining ingredients, except the cornstarch, over medium heat and simmer until the onions are transparent.

In a cup, whisk together the remaining 1 cup of water and the cornstarch until combined. Add to the skillet and bring the mixture to a boil, stirring occasionally, until bubbles break on the surface. Remove the pan from the heat and let cool.

Transfer the mixture to a blender and puree until smooth. Spoon the puree, dividing it into 6 ovals, each about 4 inches long and 3 inches wide, onto lightly oiled solid leather sheets. Place the drying sheets in the dehydrator. The drying time will depend upon the make of dehydrator you are using and the thickness of the mushroom mixture: Allow about 5 hours for drying the first side. Turn the chips over and dry another 5 hours, or until they can be peeled off easily. Store as directed on page 121.

Makes 6 chips

To use mushroom leather chips: Rehydrate a leather chip by cutting it into ¼-inch pieces with a pair of scissors. In a small saucepan, combine the leather pieces with ¼ cup boiling water. Cover and let sit for 15 minutes to rehydrate. Uncover and bring the mixture to a boil over medium-high heat, stirring vigorously with a wire whisk to break up the leather completely. Use to flavor gravies, sauces, or soups. Makes 3 tablespoons mushroom flavoring.

~~~

Real Corn Chips

The challenge of creating a crunchy corn chip, those positively addictive ones that are usually deep-fried in oil, may not seem a big deal. But to home-dried food devotees, namely myself and my friend Betsy, perfecting a healthful chip for Betsy's husband, Jim, has taken years. First, the chips had to hold together and keep their shape; then we had to get them not to crack, to be sweet enough, to have color—all without using oil. Here's our creation—and we are still fine-tuning it. However, not a drop of oil was added; and we even came up with a variation! Just so you know, the chips are yellow in color, and while they do not snap when broken, they are deliciously chewy.

3 dried tomato slices
1 teaspoon dried onion pieces
1 teaspoon dried red or green bell pepper pieces
2 cup cooked fresh or frozen corn
¼ cup plain yogurt
½ cup water
⅓ cup dried cornmeal (made from grinding ⅓ cup dried corn kernels)
½ teaspoon chopped garlic
½ cup shredded mozzarella cheese
½ teaspoon salt, plus additional for sprinkling

In a blender, grind the dried tomato slices, the dried onion pieces, and the dried bell pepper pieces to a coarse powder. Add the fresh or frozen corn and the yogurt, and puree. Add the water, the cornmeal, the garlic, and the ½ teaspoon salt, and blend until the mixture is combined. Stir in the mozzarella.

Spread the puree by the teaspoonful onto a lightly oiled solid leather sheet, using the back of the spoon to smooth the puree into 1- to 2-inch rounds, and leaving 1 inch between them. (You may have to add water, 1 tablespoon at a time, to the puree to thin it to spreading consistency.) Sprinkle the rounds with salt.

Place the drying sheet in the dehydrator. The drying time will depend upon the make of dehydrator you are using and the thickness of the rounds: Allow anywhere from 10 to 14 hours total. Turn the chips over after 6 to 8 hours and sprinkle the other side with salt. Dry the chips for 2 to 4 hours more, or until firm. Store as directed on page 121.

Makes 36 chips

Corn Carrot Chips: Here's a nice variation on a theme: Reduce the fresh or frozen corn measurement to 1½ cups and add either ½ cup grated carrots or carrot pulp left over from your juicer. Spoon the puree onto a prepared solid leather sheet and sprinkle the rounds with Cheddar cheese powder, crushed dried herbs, or commercial taco flavoring from a packet. Dry as directed.

Chapter 9

Trail Food: Backpackers Take Note

*I*f you are a backpacker (as I am), canoeist, kayaker, or outdoor enthusiast of any kind, you undoubtedly already know how taking dehydrated foods on your trip can help to lighten your load. Even if you pursue more traditional modes of traveling, but dietary restrictions or food allergies necessitate taking your own supply of foods, you know what I am talking about. Foods, fresh or canned or packaged, weigh a lot and take up valuable space; dried foods weigh a lot less and are remarkably packable. Rid of water and heavy protective packaging, dried foods make the perfect traveling companions. Dried foods high in nutritional values supply the energy you need for a day of strenuous physical activity. And by drying your own food at home and packing it yourself, you have direct control over what it is you will eat, because you've made the meals and planned the menus. No longer are you limited to ready-made mixes or someone else's idea of what's good for you out on the trail.

The recipes throughout this book can be used to plan meals away from home, but this chapter, in particular, will show you some special combinations to prepare and dry—foods that you might not think of cooking at home, but that are worth their weight in gold out in the wilds. For example, consider dried wheat gluten as a high-protein meat substitute, or dried tofu, or already cooked dried grains a nourishing meal, with the addition of vegetables.

I believe the reasons some us of us want to live temporarily (at least) in the outdoors, to sleep under the stars, to breathe crystal-clear air, to view still wide-open unpeopled spaces are highly personal. There is the challenge of doing it, of course, and the knowledge of the dramatic effect nature has on our senses. Whatever the reasons for outdoor adventuring, of this I am sure: The same foods we eat at home seem to taste much better and are much more appreciated when eaten in the outdoors away from home.

There are those moments, though, when you are camping and it starts to rain. You are dripping wet, having lugged thirty-five pounds of gear all day on your back, and you still can't find a suitable place to camp for the night. It's at those times, when all I can think about is my cozy Victorian bed with fresh, clean linens waiting for me at home, that I ask myself, "Why do I do this?"

The answer lies in how the experience helps me grow. I see the spaciousness of life; old problems disappear as new insights are made. With my eyes and ears and nose, I respond afresh to everything—especially food. Eating is a great part of the fun of adventuring.

What follows are some of my more practical insights on the foods you can take backpacking. They involve, not surprisingly, having used your dehydrator before leaving on the trip!

YOUR FOOD SUPPLY: WHAT TO TAKE

To sustain yourself, you need foods that are high in protein, fruits, vegetables, and starchy and sweet foods, but none of these can weigh too much. Dried foods are the obvious and practical choice. Among the nutritious dried foods I particularly like to carry are leathers, instant (cooked and dried) grains, and just-add-water-and-cook one-pot meals. When you dry your own foods, you are able to provide yourself on the trail with a variety of tastes, including nutritional options, that are very hard to come by if you rely exclusively on commercially prepared trail foods. And the difference in cost between the two is considerable. Here are several extremely viable sources of dried foods.

Canned Foods

Few people realize that canned foods can be dried and that many of them are delicious when rehydrated. Just as important as their taste is how transportable they become when dried. Take these simple examples:

A 1-pound 5-ounce can of fruit cocktail when dried reduces to 3 ounces and tastes just like fruit candy. And it needs no rehydrating to be enjoyed!

A 13-ounce can of cream soup reduces to 3 ounces dried.

A 6⅛-ounce can of water-packed tuna dries to 1 ounce.

The fact that a 1-pound 9-ounce jar of spaghetti sauce when dried reduces to 3 ounces may seem impossible to believe when you taste that reconstituted sauce, atop a plate of hot pasta.

How to Dry Canned Foods

Foods packed in water or juice, like canned peaches or mandarin oranges, should first be drained, then arranged in a single layer on mesh-lined drying trays. Dry until bendable to the touch.

Canned cream or stock-based soups or sauces, such as spaghetti sauce, canned tomato paste, or even ketchup, should be dried on lightly oiled solid leather sheets until the food can be peeled off. Don't be surprised if certain foods don't hold their shape when dried; they are still very usable.

When drying tuna, I prefer to use tuna packed in water, not oil, as oil-packed foods do not dry in home dehydrators as completely as water-packed ones do. Drain the tuna well before spreading it on the solid leather sheet. If you flake it into pieces or chunks, the tuna will dry faster, about 4 to 6 hours, depending on the make of dehydrator.

Depending upon the type of canned food, you can either eat it out of hand, like the dried fruit cocktail, or rehydrate it in water, juice, or milk.

Frozen Food

If you are in a hurry to leave on an outing and you haven't time to buy fresh ingredients for home drying, simply go to the frozen food section of your supermarket and pick up a selection of ready-to-eat frozen fruits and vegetables. The supply in your own freezer may also be another much closer source! To give you some idea of what you will be carrying, a 30-ounce package of mixed frozen vegetables when dried weighs all of 5 ounces.

141

How to Dry Frozen Foods:

If the frozen food is encased in ice crystals, remove as many crystals as you can before arranging the food on drying trays in your dehydrator. If you don't remove the ice buildup, you run the risk of flooding the machine when the ice starts to melt. Spread the frozen vegetable or fruit on the drying tray and give it a shake to jostle the pieces loose from each other. Let the tray stand at room temperature for several minutes to partially thaw, drain off any excess water, then put the tray in the dehydrator.

Leftover Food

At some point in time, everyone has some food left over. My advice is, do not discard leftovers. They can be dried very successfully and taken on camping or backpacking trips. Moreover, in drying leftovers you are doing a little something extra to extend your end of the food chain.

How to Dry Leftovers:

Select only those leftovers that appeal to you and dry them individually in your dehydrator. When dried, put each food in an airtight freezer bag, label and date the bag, and note the number of servings it contains. Place the food in a section of the freezer reserved for dried leftovers. Continue doing this over the course of a year. When you take a trip requiring lightweight food, it will be waiting for you in the freezer.

When drying a dish that contains food in different-sized chunks, like beef stew, I have found that it is better to separate the pieces of meat and/or vegetables from the gravy and dry each component separately. In the same fashion, store each component in its own separate freezer bag. When you're ready to combine them for rehydration, each ingredient will have been dried for the proper amount of time.

I also advise you not to try to dry casseroles containing cooked noodles or pasta dishes, because the noodles break down during the drying/rehydration processes. It's a better idea to take the sauce ingredients and the dry cooked noodles separately and combine them when ready to serve.

142

PROTEIN AND FAT

Now that you know what sources, besides the obvious fresh ones, you can draw on to dry foods for outdoor adventuring, it is important to address sources of protein and fat, both of which you will need in good supply on your journey. By protein, I mean eggs and milk, and by fat, I am talking here about butter, margarine, oil, or cheese.

Eggs

It is not possible to dry raw eggs in a home food dehydrator without running the risk of salmonella contamination. When backpacking or camping, therefore, I take dried egg substitutes, which can be purchased at some commercial bakeries or large grocery stores.

In general, 5 tablespoons of dried egg substitute equal 2 medium eggs, beaten.

You can dry your own eggs at home provided they are completely cooked. Repeat: Home-dry *cooked* eggs only. Scramble eggs as you would normally in a skillet, then dry them in your food dehydrator at a temperature of at least 140°F until hard, 6 to 10 hours, depending on the make of dehydrator. Let them cool and pulverize them in a blender. Dried cooked eggs are not a substitute for raw eggs.

This brings to mind another important point about trail food. Know the foods you are taking on the trip and how they combine. Do not experiment out in the wilds. Test out combinations at home before you leave, then take only your successes along in your food pack.

Milk

Buy dry milk to take with you on the trail. Whether dry or powdered, instant or noninstant, reconstitutable milk is abundantly available in supermarkets and grocery stores.

For 1 cup milk: Stir ¼ cup dry milk into 1 cup cold water and let sit for at least 15 minutes before using.

You may also want to purchase dried buttermilk, which cannot be dried at home because of its oil content. In cooking or

143

baking, buttermilk adds a lighter texture to the finished product and increases its nutritional value. In recipes, combine dried buttermilk with the other dried ingredients, then add liquid.

For 1 cup buttermilk: Stir ¼ cup dried buttermilk into 1 cup water.

Fats—Butter, Margarine, and Oil

Oil is not water and, as a consequence, does not dry well in a home food dehydrator. Therefore, you will have to purchase commercially dried butter buds or butter-flavored granules to take with you camping. While these dried products, including commercially dried oil, are good for cooking and baking, they do not work well for sautéing. On the trail, you may simply prefer to take olive oil. Always carry it in a spill-proof plastic container, as plastic bags invariably leak.

Although I do not recommend dehydrating milk, I was curious whether ice cream could be successfully dried. I dried three different flavors, on oiled solid leather sheets, by the tablespoon. Both the vanilla and strawberry ice cream turned into chalky powder, and the chocolate, when dried, was sticky on the bottom with the chalky powder on top. Beyond the sheer experience of it—could ice cream even be dried because of its high oil content?—I could not find a use for the powder, aside from a topping for other frozen desserts to add sweetness. Only the dried chocolate ice cream had any substance to speak of, and most of it was sticky.

Cheese

Cheese is a good source of both protein and fat, and unlike raw eggs and milk, certain types of low-fat cheese can be home-dried, including Parmesan, Romano, Asiago, and even low-fat cottage cheese.

How to Dry Low-Fat Cheese:

Cut the cheese into ⅛- to ¼-inch-thick slices and dry as described for other fatty foods, such as bacon or ground beef (pages 91 and 95).

144

OTHER HIGH-ENERGY TRAIL FOODS

Wheat Gluten

No discussion of high-energy foods appropriate for backpacking or camping would be complete without mention of wheat gluten, a protein or meat substitute known to vegetarians and other health-food enthusiasts. Most likely you have heard of gluten as the stretchy substance in bread dough that provides the elasticity that allows the dough to rise. If "overworked," the gluten tightens up, toughening the loaf.

Gluten can actually be separated out of a mass of dough, dried, and used as a meat substitute or extender. If you are a fan of Vietnamese cooking, you already know that gluten appears in that cuisine as "mock duck"—quite a stretch when you think of what gluten actually is!

When incorporating gluten into your own cooking, no matter the guise, it is important to remember that it is an incomplete protein and should always be served with another protein like eggs, milk, cheese, or meats. And because it has practically no taste of its own, you can add it to soup and let it absorb the flavor of the soup's ingredients and base, or add herbs and spices to the gluten itself.

To Separate Gluten from Dough:

Begin by making the dough. I like to grind my own wheat, hard red winter wheat, which I buy at the health-food store. Mix 2 cups flour with 1 cup water and knead, either by hand or in a bread mixer, until satiny and smooth. Shape the dough into a ball, put the dough in a bowl, and cover the dough with water. Let sit for 1 hour. As the dough sits, you will see the bran and starch begin to separate from the mass.

Remove the dough from the water and wash it under running lukewarm water. The bran will wash off, leaving a tight, elastic ball of gluten. Let the raw gluten relax for about 5 minutes before you dry it.

To Dry and Grind Wheat Gluten:

Form the raw gluten into 2- to 3-inch patties and place the

145

patties on a greased baking sheet. Bake in a preheated 250°F oven for 30 minutes.

Put the dried gluten patties through a meat grinder or grind them in a blender until the gluten has the texture of ground meat. (It should look like hamburger.)

To Dehydrate Wheat Gluten:

Put the ground gluten on a leather sheet and dry in a dehydrator 4 to 8 hours, depending on the make of dehydrator, until hard.

To Use Dried Wheat Gluten:

Add it to Backpacker Spaghetti Sauce (page 161) or to the meatless variation (page 163). Or incorporate it into soup. Because wheat gluten is dried until hard, you will need to allow additional time for it to rehydrate in liquid.

Tofu

Like wheat gluten, tofu is high in protein. Tofu is bean curd cake made from soybeans. It comes in squares that are packed in water and it is sold in Asian markets, health-food stores, and large supermarkets. Tofu is rich in nutrients, free of cholesterol, and low in saturated fats and calories. It contains all eight essential amino acids in a configuration that is readily usable by the human body. And if that were not enough, it has about 35 percent more protein than any other unprocessed plant or animal food. Dried tofu can be a nutritional godsend for vegetarians and non-vegetarians alike when trekking away from home.

Tip: Because tofu, like gluten, has little flavor, I like to slice it and then marinate it in 1 part soy sauce to 4 parts water before drying it. Add dried herbs, such as dill and basil, plus ground pepper to the soy sauce for additional flavor.

To Dry Tofu:

- Cut the fresh, drained tofu into ⅛- to ¼-inch slices and place the slices on the drying tray of your dehydrator. Dry for 4 to 8 hours, depending on the make of dehydrator, until brittle.
- Or slice the tofu as described above and arrange it on a paper-towel–lined layer of newspaper. Cover the tofu with another layer of paper towels and newspaper, then place a weight—a

cast-iron skillet, for example—on the paper layer. Press for 4 to 8 hours. Remove the weight and toweling, then place the tofu slices on dehydrator trays. Dry until crackerlike and brittle.

• Or arrange slices of tofu on a baking sheet and freeze them for a minimum of 8 hours. Transfer the frozen tofu slices to your dehydrator and dry until crackerlike and brittle.

One pound fresh tofu equals 3 ounces dried.

To Use Dried Tofu:

• Enjoy herbed marinated dried tofu slices as crackers.
• Rehydrate dried tofu slices by covering them with hot water and letting them sit for several hours to rehydrate. Drain, chop, and add to soups, casseroles, salads, egg or rice dishes, or sauces.
• Rehydrate dried tofu and use it as an egg substitute: Allow ⅓ cup mashed rehydrated tofu for each whole egg in a given recipe.
• Grind dried tofu slices into powder and use as a flour or cheese substitute.
• Make Tofu Soup (page 191) or Eggs with Tofu and Fresh Asparagus (page 207).

RICE AND OTHER GRAINS

Grains not only add needed nutrients to your diet when you are out on the trail, but they are also superb filler-uppers—an attribute that should never be underestimated when you are putting together a food pack. Just as pasta or noodles hit the spot when you are hungry or cold (or both), so does a nourishing bowlful of rice. Furthermore, rice and other grains can be added to "stretch" certain dishes that might not quite go all the way around those empty plates by the campfire. Take it from me, you do not want to run the risk of shortchanging hungry campers.

Carrying dried cooked grains, and I emphasize the word "cooked," in your food pack has several advantages. By drying the grain after it is cooked, you eliminate the long cooking time and, as a consequence, save on fuel. Depending upon the size

147

and texture of the grain, as well as the altitude, rehydration of cooked dried grains can range from minutes to hours.

To Cook and Dry Short-Grain Brown Rice:

Cook 1 cup short-grain brown rice in 2 cups boiling water until tender, about 30 minutes. Let cool and spread the rice in an even layer on mesh sheets on solid leather sheets in the drying tray. Place the trays in the dehydrator. Dry for 6 to 10 hours, depending on the make of dehydrator, or until hard.

To Rehydrate Dried Cooked Rice:

Combine equal amounts of rice and hot water in a saucepan and let sit for several minutes to rehydrate. Place the pan over medium heat and bring the water to a boil. Remove the pan from the heat, cover the pan, and let stand until the rice is soft. Or to quicken the process, simmer the rice, adding more liquid as necessary. Dried cooked rice will rehydrate in about a half hour.

Of course, you can also rehydrate dried cooked rice in bouillon or meat or vegetable stock, making it a natural addition to certain soups, like Backpacker Vegetarian Tomato Soup, page 155.

TRAIL BAKING

While you may have willingly decided to leave behind heavier foods, even some favorites, while you are on the trail, you do not have to do without bread, the staff of life. In fact, not only can you take it with you in the form of flour tortillas, bagels, bagel chips, muffins or crackers, but you can bake bread over the campfire. Being able to bake bread outdoors is just one more incredible aspect of adventuring out-of-doors. To be able to look forward to fresh bread at mealtime at the end of the day is worth every last one of those exhausting steps to the campsite! And warm bread in the morning, now that's something to get up for.

Experienced backpackers and campers, devoted to making bread on the trail, already know that there is a dried sourdough starter called Goldrush Old-Fashioned San Francisco–Style Sourdough Starter Packet (net weight, ½ ounce), available at health-food stores. The starter makes easy work of biscuits and pancake batter. If you choose to dry your own starter, remember to dry it at 90°F; higher temperatures will kill the culture.

There is another way to have your bread and eat it, too, on the trail. It's called stick baking: Bread dough cooks on a stick; it's as easy, and wonderful, as that.

Stick Baking

Begin by selecting green sticks, each about 2½ feet long and about 1 to 1½ inches thick, and peel back the bark about 6 inches on one end of each stick. Make the dough (recipe follows), then wrap it around the prepared end of the stick. Rotate the stick over the fire for 8 to 10 minutes. You've just made stick bread! The finished loaf will be dark on the outside, with a hole in the middle that can be filled with stew or spaghetti sauce or a sweet.

~~

Stick Bread

2 cups Bisquick
½ cup cold water
4 prepared sticks

Have a good fire of hot coals ready and waiting.

In a bowl, stir the Bisquick and the water together until a soft dough forms. Divide the dough into 4 equal pieces.

Wrap 1 piece of the dough around the prepared end of each stick, place the dough over hot coals, and rotate the sticks for even baking. (If you heat the sticks first over the fire, the part of the dough next to the stick will cook better, but be careful of burning the sticks!) Cook for about 8 to 10 minutes, or until crisp on the outside but not burned.

Makes 4 stick breads

Vegetable Stick Bread: Rehydrate 1 tablespoon small pieces of dried tomato and 1 teaspoon each dried bell pepper pieces and dried onion in 2 tablespoons water until softened. Add the vegetable combination to the cold water before adding it to the Bisquick.

Fruit Stick Bread: Knead small pieces of dried fruit—apples, figs, dates, or fruit leathers (see pages 120–121)—into the dough before dividing it into pieces.

Jerkied Stick Bread: Work ½ cup pieces of jerky (¼-inch size) into the dough before dividing it into pieces.

PLANNING TRAIL MEALS

A day's supply of dried food for one person will weigh 1 to 1½ pounds and provide 4,000 to 5,000 calories. Take enough food to share with travelers you meet along the way and always factor in emergency rations in case of bad weather or the loss of a food pack.

Many backpackers and campers find that they function better on the trail if the meals they eat do not differ greatly from those they have at home. Keep this in mind when you cook beforehand, and start a list of menus that could be replicated for your next outing. When you find a recipe that works for you, experiment with it: Try substituting beef jerky one time, chicken jerky the next. The same basic recipe, like Backpacker Jerky Stew (page 157), will taste different each time. And if it is good at home, it will taste wonderful in the great outdoors!

The recipes in this chapter should serve as just the start of your repertoire of trail food combinations. Read through the other chapters, write down the recipes that appeal to you, their ingredients, and what you will need to dry. Then try those recipes at home.

For a three-day trip, here are some menus that use recipes from the book. As to beverages, I leave the selections up to you. Hot chocolate, coffee, or herbal tea are all good (and warming) options.

DAY 1

Breakfast
  Granola with Dried Fruit (page 239)
  Dried Apple Slices (page 47)
  Orange-Carrot Juice (page 247)

Lunch
  Potato Soup (page 188)
  Assorted Crackers

Snacks
   Assorted Fruit Leathers (pages 125–129)
   Vegetable Gorp (page 241)

Dinner
   Backpacker Jerky Stew (page 157)
   Stick Bread (page 149)
   Backpacker Yogurt Rice Pudding (page 165)

DAY 2

Breakfast
   Pancakes with Apricot Leather Syrup (page 248)

Lunch
   Backpacker Tuna à la King (page 158)
   Aunt Grace's Apple Raisin Cookies (page 238)

Snacks
   Fruit Gorp (page 241)
   Basic Beef Jerky (page 87)
   Real Corn Chips (page 137)

Dinner
   Spaghetti with Backpacker Spaghetti Sauce (page 161)
   Vegetable Stick Bread (page 149)
   Backpacker Trail Pudding (page 164)

DAY 3

Breakfast
   Fruit Leather Breakfast Cookies (page 131)
   Eggs with Tofu and Fresh Asparagus (page 207)

Lunch
   Backpacker Fancy Macaroni and Cheese (page 160)

Snacks
    Chocolate or Butterscotch Pudding Leather Cookies (pages 129, 130)
    Basic Chicken Jerky (page 89)

Dinner
    Simple Dried Veggies and Brown Rice (page 206)
    Cottage Cheese and Fruit Leather (page 129)

OTHER TRAIL FOOD IDEAS

Be sure to take foods high in fiber on the trail, for example, Granola with Dried Fruit (page 239).

To replace the salt and potassium you lose through perspiration, eat dried meats, bananas, apricots, raisins, and nuts.

Although nuts are heavy to carry, they provide a good amount of protein, besides crunch and flavor.

Seeds also perk up mealtimes and make good snacks on the trail. Take along sunflower, sesame, and pumpkin seeds.

If preparing an entire home-dried recipe is too time-consuming, add home-dried items to packaged food. Add pieces of dried beef or chicken jerky to a box of packaged fried rice. Or combine dried meats or vegetables and packaged noodle dishes: See Backpacker Fancy Macaroni and Cheese (page 160).

Dried yogurt (for procedure, see page 123) is delicious rehydrated with water and added to drinks or sauces. Or partially rehydrate it and spread it, like cream cheese, on crackers or fruit leathers.

Jerky is an excellent source of protein and very easy to carry, making it superb trail food. See pages 87–97 for its many variations.

Miso, soybean paste made from cooked fermented grains mixed with salt and water, is available fresh or dried from natural-food stores and can be used in the same way as ketchup as a substitute for salt, soy sauce, or bouillon for flavoring. To dry miso, see page 192.

HOW TO PACK DRIED MEALS FOR THE TRAIL

Some outdoor adventurers prefer to pack their food in bulk, others opt to pack each meal separately, and still others make up daily packs. While packing in bulk will probably add to the over-all weight you will be carrying, a choice of foods will very likely inspire creativity.

One-pot meals are the easiest to prepare, and they offer unlimited ways to use dried foods. Good one-pot meals include Backpacker Jerky Stew (page 157), Backpacker Jerkied Tomato Rice (page 159), and Fancy Macaroni and Cheese (page 160). Another option is to prepare a main-course dish like Simple Dried Veggies and Brown Rice (page 206) at home, then dry it in your food dehydrator. Pack the meal in a heavy-duty Ziploc bag, and stow it in your food pack. Then, on the trail all you have to do is rehydrate it, heat it, and enjoy.

I repeat, use heavy-duty plastic bags for carrying trail food and organize your food pack carefully and intelligently. As efficient as plastic bags are, animals can still smell the food in them. To really be on the safe side and to outwit any foraging forest animals, you could also vacuum-pack your dried food meals. The food will be sealed airtight, eliminating any possibility that an animal could pick up the scent.

Food is definitely part of the fun of outdoor adventuring. The more creatively you eat on the trail, the more profound the experience. Dried foods add variety, and there is a lot to be said for variety! And they lighten the load.

FOOD REHYDRATION ON THE TRAIL

While on the trail, plan far enough ahead to integrate food rehydration time into the day's activities. There is little that is more disheartening than having to wait and wait and wait for a meal when you're hungry. So after lunch on any given day of camping, anticipate dinner by combining a dried soup or dried cooked rice with a little water in a sealable plastic bag or container with a tight-fitting lid. As the afternoon passes, add more water as needed; the item will be rehydrated by dinnertime. By adding boiling water you can speed up the process. A clear plastic 18-ounce peanut butter jar weighs 2 ounces when empty and makes a great container for rehydrating dried foods. And you're doing your part in the recycling process! For a more in-depth discussion of rehydrating dried foods, see Chapter 10, pages 169–173.

What's on Your Back

Approximate weight of foodstuffs common to food packs

4 cups dried cooked brown rice	= 1 pound
6 cups oatmeal	= 1 pound
3 cups powdered milk	= 1 pound
3 cups raisins	= 1 pound
4 cups granola	= 1 pound
6 cups home-dried bananas	= 1 pound
8 cups home-dried tomatoes	= 1 pound
8 cups home-dried peaches	= 1 pound
2½ cups home-dried celery powder	= 1 pound
4 cups applesauce leather, cut into 1-inch squares	= 1 pound

Water takes longer to boil at higher elevations, and rigorous boiling can quickly break food into pieces. As a consequence, don't walk away from the pot on the fire. It may need some of your attention, even if you're having only a simple one-pot meal.

Although you have read this many times already in this book, I will say it again: The larger the piece of dried food, the longer it takes to rehydrate. Break leathers into 1- to 2-inch pieces. And by completely rehydrating dried foods, you can conserve the amount of fuel you need for cooking.

TRAIL COOKING

When you are getting ready to cook over a campfire, you can get an idea of how hot the coals are by holding your hand over the fire, about two feet above it. Then count the seconds it takes until you must pull your hand away. Calculate the temperature as follows:

1 to 2 seconds = 500°F
3 to 4 seconds = 400°F
5 to 6 seconds = 300°F
7 to 10 seconds= 200°F

I hasten to add that I make no claims as to the accuracy of this system! I do know that it is fun to try, and is a proven hand warmer-upper when the temperature drops!

Here are a few other practical tips:

If the wood for the fire is all the same size, the coals will burn at the same rate.

When the flames have burned down and the coals are ashy gray on top and red hot beneath, start cooking.

If all you are cooking is eggs, the coals should be no bigger than the size of your thumb and about 1 inch deep; if you are baking, as with Stick Bread (page 149), the coals must be larger, about the size of a piece of charcoal and about 3 inches deep.

TRAIL FOOD RECIPES

~~~

Backpacker Vegetarian Tomato Soup

If you've been using your food dehydrator, you will have all, or most, of the ingredients on hand to make this warming combination. The ingredients weigh all of 3 ounces, which means you can take a lot of it along on your trip!

1 ½ cups water, plus ½ cup
¼ cup dried tomato powder
¼ teaspoon dried bell pepper powder
⅛ teaspoon dried onion powder
⅛ teaspoon dried garlic
⅛ teaspoon dried basil
Pinch of dried celery powder
½ cup powdered milk

In a camp pot, combine the 1½ cups water and all the remaining ingredients except the ½ cup water and the milk. Let sit, covered, for 15 minutes. Bring the mixture to a boil over high heat, lower heat to medium, and simmer for 5 minutes.

In a cup, combine the remaining ½ cup water and the milk. Stir and add to the soup base. Remove the pot from the heat, cover, and let sit for 10 minutes.

Makes 1¾ cups, or 2 servings

Variation: Add ¼ cup cooked dried short-grain brown rice and let it rehydrate in the soup base.

———

Backpacker Rice Balls Wrapped in Nori

This appetizer might not strike you as camp food, but I am including it because it is so different, exotic even. The rice balls are extremely low in fat, and if you like *nori*—dried seaweed— an Asian ingredient that can be found at Japanese or Asian markets, this is a way of having it out on the trail. Be careful to carry these so that they remain flat; if crushed or jostled, they break apart.

You can make the *nori* even more fragrant by toasting sheets of it over an open flame until slightly darker in color. For an interesting variation, try pieces of rehydrated dried apple or plum instead of tomato.

Total weight: 4 ounces.

1 cup cooked dried short-grain brown rice (for procedure, see page 148)
2 cups water, divided
16 dried tomato pieces (½ inch in diameter)
16 strips of *nori* (Japanese dried seaweed), each strip 1½ inches wide by 5 inches long

In a saucepan, combine the rice with 1 cup of the water and bring the water to a boil over medium-high heat. Remove the pan from the heat, cover, and let sit for at least 15 minutes to rehydrate.

Place the pan over medium heat and bring the rice to a boil. Cover partially and simmer until the rice is tender, about 15 to

30 minutes. If you have to add additional water, add 1 table-spoon at a time.

As the rice is finishing cooking, combine the dried tomato pieces in the remaining 1 cup water and let sit for 5 minutes to rehydrate.

Let the rice cool, and drain the tomatoes. Press the rice into 16 balls, each the size of a golf ball. In the middle of each rice ball enclose 1 piece of softened dried tomato. To prevent the rice from sticking to your hands, dip your hands in water every now and then. Wrap each ball in a strip of *nori*, encasing it completely and sealing the edges by rubbing the seaweed with water and pressing down firmly. Pack, seam side down, in a covered container.

Makes 16 appetizers

Backpacker Jerky Stew

This stew, one of my favorites, is great to take backpacking because it is made with all dried ingredients. Feel free to double or triple the recipe. At home you can make it in a slow cooker: Combine all the ingredients and let them bubble away on medium heat for 2 to 3 hours, or over low heat for 6 to 8 hours. Add dried corn, dried peas, or dried green beans to the vegetable/jerky rehydration combination whether making this over a campfire or on the top of the stove.

I have provided the option of adding a fresh carrot for crunch. It adds a nice touch, and because you have reduced the weight of your pack by taking along dried foods, you can afford the luxury of carrying a few fresh fruits and vegetables.

Total weight: 4 ounces.

4 cups water, divided
1 cup dried tomato pieces (about 20 slices, broken)
1 cup beef jerky pieces (½-inch size)
1 cup dried peeled potato slices
1 tablespoon dried bell pepper pieces
1 tablespoon dried onion pieces
½ teaspoon dried basil
½ teaspoon dried oregano
½ teaspoon dried garlic

Salt and pepper to taste
1 fresh carrot, sliced (optional)
1 cup cooked dried short-grain brown rice
(for procedure, see page 148)

In a large saucepan, combine 3 cups of the water and all the remaining ingredients except the carrot, if using, and the rice. Let sit for 30 minutes to rehydrate.

Place the pan over medium heat and bring the mixture to a boil. Simmer the stew for 30 minutes to 1 hour, or until the jerky is tender. If desired, add the fresh carrot when the stew comes to a boil.

While the stew is cooking, in a pan combine the rice with the remaining cup of water and bring the water to a boil over medium-high heat. Remove the pan from the heat, cover, and let sit for 15 minutes to rehydrate. Place the pan back over medium heat and bring the rice to a boil. Cover partially and simmer until the rice is tender, about 15 to 30 minutes.

Serve the stew over the hot cooked rice.

Serves 2 to 4

~~~

Backpacker Tuna à la King

This recipe, which combines commercially prepared foods with interesting dried foods, is for all those who camp or backpack in the mountains, and want a truly hearty, nourishing, and healthful meal at the end of a strenuous day. Who would have thought that you could enjoy tuna à la king out in the wilds? And if you're really organized, you will also have made noodles to take on the trip (see page 214).

The dried ingredients, not including the noodles, weigh a mere 8 ounces.

2 tablespoons dried peas
1 tablespoon dried mushroom pieces
1 teaspoon dried bell pepper pieces
1 teaspoon dried onion pieces
1 teaspoon dried celery powder
5 cups water, divided

½ cup flaked dried tuna fish (for procedure, see page 141)
½ cup 1-inch pieces dried cream of mushroom soup, crushed
(for procedure, see page 141)
1 cup milk (made by combining ¼ cup powdered milk with
1 cup water)
2 cups narrow dry egg noodles
2 tablespoons grated Parmesan cheese
Salt and pepper to taste

In a saucepan, combine the dried peas, the mushroom pieces, the bell pepper pieces, the onion pieces, and the celery powder with 1 cup of the water. Let the mixture sit for 30 minutes to rehydrate.

In a bowl, combine the dried tuna and the dried soup with the milk. Let sit for 30 minutes to rehydrate.

Place the saucepan over medium heat and bring the mixture to a boil. Reduce the heat to low and simmer the vegetables until the peas are cooked, about 30 minutes, adding more water if necessary. Add the tuna fish-mushroom mixture and bring the mixture to a boil. Simmer until it thickens, about 15 minutes.

In another saucepan, bring the remaining 4 cups water to a boil. Add the egg noodles, and cook until they are tender. Drain the noodles well. Return the noodles to the pan, add the egg noodles, and combine the mixture well. Stir in the Parmesan cheese and season with salt and pepper.

Serves 2 to 4 (depending upon how far you have hiked that day)

Tip: Dried turkey, chicken, or salmon can be substituted for the dried tuna. Dried shredded carrots are nice too. And dried tomato pieces add lovely color, too.

⌒⌒

Backpacker Jerkied Tomato Rice

This dish combines meat, vegetables, and a grain—a nutritious triumvirate—and all you have to do to prepare it is to use your dehydrator before you hit the trail. When you're tired, cold, and wet—and what backpacker doesn't know that feeling?—this is the dinner to have.

The packet of dried ingredients weighs 10 ounces, and every ounce of it is flavor- and power-packed.

1 cup ½-inch pieces Ground Beef Jerky (Taco, page 97, or Spicy, page 96)
3 cups water
¾ cup cooked dried short-grain brown rice (for procedure, see page 148)
½ cup dried tomato powder
1 teaspoon dried onion pieces
1 teaspoon dried celery powder
1 teaspoon dried bell pepper pieces
1 teaspoon light brown sugar
½ teaspoon dried mustard
Salt and pepper to taste

In a saucepan, combine all the ingredients. Let sit for 1 hour to rehydrate.

Place the pan over medium-high heat and bring the mixture to a boil, stirring occasionally. Boil for 5 minutes. Remove the pan from the heat, cover it, and let the rice sit for at least 30 minutes until it fully rehydrates and all the ingredients have softened.

Serves 4 as a main course

Backpacker Fancy Macaroni and Cheese

"Fancy" may not be quite the appropriate word here, but what I am hoping to convey is the notion that macaroni and cheese, the great comfort food that it is, can be enhanced with different kinds of dried foods to make it a particularly healthy and tasty dish especially if you're traveling with children. And the grown-ups will like it, too! Here, dried bacon bits add the spark. In addition to (or instead of) the bacon, you can add dried tomato flakes, dried onion pieces, and/or dried mushroom pieces. Rehydrate these in the milk, as you do the bacon. Double or triple this recipe if you're trekking with carbohydrate lovers.

Total weight of the dried ingredients, including the noodles, equals 8 ounces: Now, that's portable!

1 tablespoon powdered milk, dissolved in ¼ cup water
2 tablespoons dried bacon bits, crumbled
One 7¼-ounce box of macaroni and cheese dinner
6 cups water
2 tablespoons butter
Salt and pepper to taste
Dried herbs of choice to taste

In a small bowl, combine the milk with the bacon bits and stir in the packet of dried cheese sauce from the macaroni and cheese dinner. Let sit for 10 minutes to rehydrate.

In a large saucepan, bring the 6 cups water to a boil, add the noodles, and boil, stirring occasionally, for 7 to 10 minutes. Drain the macaroni and return it to the pan. Add the butter and stir until melted. Add the rehydrated cheese sauce, salt, pepper, and herbs of choice, and combine the mixture thoroughly.

Serves 2

~

Backpacker Spaghetti Sauce

As you already know, homemade or store-bought spaghetti sauce can be dried into leather and then rehydrated, making it ideal for taking along on a camping trip. Generally, 24 ounces of spaghetti sauce weigh 3 to 4 ounces dried into leather. When broken into 1-inch pieces, 3 to 4 ounces of the leather yield 2 cups. Not incidentally, 1 pound lean ground beef dried weighs 5 ounces and equals ¾ cup. Both the sauce and meat weigh so little it's almost impossible not to stow them in your food pack! And who doesn't like spaghetti?

Besides being very easy to transport, the ingredients here render a truly good sauce. All that is required is a little preplanning, but when done and the sauce tops hot cooked pasta, you have a nourishing, good meal, the kind hungry campers can really tuck into.

Total weight equals 12 ounces, not including the pasta, or the cheese.

For the beef:

¾ cup dried lean ground beef (for procedure, see page 95)
1 cup water

For the sauce:

2 cups 1-inch pieces dried spaghetti sauce leather (for procedure,
    see page 123)
½ cup dried tomato pieces (about 10 slices), torn into quarters
¼ cup small dried mushroom pieces
1 teaspoon dried onions
1 teaspoon dried bell pepper pieces
½ teaspoon dried celery powder
½ teaspoon dried oregano
½ teaspoon dried basil
½ teaspoon dried garlic
3 cups water

Prepare the beef: In a large saucepan, combine the dried beef
and the 1 cup water. Let sit for at least 1 hour to rehydrate. (To
speed up the process, combine the beef with 1 cup boiling water
and cook for about 2 minutes. Cover and let sit for about 30
minutes, or until the meat is softened.)

When the beef is rehydrated, add the spaghetti sauce leather
pieces with the dried tomato pieces. Stir in all the remaining
ingredients, including the 3 cups water, and let sit for at least 1
hour.

Place the pan over medium heat, bring the sauce to a boil, and
simmer it, stirring occasionally, for about 30 minutes, or to the
desired thickness, adding more water if necessary.

Serve over hot cooked pasta, with grated Parmesan cheese as
an accompaniment.

Serves 4

Backpacker Meatless Spaghetti Sauce: If desired, eliminate the
dried ground beef and the water needed for rehydration. The
rehydration time for the sauce, as well as the cooking time, will
be reduced by about one third. For a really thick sauce, add only

2 cups water to the recipe, reserving the remaining 1 cup water to thin the sauce if needed.

~~~

OTHER BACKPACKER OPTIONS FOR TOMATO SAUCE

As long as you have dried tomatoes on hand at home, you have several options for taking them along as trail food. The dried tomatoes can be in powder form, leather form (see Tomato Leathers, page 132–135), or in pieces. With any or all of these, tomato sauce is very easy to make. To make tomato paste, use half the recommended amount of water.

To Season Tomato Sauce or Paste: Add dried herbs, such as basil or oregano; celery powder, onion powder, or bell pepper powder; garlic, salt, pepper, and a pinch of sugar, if desired.

Other options: Add dried mushroom pieces, dried zucchini pieces, or dried spinach pieces.

~~~

Tomato Sauce (from Dried Tomato Powder)

½ cup dried tomato powder
1 cup water

In a small camp pot, combine the tomato powder with the water and bring the sauce to a simmer. You have just made practically instant tomato sauce.

Makes 1 cup

~~~

Tomato Sauce (from Dried Tomato Leather)

½ cup dried tomato leather pieces (1-inch size or smaller)
1 cup water

In a camp pot, combine the tomato leather pieces and the water, and bring the mixture slowly to a simmer. Use a spoon or wire whisk to break up the leather pieces and simmer, stirring, until saucelike.

Makes 1 cup

~~~

Tomato Sauce (from Dried Tomato Pieces)

1 cup tomato pieces
1 cup water

In a camp pot, combine the tomato pieces and water. Let sit for about 15 minutes until rehydrated.

Makes 1⅓ cups

~~~

Backpacker Trail Pudding

Here's an easy-to-make, light-to-carry, good-to-eat-on-the-trail combination that blends real food (in the form of dried fruit powder) with a packaged mix. And it makes a fast dessert at home, too.

2 cups water
1 cup powdered milk
One 3.4-ounce box vanilla instant pudding
2 tablespoons dried fruit powder, such as strawberry, apricot, peach, or banana

In a camp pot or container, combine all the ingredients and stir until completely blended. If desired, divide the pudding among juice cups and let stand for at least 10 minutes, or until thickened.

Serves 4

On the Trail: A Longing for Green

If you're anything like me, there comes a time out on the trail when, no matter how well and interestingly I've been eating, I long for something green. Because the idea of carrying a head of lettuce in my pack was a little ridiculous, I had to come up with something else. And I did. Don't laugh when you read about how I carry this little bit of green with me. It's lightweight and it works! Here's my high-energy, low-calorie, high-in-protein discovery.

(There is one special item you will need: a lady's nylon stocking!)

Sprouts for the Trail

1 nylon stocking
1 ounce alfalfa sprouts, sunflower seeds, chia seeds, mung beans, or green lentils

Cut off the foot and tie a knot at the bottom of the stocking. Put the sprouts in the leg of the stocking and tie another knot at the top. Place the stocking in a plastic bag of water and tie the bag to the outside of your pack. Let soak overnight.

Remove the stocking from the bag and rinse the sprouts. Attach the stocking to your pack and each day rinse the sprouts in water. Anywhere from 3 to 5 days later, you will have green sprouts. What a treat!

Backpacker Yogurt Rice Pudding

Except for the milk, you can combine and carry all the ingredients for this pudding in one very small plastic bag. Allow about 1½ hours to prepare it from start to finish, and up the nutrients by adding nuts or other dried fruits, such as apricots, cherries, or cranberries. The recipe doubles well.

1 cup milk (made by combining 1 cup water and ¼ cup powdered milk)

½ cup cooked dried short-grain brown rice (for procedure, see page 148)

½ cup dried plain or vanilla yogurt pieces (for procedure, see page 123)

¼ cup dried grapes (raisins) or other dried fruit

1 tablespoon brown sugar

½ teaspoon powdered ginger or tiny pieces of candied dried ginger (page 44)

⅛ teaspoon ground cinnamon

⅛ teaspoon ground nutmeg

In a saucepan, combine the milk with all the remaining ingredients. Let the mixture sit for at least 1 hour to let the rice plump up.

Place the saucepan over low heat and simmer it slowly for 5 minutes. Increase the heat to high and boil the mixture for 5 minutes, stirring often to prevent scorching. Remove the pan from the heat. Cover and let the pudding sit for 15 to 30 minutes to allow the rice to rehydrate completely. You may have to add more milk. Serve warm or chilled.

Serves 2

Part Two

THE RECIPES

Chapter 10

Cooking with
Dehydrated Foods

$\mathcal{N}$ow that you have a supply of dried foods in your pantry, you can begin to cook and/or bake with them. Of course, you have probably already discovered that some, like fruits and vegetables, jerky, and certain leathers, need no reconstitution to be enjoyed. A handful of dried grapes, otherwise known as raisins, or vegetable chips, or a piece or two of taco or spicy beef jerky prove that. But other dried foods need to be rehydrated before they can be eaten or used in recipes.

HOW TO REHYDRATE DRIED FOODS

Rehydrating, reconstituting, and refreshing are different words for the same process: adding liquid back to dried foods to prepare them for consumption. In short, by returning liquid to the dried food you are reversing the dehydration process.

How much liquid do you add to rehydrate a dried food? The general rule is to use an equal amount of liquid to the amount of food you are drying. Add the liquid little by little and try not to use more than is necessary. If you have added too much, drain it off and reserve it for cooking: Rehydration liquid contains nutrients from the food that has been soaked in it. When you become really experienced at cooking with dried foods, you will look at a recipe, gauge the amount of liquid in it, figure out how and when to add a dried ingredient, and retain the rehydration liquid for its nutritional value.

How much time does it take to rehydrate a dried food? The amount of time required for rehydration depends on different factors that include:

- the size of the piece of food
- the type of food and whether it was fresh, frozen, or canned before being dried
- whether the food was blanched before being dried
- the degree of dryness of the food
- the temperature of the liquid used for rehydration: *the hotter the liquid, the faster the rehydration*

Small pieces of dried food, and obviously powders, rehydrate almost instantly. Larger pieces may take 30 minutes to several hours. Unblanched foods will unfailingly take longer to rehydrate than ones that have been blanched, because blanching breaks down the cell structure, thus promoting faster reconstitution. Foods that have been dehydrated until hard, such as rice and tofu, will take more time to rehydrate. When the rehydration process takes longer than 2 hours, the bowl of food being rehydrated should be placed in the refrigerator.

What does rehydrated food look like? Most rehydrated foods regain their original size, form, color, and appearance. It is almost impossible to taste the difference between cooked fresh spinach and rehydrated cooked spinach. Carrots will not only regain their crunch, but they will also taste a little sweeter after rehydration because the sugars in them are intensified in the dehydration process. Apple pie made with dried apples (see recipe, page 226) is absolutely delicious, if I say so myself!

Other foods, such as watermelon, for example, will not return to their original form because their cell structure has collapsed. Rehydrated tomatoes are not going to look exactly like the tomatoes you picked from your garden. However, I have used dried tomatoes in everything but BLTs, and many people have told me that they would rather used dried tomatoes in sandwiches than the anemic tomatoes available during winter in most grocery stores.

METHODS OF REHYDRATION

There are a handful of different methods of rehydration. I begin with the most straightforward ones.

Hot Water: Soak 1 cup dried fruit or vegetable in 1 cup water that has been brought to a boil, then remove the pan with the rehydrating dried food from the heat for 5 minutes to 1 hour, depending upon the size of the pieces. Remember that boiling and hot-water soaks speed up the rehydration process.

Cold Liquid: Although water may be the most common liquid used for rehydration, fruit juice, cider, vegetable juices, consommé, milk, yogurt, wine, liquor, even vinaigrette may be used. Place the dried food in a container and barely cover with the liquid of choice. Depending upon type and size, the food will rehydrate in minutes or hours. Refrigerate foods that are being reconstituted in milk or other perishable liquids or if the rehydration time takes longer than 2 hours.

• If you use hot or cold liquid to rehydrate dried foods, you can add most flavorings, such as spices or herbs, at any point during the rehydrating process. Add salt or sugar only at the end of the rehydrating time. (See Tips on Rehydration, page 173.)

Cooking: Most dried vegetables need a few minutes to absorb liquid before the cooking process begins or they may toughen as they cook. For the best results, allow dried vegetables to soak in liquid until their color begins to change and they plump up. Then add them to the other ingredients in the recipe and start the cooking process. Other types of dried foods can be cooked without first being rehydrated, although dried fruits become more tender if soaked and/or simmered, then cooked.

Steaming: This method of rehydration prevents the loss of nutrients that occurs when foods are submerged in liquid to rehydrate them. To steam, place the dried food in a steaming basket and place over boiling water until the food softens. Allow anywhere from 5 to 30 minutes, depending upon the size of the pieces. Steaming is often used to soften dried foods prior to their being chopped or blended.

Standing: This method is as simple as it sounds. Some dried foods can literally stand in a place with high levels of humidity, and they will soften. A cup of dried apples left uncovered on the kitchen counter on a humid day will absorb some moisture from the air. However, do not leave the dried food out for too long or it will absorb enough moisture to spoil.

Another option is to soften dried foods to be eaten as snacks by placing them in a plastic bag with 3 or 4 drops of water. Seal the bag and refrigerate it for a couple of hours.

Microwaving: To those who use microwave ovens, it comes as second nature to rehydrate dried foods in them. Here is how to reconstitute 1 cup blanched dried corn: Put the corn in a microwave-safe container, add 2 cups water, and cover the container. Microwave at 100 percent (high power) for 2 minutes. Remove the container, stir the corn, and cover. Repeat the process. Remove the container, stir, then let the corn sit for 2 minutes. This is only the rehydration process; additional cooking time will be needed. In general, when using a microwave oven for rehydrating dried foods, remember that the bigger the piece of food, the longer it will take to become reconstituted. Pretreated, blanched food will rehydrate faster.

Tips on Rehydration

To Rehydrate Dried Fruits: Use a boiling, hot, or cold-water soak. Or steam them. You can also sprinkle the dried fruits with liquid and let them stand until soft. The amount of time needed for rehydration will depend upon the temperature of the liquid you used—boiling water being the fastest catalyst—and the size and type of the pieces of fruit.

To Rehydrate Dried Vegetables: Some vegetables, carrots, green beans, and corn, tend to toughen when placed directly in boiling liquid. Therefore, when adding dried vegetables to a soup or stew, turn off the heat, then add the vegetable and let stand at least 5 minutes. The vegetable will swell and lighten in color. Resume cooking. The vegetable will fully rehydrate as the dish finishes cooking.

To add small pieces of vegetable, such as dried tomatoes, to a salad, put them in the salad dressing.

Dried vegetables and dried rice can be soaked separately, then cooked together.

To Rehydrate Dried Meats and Fish: Jerky, made of meat or fish, is most commonly eaten dry. However, should you want to add jerky to a stir-fry, for example, rehydrate it in an amount of liquid equal to the amount of jerky. You can also add jerky to soups, stews, or casseroles if there is sufficient liquid in the dish for the jerky to rehydrate.

To Rehydrate Food Leathers: Both fruit and vegetable leathers are great eaten just as is, as snacks, or rehydrated into beverages, soups, and sauces. Leathers rehydrate much faster if they are torn into 1-inch pieces before soaking.

To Rehydrate Dried Herbs and Flowers: Both dried herbs and dried flowers rehydrate almost instantly. Or you can crush them or pulverize them in a blender.

If you are adding salt or sugar, do so at the end of the rehydration period as both may interfere with the dried food's absorption of liquid and thus toughen the food.

Key Technique 12: To Rehydrate and Cook Dried Corn

1. In a saucepan, combine ¼ cup dried corn with 1 cup hot water. If the corn has been blanched, it will rehydrate in 5 to 10 minutes, whereas unblanched corn will take about 30 minutes or longer.
2. Bring the rehydrated corn to a boil and cook for 3 to 5 minutes. Cover and let sit for 5 minutes.
3. Drain. Add salt and pepper and butter to what is now ¾ cup cooked corn. Serve immediately or use as below.

Example: Creamed Corn

Years ago, when I first made this recipe, my mother and father came for lunch. Dad took one bite of the corn and said, "This is how it used to taste." In his youth, he had lived on a farm, where his mother dried corn on pans in the attic and used it to make creamed corn on toast, a family favorite.

1 tablespoon butter
1 tablespoon all-purpose flour
½ cup milk
¼ teaspoon sugar
¾ cup cooked dried corn (see above)
½ teaspoon dried celery powder
Pepper to taste

In a saucepan, melt the butter over low heat. Sprinkle in the flour and stir with a wire whisk until blended. Slowly add the milk and the sugar, stirring constantly. Add the cooked corn, celery powder, and pepper, and remove the pan from the heat. Top with more celery powder or a dusting of Parmesan cheese.

Serves 2

Tip: Rehydrate small pieces of dried green bell pepper with the corn and cook them together.

COOKING WITH REHYDRATED FOODS

Once a dried food has been rehydrated, the cooking process is basically the same as with any fresh, frozen, or canned food, although a rehydrated food may cook more quickly than a fresh food, especially if it was blanched before being dried. It is always recommended to try to cook the dried food in the liquid in which it was rehydrated. Also, it is better to add liquid during the cooking process than to start out with more liquid than is needed. Like fresh foods, dried foods, if overcooked, lose both texture and flavor.

Slow cookers work beautifully with all dried foods. Their low temperatures and long cooking times give flavors a chance to mingle; steam collects on the lid and drops back into the pot, keeping the foods moist and nutritious. When using a slow cooker, it is important to make sure that you have enough liquid. I do not rehydrate dried foods before cooking them in a slow cooker.

Another discovery I have made is that in specific instances I will get a better finished product if I allow the combined mixture to sit a few minutes before cooking. Take, for example, Carrot Cake with Cream Cheese Frosting (page 222). I assemble the batter, put it in the prepared pan, and then let the pan sit at room temperature for about 10 minutes before I put it in the oven. The flavors mellow during that time, and the recipe, plain and simply, turns out better.

Another observation that I can make about using dried food as opposed to fresh in recipes is that I generally use more of the dried food. When I make the carrot cake recipe, for instance, with fresh grated carrots, I use 3 cups; whereas when I make it with dried carrots, I use the equivalent of 4 cups fresh. This means that you utilize more fruits and vegetables in your preparation when you cook with dried foods.

It is also interesting to note that when rehydrating dried foods, you often use less liquid to cook them. Do not feel that you have to compensate for all the water that was removed from the dried foods. You do not, which gives you much more control over the amount of liquid in a recipe. I find this an asset, and it is a creative way to control the finished products.

When it comes to baking with dried foods, trust your instincts. You have probably added a dried food to a batter, in the form of raisins, more times than you can remember. Similarly, you can add your favorite home-dried fruit in pieces, as is, to a batter. Or you can rehydrate the dried fruit, then add them to the recipe. Or you can rehydrate the fruit in the liquid in the recipe. Or you can dust the fruit pieces with flour to prevent them from sinking in the batter, then add them. If you substitute one fruit for another, adjust the spices in the recipe and note that dried fruits have a high sugar content, which means that the sugar measurement in some recipes can be reduced.

And whatever you do, don't forget this old trick: Add your own dried fruits to packaged cake and cookie mixes for quick treats with a personal touch.

The Power of Pulverization

There is no way to overstate the rewards of pulverizing dried foods. To begin with, the flavors are intense—so pure, in fact, that celery powder, for one, can readily substitute for salt, and many other pulverized vegetables can be used as nutritious seasonings. Second, pulverizing is a means of using a dried food product that may not be quite up to your standards.

Dried fruit or vegetable powders can be used for making soups and juices, as natural food colorings, and even as a supplement to flour: add ½ cup dried powder to each cup flour in a recipe, and add 2 tablespoons additional liquid.

To grind dried fruits or vegetables to a powder, be sure that they have been dried hard; otherwise they can gum up your blender. A reminder: Putting dried foods in the refrigerator or freezer for 15 to 30 minutes before pulverizing them turns them crisp and they become easier to pulverize.

Prepare Your Own Baby Food

With dried foods on hand, you won't believe how easy it is to prepare baby food. In many cases, all you need do is soak the dried food, then blend it.

Pulverize dried foods to reconstitute them for infants (see pages 80 and 176). As your child grows, pulverize dried foods to a coarser texture. Use single-item powders, then combine powders as you introduce new foods. If your child is food sensitive, dried, pulverized foods can be very helpful because you control the ingredients.

Three points to remember when you are preparing pulverized food for your child:

- Start out with a small amount of liquid and gradually add more until the desired consistency is achieved. It is best to add liquid to the dried food just before using it.
- Store rehydrated foods, including baby food, in the refrigerator.
- Discard any leftover baby food that has been at room temperature for more than an hour.

MICROWAVE-COOKING DRIED FOODS

The basic principles of microwave cooking apply when cooking dried foods in a microwave oven. In other words, remember that microwaves cook foods by heating the water inside them. Dried foods have no water in them, thus they must first be rehydrated. The amount of water to add and the cooking time will vary, depending upon how dry the foods are, the size of the pieces, and the way the foods were dried.

Here are a few obvious, very general pointers when cooking dried foods with your microwave:

- Watch the cooking time carefully. Overcooking is the most common error when using a microwave.
- Always put the food in a microwave-safe container and be sure that it is large enough. A good rule-of-thumb is that the container have twice the capacity of the dried-food measurement.
- Large pieces of food should be stirred once or twice during cooking to ensure even cooking throughout.

Chapter 11

Soups and Starters

$\mathcal{T}$he most obvious, and wonderful, aspect of using rehydrated foods to make soup is that no presoaking of dried ingredients is needed because the soup base acts as the rehydration liquid! Of course, the better the stock or broth you use, the better the soup. Also, the more dried ingredients you have on hand—soup making being something of an improvisational art—the better the flavor.

This chapter begins with Basic Chicken Vegetable Soup. Loaded with dried tomatoes, carrots, peas, corn, and beans, any of which you can vary according to taste, and fragrant with herbs that you have dried yourself, this favorite can serve as a first course, a Sunday night supper, or as a welcome pick-me-up any time of the day. Its ingredients are also lightweight and convenient to take on a camping or hiking trip when the long-range weather forecast suggests rain. Old wives' tale or not, when a chill sets in, chicken soup hits the spot.

Dehydrated vegetables enhance cream soups as well. Of the handful of tempting recipes included here I urge you to try Cream of Tomato. You can make it with dried tomato pieces, with powder, or with leather, for this soup is a perfect example of the fascinating options available to the cook once a vegetable has been dried. And if you have grown your own tomatoes, you will not believe how great that first spoonful of your own home-grown tomato soup tastes. In the same way, Creamy Mushroom Soup bursts with flavor, especially when made with dried shiitake mushrooms or morels. Try rehydrating the mushrooms in dry white wine for extra-special flavor.

Soup for dessert is traditional in Wisconsin, settled as it was by Scandinavian homesteaders who brought this culinary cultural folkway with them when they came to this country. Two fruit soups appear here—one creamy, rich, and cool; the other juice-based, clear, and refreshing served either hot or cold. Each relies upon a store of dried fruits—memories of summer—which no longer have to be seasonal.

Fresh-baked bread, or salad, is often all you need by way of accompaniment. However, I urge you to consider one of the starters included at the end of this section: Party Brie, Baba Ghanouj, or Vegetable Loaf. I am sure you will find a remarkable number of reasons for making one or all of them at a moment's notice.

Which brings me full circle: With dried foods on hand, you can very easily create a variety of simple, good-tasting foods that are good for you. The soups and starters that follow attest to that.

Basic Chicken Vegetable Soup

Here's a good basic soup, to perk up your spirits and warm you right down to your toes. Note the number of dried vegetables in it. To speed the prepreparation along, know that a 16-ounce (1-pound) bag of mixed frozen vegetables—carrots, corn, peas, and green beans—will dry in anywhere from 8 to 24 hours. However, at the end of that time you will have four different vegetables ready for soup making.

2 cups chicken, beef, or vegetable stock
2 cups water
1 cup small raw chicken pieces
½ cup dried tomato slices, broken into ½-inch pieces
¼ cup dried carrots
¼ cup dried peas
¼ cup dried corn
¼ cup dried green beans
1 tablespoon dried onion pieces
1 tablespoon dried bell pepper pieces
1 tablespoon dried mushroom pieces

1 tablespoon dried celery powder
1 teaspoon Worcestershire sauce
½ teaspoon dried basil
¼ teaspoon dried thyme
1 teaspoon chopped garlic
1 bay leaf
½ teaspoon salt
¼ teaspoon pepper
A fresh vegetable of choice, with crunch, like sliced celery

In a saucepan, bring the chicken stock and the water to a boil, and remove the pan from the heat. Add all the remaining ingredients, except the salt, pepper, and fresh vegetable, and let sit, covered, for at least 30 minutes to rehydrate.

Bring the mixture to a boil, reduce the heat to low, and let the soup simmer, partially covered, for 30 minutes until the vegetables are tender.

Add a fresh vegetable of choice, the salt and pepper, and serve.

Serves 4

～

Good Dried Bean Soup

This is a soul-satisfying soup filled with beans and vegetables, then flavored with a little bit of cooked chicken. Letting the soup simmer gently for a long time results in a richer, more flavorful taste. Add water during cooking as needed. For accompaniment, serve your favorite bread and a pleasing dessert, like Dried Apple Pie (page 226) or Carrot Cake with Cream Cheese Frosting (page 222).

¼ cup dried pinto beans
¼ cup dried kidney beans
¼ cup yellow split peas
4 cups chicken stock, divided
7 cups water, divided
1 tablespoon dried celery powder
1 bay leaf
2 tablespoons dried onion pieces
1 teaspoon Worcestershire sauce

1 teaspoon chopped garlic
½ teaspoon dried dill weed
½ teaspoon salt
¼ teaspoon paprika
¼ teaspoon pepper
¼ cup dried green beans
¼ cup dried peas
2 tablespoons dried shredded carrots
1 tablespoon dried bell pepper pieces
1 cup cooked chicken pieces

Rinse each type of bean separately in cold water. In a soup kettle, combine the rinsed pinto beans, 2 cups of the chicken stock, 2 cups of the water, the celery powder, and the bay leaf. Bring the liquid to a gentle boil over medium-low heat, cover partially, and cook the beans for 1 hour.

Add the remaining 2 cups chicken stock, 2 more cups water, the rinsed kidney beans, the dried onion pieces, the Worcestershire sauce, and the garlic to the kettle. Cover partially and cook over medium-low heat for 1 hour.

Add 2 more cups water, the rinsed yellow split peas, the dill weed, the salt, the paprika, and pepper, and cook, partially covered, for 30 minutes.

In a saucepan, combine the dried green beans, the dried peas, the dried carrots, the dried bell pepper pieces with the remaining 1 cup water, cover, and cook over medium-high heat for 30 minutes. Add the rehydrated vegetables and the liquid to the kettle. Cover the kettle and let sit for 15 minutes. Add the chicken, return the kettle to the heat, and simmer, partially covered, for about 30 minutes until the vegetables are soft.

Serves 6 to 8

~~~

Fish Chowder

Here's a recipe for fisherfolk and for chowder and soup lovers alike. The fish I prefer to use here is dried white fish, and if you like to fish and home-dry your catch, you may well have plenty of it on hand to make this hearty combination.

The basic chowder recipe can be turned into corn chowder with just a few substitutions: Replace the ½ cup dried fish with

182

1 cup dried corn; add ¼ cup dried shredded carrots, and replace the dill weed with the same amount of dried rosemary. Prepare as below. And enjoy.

2 cups water
½ cup dried fish pieces (½-inch size)
½ cup small dried potato pieces
1 tablespoon dried onion pieces
1 teaspoon dried green bell pepper pieces
1 teaspoon dried celery powder
1 teaspoon dried dill weed
1 tablespoon butter
1 tablespoon all-purpose flour
2 cups milk
½ cup dried potato flakes (for procedure, see page 189)
Salt and pepper to taste

In a saucepan, combine the water with the next 6 ingredients. Let sit for 1 hour to rehydrate.

Bring the mixture to a boil over high heat and simmer gently for 5 minutes. Reduce the heat to low and simmer the soup gently for 30 minutes, adding more water, if necessary, until the fish and vegetables are tender.

In a small saucepan, melt the butter and whisk in the flour. Whisk in the milk gradually, stirring constantly to prevent any lumps from forming, until the mixture is smooth and thickens, about 3 or 4 minutes. Stir the white sauce into the chowder base and add the potato flakes. Cook for 5 to 10 minutes until thickened. Add salt and pepper to taste and serve.

Serves 4

~~~

Root Soup with Ham

The roots in this soup include potatoes, parsnips, and turnips, assisted by quite a few other vegetables plus ham for flavoring. Vary the vegetables as you like: Two very good alternatives are dried rutabaga slices and shredded cabbage. An honest, nourishing Sunday night supper–type soup like this goes particularly well with Corn Bread (page 233), still warm from the oven. Serve the bread with a small dish of honey, which complements the saltiness of the ham and the sweetness of the root vegetables.

2 cups fully cooked ham cubes
6 cups water
½ cup dried potato slices
½ cup dried parsnip slices
½ cup dried turnip slices
¼ cup dried green beans
¼ cup dried Brussels sprouts slices
1 tablespoon dried onion pieces
1 tablespoon dried shredded carrots
1 tablespoon dried green bell pepper pieces
½ tablespoon dried celery powder
1 teaspoon chopped garlic
1 teaspoon Worcestershire sauce
½ teaspoon celery seed

In a large saucepan, bring the ham and water to a boil and cook for 10 minutes. Add all the remaining ingredients and bring the mixture again to a boil. Remove the pan from the heat, cover the pan, and let sit for at least 30 minutes to rehydrate.

Return the pan to the heat, bring the mixture to a boil, and simmer the soup about 30 minutes until all the vegetables are tender, adding more water if necessary.

Serves 6

~~~

Borscht

This chilled soup, so good on a hot summer's day, is virtually fat-free. Further, beets are a good source of potassium. You can also make this borscht with dried beet powder—2 cups dried beet slices reduce to ½ cup beet powder. The soup will still have little bits of beets in it if you use the powder; it also remains a beautiful rosy color and is light and refreshing on the palate. If you are a beet fan, like me, you will want to serve this soup hot in the winter, with a good loaf of fresh-baked bread.

2 cups dried beet slices
2 cups chicken stock
Pinch of dried dill weed, plus 1 teaspoon

Half a lemon for juicing
2 cups water
2 tablespoons white or wine vinegar
1 tablespoon honey
¼ teaspoon salt
Sour cream or dried plain yogurt pieces for garnish

In a soup kettle, combine the dried beet slices with the chicken stock, the pinch of dried dill, and a squeeze of lemon juice. Let sit about 30 minutes to rehydrate. Transfer half of the rehydrated beet mixture to a blender and chop to small pieces. Return to the kettle. Repeat with the remaining mixture, but in this batch leave bigger pieces of beet. Return to the kettle.

Pour the water into the blender and blend to loosen any remaining puree in the container. Add the liquid to the kettle. Stir in the vinegar, the lemon juice, the honey, the remaining dill weed, and the salt, cover the kettle, and simmer the soup slowly, stirring often and adding more liquid if necessary, until the beets have softened, about 30 minutes.

Let the soup cool, then refrigerate it until chilled. To serve, top each serving with a dollop of sour cream or pieces of dried yogurt and another sprinkling of dried dill.

Serves 6

~~~

Cream of Tomato Soup

My love for tomatoes extends to growing them, eating them, cooking them, and, of course, drying them and using them in all their different, compelling dried forms. This soup (one of my favorites of the entire collection) can be made with tomatoes in all their dried variations: slices, torn in pieces; powder; or leather, also torn in small pieces. The leather will take the longest time to rehydrate; the small pieces take slightly less time; the powder is the quickest to rehydrate.

Whatever type of dried tomato you use, you can add ¼ cup cooked rice or some dried vegetables or vegetable flakes at the end. Precooked dried beans are nice, too. What you have here, additions or not, is the wonderful taste of tomatoes in a light cream soup.

1 cup water
1 cup dried tomato slices, broken into quarters; *or* ¼ cup tomato powder; *or* ½ cup tomato leather, in pieces
1 bay leaf
¼ teaspoon dried celery powder
¼ teaspoon chopped garlic
⅛ teaspoon dried basil
Pinch of dried oregano
1 cup milk
½ cup heavy cream or sour cream
Salt and pepper to taste

In a saucepan, combine the water and the next 6 ingredients, and let sit for at least 5 minutes to rehydrate.

Bring the mixture to a boil and simmer for about 5 to 10 minutes, or until the tomato pieces are softened. Use a whisk or fork to break up the tomato pieces or leather. Stir in the milk and cook over low heat, stirring often to prevent scorching, for about 5 minutes. Add the heavy cream. Season with salt and pepper, and heat until heated through.

Serves 2

Creamy Mushroom Soup

This is a rich, marvelously flavored soup that can easily be doubled or even tripled if you want to serve it to company. Dried shiitakes or morels are the mushrooms of choice, as both are packed with flavor. Should you want a smoother-textured soup, simply puree the mushrooms after sautéing them.

1 cup dried mushroom slices (preferably shiitakes or morels)
1 cup dry white wine
3 tablespoons butter, divided
2 tablespoons all-purpose flour
1 cup milk
1¼ cups chicken stock
¼ teaspoon ground nutmeg
½ cup sour cream or 4 ounces cream cheese, softened
1 tablespoon finely chopped fresh green onions for garnish

In a bowl, combine the dried mushrooms with the wine and let sit for 15 minutes until softened. Drain the rehydration liquid into a bowl, reserving 2 tablespoons.

In a small skillet, heat 1 tablespoon of the butter until hot, add the mushrooms and sauté them.

In a saucepan, melt the remaining 2 tablespoons butter over medium heat. Sprinkle in the flour, and stir to combine. Pour in the milk slowly, stirring constantly with a wire whisk to eliminate any lumps. Cook, whisking, until thickened to a saucelike consistency. Add the chicken stock and the nutmeg, continuing to whisk to prevent scorching, until the soup thickens as desired. Add the sautéed mushrooms and reserved rehydration liquid. Stir in the sour cream and heat, being careful not to let the soup boil.

To serve, divide the soup among bowls and garnish each serving with a sprinkling of chopped green onions.

Serves 2

Cream of Broccoli Soup

This appealing soup can be made with dried cauliflower instead of dried broccoli. You can serve it either hot or chilled, as a first course, or even as a main course during the warmer months of the year. You might consider adding dried Swiss chard and spinach leaves—about ¼ cup each—to lend a nice greenness to the color and tanginess of the soup. This recipe doubles very successfully.

1 cup dried broccoli pieces
¼ cup dried mushrooms
¼ cup dried shredded carrots
1 tablespoon dried celery powder
1 tablespoon dried onion pieces
1 teaspoon dried green or red bell pepper pieces
1 teaspoon chopped garlic
1 teaspoon crushed dried chives
¼ teaspoon dried thyme
2 cups chicken stock
2 cups hot water
½ cup milk

½ cup heavy cream
1 heaping tablespoon all-purpose flour
1 tablespoon dry sherry
Salt and pepper to taste

In a soup kettle, combine the first 9 ingredients with the chicken stock and the water. Let sit for at least 1 hour to rehydrate.

Bring the mixture to a boil, reduce the heat to low, and simmer the soup, adding a little more water if necessary, for 30 minutes until the vegetables are tender. (If desired, let the soup cool and puree half of it to achieve a smoother consistency. Add the puree back to the kettle.)

In a small bowl, stir together the milk, the heavy cream, and the flour until smooth. Stir in the sherry. Whisk the mixture into the hot soup base, and over low heat simmer the soup, stirring often, for 5 to 10 minutes until thick. Add additional milk if needed. Season the soup with salt and pepper, and serve.

Serves 4

～～

Potato Soup

Unlike Root Soup with Ham (page 183), with its stock-style base, this soup is creamy and thick and the flavor actually improves if allowed to stand a few hours before serving. Vary the herbs as your supply or inclinations allow. Small pieces of dried jerky or bacon bits are very good added to it, too. With a salad, it makes a pleasing simple lunch or supper, particularly on a chilly fall or snowy winter day. And the recipe doubles nicely, too.

2 cups dried potato slices
3 chicken bouillon cubes
5 cups water, plus 2 cups cold water
¼ cup small dried tomato pieces
2 tablespoons shredded dried carrots
2 tablespoons dried green beans (1-inch pieces)
1 tablespoon dried bell pepper pieces
1 tablespoon dried mushroom pieces
1 tablespoon dried onion pieces
¼ teaspoon dried basil
¼ teaspoon dried oregano

¼ teaspoon chopped garlic
¼ teaspoon dried mustard
¼ teaspoon dried celery powder
¼ teaspoon celery seed
2 cups cold water
½ cup instant dry milk
1 cup dried potato flakes (store-bought or homemade; see note
  below)
Freshly grated Parmesan cheese

In a soup kettle, combine the dried potato slices, the bouillon cubes, and the 5 cups water. Let sit about 5 minutes to absorb some of the liquid. Add the dried tomatoes, the carrots, the green beans, the peppers, the mushrooms, the onions, and all the seasonings. Bring the mixture to a boil over high heat. Remove the kettle from the heat, cover it, and let the mixture sit for at least 15 minutes to rehydrate.

Return the kettle to the heat, bring the soup to a boil, and let it simmer slowly, stirring occasionally, for at least 1 hour until the vegetables are soft, adding water if necessary.

In a pitcher, stir together the 2 cups cold water and the dry milk. Bring the soup to a boil and stir in the milk. Reduce the heat to low and gradually stir in the potato flakes. Stir constantly, to prevent the soup from scorching, for about 5 minutes. Top with Parmesan cheese before serving.

Serves 4

Homemade Potato Flakes: Spread cooked mashed potatoes on lightly oiled leather sheets, place in the dehydrator, and dry. Break the sheets into chunks, put in the blender, and pulse until ground into flakes.

Dried Fruit Soup

Fruit soup is traditional in Norway and common in Minnesota and Wisconsin, which were settled by Scandinavians. Beautifully colored, thanks in large part to its cranberry juice base, this dessert soup can be served either cold or hot, with a pitcher of heavy cream on the side. If the 4 cups water are reduced to 2 cups, the mixture, which will be thicker, can serve as a filling for pies or as a pudding. Vary the fruits as you wish.

1 cup dried apple pieces (½-inch size)
½ cup dried plum pieces (½-inch size)
½ cup dried pear pieces (½-inch size)
½ cup dried peach pieces (½-inch size)
½ cup dried cranberries
3 cups cranberry juice
1 tablespoon fresh lemon juice
1 teaspoon ground cinnamon
¼ teaspoon ground cloves
4 cups water
4 tablespoons quick-cooking tapioca
½ teaspoon vanilla

In a large nonreactive saucepan, combine all the dried fruits with the cranberry juice and bring the mixture to a boil over high heat. Remove the pan from the heat, cover the pan, and let the mixture sit for at least 30 minutes to rehydrate.

Stir in the lemon juice, the cinnamon, and the cloves, bring the mixture back to a boil, and simmer it slowly for 15 to 30 minutes until all the fruit is softened. Stir in the water and the tapioca, and continue to simmer slowly until the tapioca is cooked, about 5 minutes. Stir in the vanilla. Serve hot or cold.

Serves 8 to 12

Cold Berry Soup

Here's an absolutely glorious way to remember summer—all year long. Serve this soup either as a first course, with a light entrée to follow, or as a dessert soup. This is a good recipe to make when seasonal doldrums set in: There is no cooking whatsoever involved in preparing it. And the tastes are sublime.

⅓ cup dried blueberries
⅓ cup dried raspberries
⅓ cup dried strawberries
½ cup dry or sweet red wine
Juice of 1 orange
1 cinnamon stick
4 whole cloves
½ cup heavy cream

½ cup sour cream
Honey or sugar to taste
Fresh or dried mint leaves for garnish

In a bowl, combine all the berries with the wine, the orange juice, the cinnamon stick, and the cloves, and let the berries rehydrate for 15 minutes.

In another bowl, whisk together the heavy and sour creams, and chill the mixture, covered, for at least 4 hours.

Remove the cinnamon stick and the cloves from the berry mixture, then puree the mixture in a blender, adding water if necessary for easy blending.

Stir the berry puree into the combined creams and stir in honey (or sugar) to taste. Divide the soup among chilled bowls and garnish each serving with a dollop of additional cream and either fresh or dried mint leaves.

Serves 4

~~

Tofu Soup

Dried bean curd may be an acquired taste—to Westerners—but, in fact, over a thousand years ago the Chinese discovered that fresh bean curd cakes could be frozen. It was the Japanese who discovered that frozen bean curd could then be dried, thus ensuring its preservation and year-round availability.

Healthful, simple to make, and of obvious Japanese derivation, this soup can be doubled easily. Clearly, the better the chicken stock, the better the soup. Whether you choose canned broth or homemade stock, be sure to defat it before using. You will find the Asian ingredients in well-stocked Japanese markets as well as in many natural-food stores.

2 cups chicken stock
½ cup water
¼ cup dried tofu (bean curd), cut in cubes (½-inch pieces)
½ tablespoon hijiki (dried sea vegetable in black strands), available at natural-food markets
1 tablespoon dried miso (dried soybean paste), available at natural-food markets, or see tip below
1 tablespoon chopped green onions for garnish

In a saucepan, bring the stock and the water to a boil over high heat. Stir in the tofu cubes. Remove the pan from the heat, cover the pan, and let the mixture sit for at least 30 minutes to rehydrate.

Return the pan to the heat and bring the mixture to a boil. Slowly simmer the soup for about 15 minutes until the tofu softens, adding additional water, if necessary. Stir in the hijiki and the miso, and simmer the soup slowly until well blended. Sprinkle the soup with the chopped green onions before serving.

Serves 2

Tip: Fresh miso can be spread on lightly oiled leather sheets and dried until hard. Allow about 4 hours to dry. Crush, then store in an airtight container.

Party Brie

A ready-to-eat wheel made of Brie, fresh nuts, dried grapes, dried cranberries and apricots provides all the makings of an impressive hors d'oeuvre that can be served at gatherings or taken as a hostess gift when visiting friends. It is best served on crusty rounds of French bread or crackers. You can vary the toppings as you desire. Dried chopped Bing cherries, for example, go very nicely with the creamy-tangy taste of the cheese.

1 wheel ripe Brie cheese, 8½ inches in diameter
½ cup dried Champagne grapes
½ cup finely chopped toasted almonds
½ cup diced dried apricots (½-inch size)
½ cup chopped walnuts (¼-inch size)
½ cup dried green grapes
½ cup pine nuts
½ cup finely chopped dried cranberries

With a sharp knife, trim the rind off the top of the wheel of Brie. Score the cheese into 6 equal wedges by making ⅛-inch indentations with the knife on the top of the wheel. Arrange the Champagne grapes over the top of 1 wedge. Press the bottom of an oiled spoon over the grapes to secure them in place. Do this over each wedge. On the next wedge, arrange the almonds. On the next, the apricots; and on the fourth wedge, the walnuts. Next to them, arrange the dried green grapes; and on the remaining wedge, place the pine nuts. Make a circle of the dried cranberries in the middle of the wheel. Let the Brie stand at room temperature for 1 to 2 hours before serving. Serve on rounds of French bread.

Serves up to 30

Baba Ghanouj (Sesame Eggplant Dip)

Baba ghanouj is a deservedly famous Lebanese hors d'oeuvre of roasted or baked eggplant that is pureed, then combined with garlic and tahini, the nutty, full-flavored sesame seed paste of the Middle East. My variation here incorporates plain yogurt into the dip itself, instead of serving it on the side. Healthful, wholesome, and slightly coarse in texture, this dip is superb as a filling for warm pita bread, or as an accompaniment to tabbouleh, bulgur salad, another marvelous Lebanese creation.

½ cup pulverized dried eggplant
¾ cup water
½ cup plain yogurt
1 tablespoon chopped garlic
1 tablespoon tahini (available at health-food stores)
1 teaspoon fresh lemon juice
Pinch of salt
Pita pockets
Shredded fresh carrots and zucchini, bean sprouts, and sliced cucumbers
Chopped parsley or sliced ripe olives for garnish

In a blender, combine the first seven ingredients and blend until smooth. If more liquid is needed, add 1 tablespoon at a time. The consistency should be like thickened yogurt. Transfer the dip to a bowl, cover, and refrigerate for at least 1 hour before serving.

To serve, fill pita pockets with the dip and top with the fresh vegetables and a sprinkling of either chopped parsley or ripe olives.

Makes about 1 cup dip, enough to fill two 6-inch pita pockets, halved

~~~

Vegetable Loaf

A loaf of French bread and five ingredients are all you need to make this simple healthy combination that is perfect to take on picnics or serve as an accompaniment to soup or salad. The dried peppers take 1 hour to rehydrate, and the stuffed loaf needs to chill for 4 (unattended) hours—a total of 5 hours, with a delicious reward when the time is up. Besides looking very pretty, this stuffed bread has surprisingly interesting flavor.

⅓ cup dried green bell pepper pieces
⅓ cup juice from a jar of Spanish olives
½ cup sliced Spanish olives
1 fresh onion, chopped into small pieces
1 large ripe tomato, cut into ½-inch pieces
½ teaspoon dried basil
1 loaf French bread

In a large bowl, combine the dried bell pepper pieces and the olive juice. Let sit for 1 hour to rehydrate. Add the olives, the onion, the tomato, and the basil, and combine the salad well.

Slice the bread in half horizontally and remove some of the crumb, hollowing out each half until a ¾-inch thick shell remains. Tear the crumb that has been removed into chunks and add it to the olive salad, combining it well.

Stuff each half of the loaf with olive salad. Carefully re-form the loaf, pressing the halves together, and wrap the bread in aluminum foil. Refrigerate the stuffed bread for 4 hours before slicing with a serrated knife into 1½-inch slices.

Serves 6

Chapter 12

Main Courses

W e have seen how dried foods can be incorporated into soups and even salads. Imagine, then, how they can be used to enhance main-course dishes. The eclectic grouping of recipes that follows ranges from plain to fancy, from old favorites to the untraditional. What all the recipes have in common, though, is the use of dried foods in as many innovative and pleasing ways as possible.

My discovery, years ago, that I could make soufflés with dried vegetable powders surprised me. What would the taste be like? And the texture? When you try Asparagus Soufflé (page 201), you will see how well it works. The texture is as light as air, literally (because all the water in the asparagus has been removed), leaving a concentrated essence of asparagus. With eggs on hand and dried vegetables in the pantry, you are only an hour or so away from a marvelous taste discovery, one that is also fun to make and serve.

The remaining recipes in this section are equally enjoyable. Here's a practical example: Make chili from a Sloppy Joe hamburger base; or, even easier, serve up Sloppy Joes (page 203) instead. On a much more elegant note, don't miss either Fettuccine with Creamed Smoked Chicken (page 196) or Shiitake Wild Rice Casserole (page 200). Each is wonderful for entertaining friends at home or for taking to a get-together. Another good party dish is Turkey and Vegetable Pie (page 198), which can be made in advance and only needs reheating before serving. I like to garnish it with fresh grapes and serve it with a green salad.

MARY BELL'S COMPLETE DEHYDRATOR COOKBOOK

Finally, you will note that brown rice appears in two very simple recipes that incorporate the chewy grain with dried vegetables. Serve either of the rice recipes with Meat Loaf (page 197), another of my favorites.

The ways we have thought about food are obviously changing. Dinner for some may be a salad, or soup and a salad. Main courses may be served in smaller portions, and clearly the nutritional aspects of many people's diets are of paramount importance. Here, entrées have been made with dried foods, either as main components or as flavorings. I trust you will find both the variety and flavors astonishing—and provocative. I hope the ideas inherent in these combinations will encourage you to create your own recipes, incorporating more and more dried foods.

~~~

Fettuccine with Creamed Smoked Chicken

This is an elegant, rich dish that is enhanced in flavor by dried shiitake mushrooms and in color and flavor by small pieces of beautiful olive-oil–soaked dried tomatoes. You can substitute smoked salmon or smoked tuna for the chicken for an even fancier combination. Serve with a crisp green salad with tangy mustard vinaigrette. You could even make your own noodles to accompany this. See Vegetable-Flavored Homemade Noodles (page 214).

10 olive-oil–packed dried tomato slices (page 38), torn into quarters
3 tablespoons dried onion pieces
3 tablespoons dried green bell pepper pieces
3 tablespoons dried shiitake mushroom pieces
1 cup water
2 large cloves garlic, minced
⅓ cup cooking sherry or dry white wine
1 cup whipping cream
2 cups smoked chicken pieces (bite-sized)
⅛ teaspoon white pepper
2 tablespoons fresh lemon juice
½ pound cooked hot fettuccine, drained

In a small bowl, combine the dried tomato pieces, the dried onion pieces, the dried green pepper pieces, and the dried shiitake mushroom pieces in the 1 cup water. Let sit for 15 minutes to rehydrate. Drain and discard liquid.

In a skillet, combine the garlic and the cooking sherry, and reduce the sherry over high heat by half, about 5 minutes. Add the cream, lower the heat to medium, and reduce the cream by half, about 10 minutes. Add the rehydrated vegetables and cook for 2 minutes. Stir in the smoked chicken and the pepper, and cook only until the chicken is heated through. Remove the skillet from the heat and stir in the lemon juice.

Divide the cooked noodles among dinner plates and top each serving with the creamed smoked chicken.

Serves 4

Meat Loaf

Here's another recipe that answers the question "How do I use the vegetables I've dried?" Meat loaf makes a great vehicle for dried rehydrated veggies, and by using celery powder you don't even need to use salt—celery being naturally high in sodium.

I've included this particular recipe because over thirty years ago my dad had a very serious heart attack. Following it, he stopped smoking, changed jobs (reduced his stress), and censored his intake of salt and sweets. My dad just turned eighty-five. This was one of our family's recipes that we have enjoyed for many years.

For the topping, make the tomato sauce with tomato leather and water, or use ketchup.

½ cup small pieces tomato leather
½ cup water
½ cup milk
1 egg
½ teaspoon chopped garlic
2 tablespoons dried tomato pieces
2 tablespoons dried mushroom pieces
1 tablespoon dried onion pieces
1 tablespoon dried celery powder
1 tablespoon dried bell pepper pieces
¼ teaspoon dried basil
¼ teaspoon dried oregano

1 teaspoon Worcestershire sauce
½ teaspoon prepared mustard
½ cup plain unseasoned bread crumbs
1 pound lean ground beef

Preheat the oven to 325°F.

In a small saucepan, combine the tomato leather and the ½ cup water, and bring the water to a boil. Remove the pan from the heat and let sit for 10 minutes to rehydrate. Return the pan to the heat, bring the mixture to a boil, and simmer it, stirring and mashing the leather with a fork until thick, about 5 minutes. Let the tomato sauce cool while you make the meat loaf.

In a cup, stir together the milk and the egg until combined. Add the garlic and stir again. Add all the dried vegetables, the celery powder, the basil, and the oregano, and combine well. Stir in the Worcestershire sauce and the mustard, then let the mixture sit for 10 minutes. Add the bread crumbs and the beef, and combine the mixture thoroughly. Transfer the meat loaf mixture to a 9 × 5 × 3-inch loaf pan. With the back of a fork, make an indentation down the length of the loaf, then pour the cooled tomato sauce into it.

Bake the loaf for 1 hour.

Serves 6 to 8

~~

Turkey and Vegetable Pie

I call this a pie even though the pastry is on the bottom, covered by a filling of delicious chopped turkey (or chicken) and almost any kind of dried vegetable you can think of. Make it after Thanksgiving or Christmas, when you are looking for a really pleasing way to use up the holiday bird. A big salad and a sweet dessert are all you need to complete the menu. This is comfort food, the kind our grandmothers made.

2 tablespoons dried peas
2 tablespoons dried corn
2 tablespoons dried mushroom pieces
1 tablespoon shredded dried carrots
1 tablespoon dried onion pieces
1 tablespoon dried bell pepper pieces

1 teaspoon dried dill weed
¾ cup water

For the pastry dough:

1 cup all-purpose flour
1 teaspoon baking powder
½ teaspoon salt
2 tablespoons butter, softened
1 cup sour cream

For the filling:

2 tablespoons butter
1 cup chopped fresh broccoli, stems peeled and sliced
2 cups chopped cooked turkey
One 10¾-ounce can cream of mushroom soup
¼ teaspoon pepper

In a bowl, combine the dried peas, the corn, the mushroom pieces, the carrots, the onion pieces, the pepper pieces, and the dill weed in the ¾ cup water, and let sit for 15 minutes to rehydrate.

While the vegetables are soaking, in a bowl stir together with a fork the flour, the baking powder, and the salt. Cut in the softened butter, then stir in the sour cream. Form the dough into a flat disk and chill it briefly, if desired.

Press the dough onto the bottom and up the sides of an 8-inch square baking dish and make a raised edge. Set the dish aside.

Preheat the oven to 400°F.

In a skillet, melt the butter and add the broccoli and the rehydrated vegetables, including the water. Simmer the mixture until the water has evaporated. Add the turkey, the mushroom soup, and the pepper, and combine the filling well. Pour the turkey filling into the pastry-lined baking dish and let the dish stand for 10 minutes. Bake the pie for 30 minutes, or until the edges of the pastry are golden.

Remove the pie from the oven and let it stand for 10 minutes before serving.

Serves 4

～～

Shiitake Wild Rice Casserole

Shiitake mushrooms are known as the king of mushrooms, and here they lend their wonderful woodsy flavor to another delicacy—wild rice. We serve this simple-to-make but impressive dish on special occasions. The sour cream turns it creamy and rich, the mushrooms make it exotic, and the wild rice imparts a crunchy, earthy texture.

8 cups water, divided
1½ cups wild rice
1½ cups dried shiitake mushroom slices
½ cup dried onion pieces
1 cup sliced fresh celery
1 tablespoon butter
¼ cup soy sauce
1 tablespoon dried celery powder
2 cups sour cream
2 cups chopped cooked chicken
¾ cup slivered almonds

In a large saucepan, bring 6 cups of the water to a boil. Stir in the wild rice and simmer it for 35 to 40 minutes, or until it is tender when tested. Drain in a colander and rinse.

In a bowl, combine the remaining 2 cups water with the dried mushroom slices and the onion pieces. Let sit for 30 minutes to rehydrate.

Preheat the oven to 325°F.

In a large saucepan, sauté the fresh celery in the butter for 5 minutes. Add the soy sauce and the celery powder, and stir to combine. Add the rehydrated mushrooms and onions, including the liquid, and cook until the liquid is evaporated. Stir in the sour cream, the cooked wild rice, the chicken, and the slivered almonds, and combine the mixture well. Transfer to a buttered baking dish, cover, and bake the casserole for 30 minutes.

Serves 8

~~

Asparagus Soufflé

The advantage of using a dried food product to make a soufflé—
something I'll wager many people have never done—is that because the water has been eliminated, the food is lighter. With a
soufflé, that is a very important point. Plus, you get intensified
flavor from the concentrated food: In this soufflé, you will taste
the asparagus! And when you dry asparagus to make powder,
you include the tough ends of the stalks. All in all, better texture
and flavor *and* economy, three good reasons to make soufflés
with dried vegetable powders. Try this recipe as a prototype. The
choice of vegetables and combinations is almost limitless.

2 tablespoons butter
2 heaping tablespoons all-purpose flour
1¼ cups milk
¾ cup grated Cheddar cheese
¼ cup dried asparagus powder
Salt and pepper to taste
Pinch of ground nutmeg
5 eggs, separated

In a saucepan, melt the butter, sprinkle in the flour, and remove the pan from the heat. Whisk the flour into the butter thoroughly. Stir in ½ cup of the milk and blend well. A little at a
time, add the remaining ¾ cup milk.

Place the pan over low heat and cook the white sauce, whisking, until it turns thick. Remove the pan from the heat and stir
in the grated cheese, the asparagus powder, and the salt, pepper,
and nutmeg. Let the soufflé base cool.

Preheat the oven to 400°F. While the oven is heating, put a
soufflé dish, measuring 6 inches across the top, in the oven just
to warm. Butter the warm soufflé dish.

In a bowl, beat the yolks together well and whisk them into
the cooled soufflé base. In a large bowl, beat the whites until
they hold stiff peaks.

Pour half of the soufflé base over the egg whites and fold the
base in gently but thoroughly. Add the remaining base and fold
it in gently in the same way. Do not overblend.

Pour the soufflé mixture into the prepared dish and bake for 30 minutes until puffed. Serve immediately.

Serves 4

Tip: The soufflé can be made in individual 3-inch ramekins. Warm and butter the ramekins as described above, divide the soufflé mixture evenly among them, then bake for 25 minutes.

~~~

Tomato Vegetable Quiche

Three different rehydrated vegetable powders—tomato, mushroom, and spinach—flavor the filling of this quiche, but you can substitute practically any vegetable powder combination you like. The custard here is light—not heavy with water—a result of having used rehydrated dried vegetables. The more you cook with dehydrated foods, the more you will appreciate their lightness and the intensified flavors they impart.

Serve this quiche for brunch with a nice salad—or for supper. You will also have additional dough on hand to make it again!

For the pastry dough:

3 cups all-purpose flour
1 teaspoon salt
1 cup solid vegetable shortening
⅓ cup cold water
1 tablespoon white wine vinegar
1 egg

For the filling:

¼ cup dried tomato pieces, pulverized
1 tablespoon dried mushroom powder
1 tablespoon dried spinach powder
½ cup milk
½ cup sour cream
½ teaspoon salt
½ teaspoon dried basil
¼ teaspoon pepper
¼ teaspoon chopped garlic

3 eggs, beaten
1 cup grated cheese, such as aged Cheddar or mozzarella

Make the dough: In a bowl, combine the flour and salt, and cut in the shortening in bits. Stir in the cold water and the vinegar. Add the egg and combine the mixture into a ball. Knead the dough on the countertop until it is combined and will hold together in the shape of a ball. Divide the dough into 4 equal pieces. Wrap the pieces you are not using immediately individually in plastic wrap and freeze them for later use.

Preheat the oven to 375°F.

On a floured surface roll out 1 piece of the dough to fit into a 9-inch pie plate. Transfer the dough to the plate and trim and crimp the edges.

In a bowl, combine the pulverized tomatoes and the mushroom and spinach powders with the milk. Stir in the sour cream, the salt, the basil, the pepper, and the garlic, and let the mixture sit for 10 minutes to rehydrate. Stir in the beaten eggs, add the grated cheese, and combine the filling well.

Pour the filling into the dough-lined pie plate and bake the quiche for 20 minutes. Reduce the oven temperature to 350°F and bake the quiche 25 minutes longer, or until a toothpick inserted in the center comes out clean. Let the quiche cool slightly before slicing.

Serves 4 to 6

Sloppy Joes

Whether this tried-and-true combination was made by "Joe," and in the process it made him "sloppy" is not clear to me! What is clear is that it's a wonderful way to use dried tomatoes, onions, and bell peppers. It's also simple to make and both kids and grown-ups like it. If you really want to go the nine yards, you can make your own tomato sauce.

½ cup dried tomato pieces (¼- to ½-inch pieces)
1 teaspoon dried bell pepper pieces
½ cup water
1 pound lean ground beef
1 tablespoon dried celery powder
1 tablespoon dried onion pieces
1 tablespoon prepared mustard

1 tablespoon Worcestershire sauce
1 tablespoon brown sugar
1 teaspoon chopped garlic
½ teaspoon salt
One 8-ounce can tomato sauce
1 package hamburger rolls

In a small bowl, combine the dried tomato pieces and the bell pepper pieces in the ½ cup water, and let sit for 10 minutes to rehydrate.

Meanwhile, in a skillet, brown the ground beef, then drain off and discard any fat in the skillet. Over low heat, stir in the celery powder, the onion pieces, the mustard, the Worcestershire sauce, and the brown sugar. Add the garlic and the salt, and combine the mixture well.

Add the rehydrated tomato and pepper combination to the meat base and stir in the tomato sauce. Simmer the mixture, still over low heat, to the desired consistency, about 10 to 15 minutes.

To make Sloppy Joes: Split the hamburger buns, put the halves on plates, and top the buns with a spoonful or two of the meat mixture.

Serves 6 to 8

~~

Sloppy Joe Chili

Here's a recipe I serve at a party we have each year between Christmas and New Year's. Chili is perfect wintertime cold-weather fare. I like to ladle this into bowls for eating around the fire. All you need is a salad and a basket of bread—Corn Bread (page 233) is nice—as accompaniments.

I've taken quite a few shortcuts in making this chili and loaded up on the carbohydrates by adding pasta to the meat and bean mixture. Make this as hot as you like by adding more chili powder or Tabasco sauce plus some garlic, as I do. Remember that chili improves in flavor the day after it is made.

Sloppy Joes (page 203), meat mixture only
4 cups V-8 juice
One 15-ounce can kidney beans, drained and rinsed
1 teaspoon chili powder, or more, if desired

1 cup uncooked pasta of choice
Grated Cheddar cheese for topping
Chopped fresh onion for topping

To the meat mixture in the saucepan, add the V-8 juice, the kidney beans, and the chili powder, and simmer gently, stirring to prevent scorching, until the flavors are blended. Remove the pan from the heat and add the pasta. Cover the pan and let the pasta cook in the sauce until tender.

To serve, transfer the chili to a serving bowl and top it with the grated cheese and chopped onion.

Serves 4 to 6

~~~

Brown Rice and Vegetable Stir-fry

If there's one recipe that my friends and family make most often it's some combination of vegetables and rice. Everyone does it a little differently, but here's my version. If you omit the jerky, you have a wonderful vegetarian main course.

¼ cup dried mushroom slices
¼ cup dried tomato slices
¼ cup dried onion pieces
¼ cup dried bell pepper pieces
¼ cup small pieces of jerky
1¼ cups water
1 tablespoon olive oil
1 teaspoon chopped garlic
1 thin slice fresh gingerroot (optional)
1 cup chopped fresh vegetable, such as broccoli, onions, celery,
    or carrots
1 tablespoon cornstarch
2 cups cooked short-grain brown rice

In a large bowl, combine the dried mushrooms, the dried to-matoes, the dried onion pieces, the dried pepper pieces, and the jerky in the 1¼ cups water. Let sit for 30 minutes to rehydrate. Drain the mixture over a bowl, reserving any water.

In a skillet, heat the olive oil over low heat and add the garlic and the ginger, if using, and cook them until fragrant. Add the rehydrated vegetables and the jerky, and sauté them. Add the fresh vegetable and stir-fry until the vegetables are just cooked.

In a small saucepan, stir the cornstarch into the reserved rehydration water until smooth. Place the pan over low heat and stir until thickened. Pour the liquid over the stir-fried vegetables and combine the mixture well. Add the rice and cook, stir-frying it, until heated through. Serve immediately.

Serves 4

~~~

Simple Dried Veggies and Brown Rice

Brown rice is one of my favorite grains—as Brown Rice and Vegetable Stir-fry (page 205) attests—and I often just combine water, rice, and dried vegetables, let them sit for a short time, then put them on to cook: One-pot cooking at its simplest! Serve the rice as is, or stretch it with chopped leftover meat or stir-fried fresh vegetables. This recipe can be doubled or even tripled, and it keeps well in the refrigerator. To reheat, add a little water and warm it over medium heat or put in the microwave.

4 cups water
2 cups short-grain brown rice
⅓ cup dried tomato pieces (6 to 8 slices)
2 tablespoons dried onion pieces
1 tablespoon dried bell pepper pieces
1 teaspoon dried celery powder
1 teaspoon olive oil

In a large saucepan, combine the water and the rice, and stir in the remaining ingredients. Let the mixture sit for 15 minutes to rehydrate.

Place the pan over medium-low heat and bring the mixture to a slow boil, stirring to prevent sticking. Simmer the rice for about 45 minutes, or until soft.

Serves 4

Backpacker Version: Use dried cooked rice for the raw rice and only enough water to rehydrate it.

~~

Eggs with Tofu and Fresh Asparagus

This is a high-protein, low-fat breakfast dish that health-conscious eaters will respond to. Tofu, bean curd, is dried, then added in powdered form to scrambled eggs that are topped with fresh asparagus. It's lightweight, high-energy food.

¼ cup dried tofu pieces (½-inch size; for procedure, see page 146)
3 tablespoons hot water
½ teaspoon soy sauce
1 teaspoon butter
2 eggs, beaten
½ cup fresh 1- to 2-inch asparagus pieces, cooked
2 tablespoons shredded mozzarella cheese

In a blender, pulverize the dried tofu pieces to a powder. In a saucepan, combine the tofu powder, the hot water, and the soy sauce. Let the mixture sit for 10 minutes.

Place the saucepan over low heat and bring the mixture slowly to a boil. Simmer the mixture slowly until the liquid has evaporated. Stir in the butter until it is melted. Add the beaten eggs and cook them, stirring, until almost scrambled. Place the cooked asparagus pieces on top of the eggs. Sprinkle the mozzarella over all and continue to cook the eggs until the cheese is melted.

Serves 2

Chapter 13

Salads, Side Dishes, and Sauces

*T*he best salads, as anyone with a vegetable garden or a good farmstand near their home will tell you, are made with fresh, just-picked produce. That's true, but it doesn't mean that dried ingredients can't be put to very good use in salads. Add them for a flavorful accent and variety. You'll be surprised at how dried vegetables, when rehydrated, can spark up a fairly ho-hum salad. And then, when the winter months set in and you're really longing for a vine-ripened tomato and what you have on hand is a home-dried vine-ripened tomato, you'll be so grateful! You can use the dried tomatoes, broken into bits, sprinkled in salads as a substitute for bacon bits.

Some of the salads here—Mushroom Garbanzo Salad (page 212) and Pasta Salad with Dried Tomatoes (page 210)—make very good main courses. If you want to serve them in smaller portions, see soups (page 179). Salads and soups—and bread (page 231)— make natural luncheon or light supper combinations.

In this section, I have included a handful of side dishes plus one of my favorite condiments, Dried Fruit Relish (page 217). These are among the recipes I make most frequently—the old standbys that everyone loves.

Using dried ingredients for salads or side dishes is second nature to me now: Over the years, as I learned more and more about food dehydrating, I looked for more and more ways to use the foods I had dried. The journey, if you will, continues. I suspect, and hope, that this will happen to you. Make and enjoy the recipes that follow and, just as important, let them serve as examples of how to incorporate dehydrated foods into your daily diet. The variety of good salads you can make with dried foods is fascinating.

~~~

Fresh and Dried Fruit Salad

When I make fruit salad, I always include dried as well as fresh fruits. Be creative in how you use the dried fruits. Substitute dried apricots, cranberries, papayas, bananas, or pears for the usual shredded coconut and raisins. Also, you can rehydrate dried fruit in fruit juice, which adds to the flavor and helps prevent the fresh fruit from oxidizing and darkening. Melon—your favorite kind or the best available locally—is always a good choice for the main fresh fruit ingredient. And if you cannot find a pear apple—a wonderful crisp fruit—substitute a ripe pear. If you're lucky enough to have some dried pear-apple pieces on hand, add them, too—they are delicious.

½ cup dried strawberry pieces
¼ cup small dried peach pieces
1 teaspoon dried shredded carrot
⅛ teaspoon dried mint
⅛ teaspoon dried lemon peel
½ cup pineapple juice
1 cup fresh pineapple cubes (1-inch pieces)
1 cup fresh melon cubes (1-inch pieces)
2 bananas, cut into ¼-inch slices
1 kiwifruit, peeled and cut into ¼-inch slices
1 pear apple
2 tablespoons sour cream
2 teaspoons brown sugar
Lettuce for serving

In a nonreactive bowl, combine the strawberry pieces, the peaches, the carrot, the mint, and the lemon peel in the pineapple juice. Let sit for 30 minutes to rehydrate.

In a salad bowl, combine all the fresh fruits. Add the rehydrated fruits and toss to combine. In a small bowl, mix together well the sour cream and brown sugar.

To serve, line a platter with the lettuce and top it with the fruit salad. Pour the sour cream dressing over the salad just before serving.

Serves 4 to 6

~~~

Dried Fruit Jell-O Mold

Drying foods is one thing; cooking and using them is another. I am frequently asked, "Now that I have a lot of dried fruits in my pantry, what exactly do I do with them?" Here's a simple recipe to start you off using dried fruits and rehydrating them. The combinations and flavors are up to you; for example, you can also use apple juice instead of the cold water.

½ cup dried fruit pieces
1 cup cold water
One 3-ounce package fruit-flavored Jell-O
1 cup boiling water

In a bowl, combine the dried fruits and the cold water. Let sit for 10 minutes to rehydrate.

Empty the Jell-O into a heatproof bowl and pour the boiling water over it. Stir until dissolved. Add the dried fruits and the rehydration water, and stir again. Pour into a 3-cup mold and refrigerate until firm.

Serves 4

~~~

Pasta Salad with Dried Tomatoes

Pasta salad is a great favorite, especially when enlivened with home-dried tomatoes (best from your own garden, of course). This is just the salad to take to a potluck or to a church supper. It's also good served to family and friends, and great for more formal occasions. For the best flavor, let the salad chill for 6 hours before serving.

1 pound shaped or short pasta of choice, such as wagon wheels
3 stalks broccoli, peeled and steamed until tender

½ cup small pieces oil-packed dried tomatoes
3–4 fresh carrots, sliced on the diagonal and steamed until tender
1 fresh green bell pepper, cored, seeded, and cut into slivers
1 small red onion, thinly sliced
1 cup grated mozzarella cheese
½ cup frozen peas, thawed
½ cup whole imported black olives, drained
1 small jar (6½ ounces) marinated artichoke hearts, drained
Dried Tomato Vinaigrette (below)
Fresh parsley sprigs for garnish

Bring to boil a large saucepan of water with salt to taste and add the pasta. Cook until al dente. Drain well and set aside, covered.

While the pasta is cooking, in a large bowl, combine all the remaining ingredients except the vinaigrette and the parsley. Add the still-warm cooked pasta to the bowl and pour the vinaigrette over all. Toss gently, cover, and refrigerate for 6 hours.

To serve, garnish with the parsley sprigs.

Serves 10 to 12

Dried Tomato Vinaigrette

I like to use olive oil to make this dressing. Try this vinaigrette on mixed green salad as well as on fresh tomatoes.

7 tablespoons olive oil
¼ cup red wine or herb vinegar
4 tablespoons drained capers
1 tablespoon oil-packed or dried tomato pieces
3 green onions, thinly sliced
1 teaspoon Dijon mustard
1 teaspoon mixed dried herbs, including oregano, marjoram, basil, and rosemary
Salt and pepper to taste

In a 1-quart jar with a lid, combine all the ingredients. Cover, then shake to combine. Taste and adjust the seasonings as desired.

Makes a scant 1 cup

~~~

My Favorite Vinaigrette

Use this hard-not-to-like dressing on salad greens or as a marinade for fresh sliced mushrooms, carrots, radishes, or onions.

¼ cup dried green bell pepper pieces
1 tablespoon water
¼ cup olive oil
1 tablespoon freshly grated Parmesan cheese
1 tablespoon white wine or herb vinegar
½ teaspoon dried garlic powder
½ teaspoon dried onion powder
¼ teaspoon dried basil
Salt and pepper to taste
Pinch of sugar (optional)

In a small bowl, let the dried bell pepper pieces rehydrate in the 1 tablespoon water for a few minutes.

In a bowl, combine all the ingredients and whisk them together until completely blended. Season to taste with salt, pepper, and the sugar, if desired.

Makes about ½ cup

~~~

Mushroom Garbanzo Salad

Garbanzos are good for you, and when combined with mushrooms, they become surprisingly elegant as well. Allow this salad sufficient time to marinate for the flavors to marry. It's best served as a main-course salad and makes a very good vegetarian luncheon or light supper, accompanied by Vegetable Loaf (page 194).

1 cup dried mushroom slices
¼ cup water
⅓ cup olive oil
3 tablespoons red wine vinegar
1 teaspoon sugar
¼ teaspoon dried mustard
¼ teaspoon salt

¼ teaspoon pepper
Pinch of dried tarragon
½ cup sliced fresh celery
⅓ cup chopped fresh onion
1 tablespoon dried parsley
1 tablespoon dried bell pepper pieces
1 teaspoon finely chopped garlic
1 teaspoon dried tomato pieces
1 teaspoon dried celery powder
One 20-ounce can garbanzo beans (chick-peas), drained and
  rinsed
¼ cup chopped black olives
Lettuce leaves
Tomato wedges
Grated Romano cheese for serving

In a bowl, let the mushroom slices sit in the ¼ cup water for 10 minutes to rehydrate.

In a large salad bowl, combine the olive oil, vinegar, sugar, mustard, salt, pepper, and tarragon. Add the rehydrated mushrooms (and rehydration liquid if any remains). Stir in the celery, the onion, the parsley, the dried pepper pieces, the garlic, the dried tomato pieces, and the celery powder. Add the beans and the black olives, and toss to combine. Cover the salad and let it marinate for several hours for the flavors to blend.

To serve, line a platter with the lettuce. Top with the mushroom and bean salad, and arrange the tomato wedges around the sides. Sprinkle with the Romano cheese to taste.

Serves 8

Broccoli and Pineapple Salad

Fresh broccoli, a good source of vitamins A and C, combines here with two unlikely ingredients—bacon and dried pineapple—to make a remarkably tempting mix. I like to take this salad on picnics or to potlucks, where I can be certain it will be a hit! Serve as a main course or in smaller servings, preceded by a simple clear soup and a warm loaf of bread.

4 cups fresh broccoli florets combined with stems, cut into ½-inch pieces
1 cup thinly sliced fresh celery
½ cup sunflower seeds
½ cup mayonnaise
1 tablespoon sugar, or to taste
2 tablespoons white wine vinegar
1 tablespoon dried onion pieces
½ cup dried pineapple pieces, cut into raisin-size bits
½ pound bacon, cut crosswise into ¼-inch strips

In a large salad bowl, stir together gently the broccoli, the celery, and the sunflower seeds.

In a small bowl, whisk together the mayonnaise, the sugar, the vinegar, and the dried onion. Add the pineapple pieces, 1 at a time, and let the dressing sit for 10 minutes.

Meanwhile, in a skillet cook the bacon until crisp. Transfer it to paper towels to drain.

Add the dressing with the bacon to the broccoli mixture and toss the salad gently to combine.

Serves 6 to 8

~~~

Vegetable-Flavored Homemade Noodles

Many's the time I've walked by vegetable-flavored noodles in fancy food shops and smiled, knowing how easy it is to make them at home. All you have to do is pulverize the dried vegetable (or vegetables) you want in the blender: You need only 2 tablespoons of powder. Making your own noodles saves you a considerable amount of money and it's fun and easy. Imagine a combination of spinach, tomato, and basil noodles. Or just tomato and basil. Or mushroom noodles. You get the idea.

For a selection of sauces to top these noodles, see pages 163–164 and 218–219.

2 eggs
2 tablespoons dried vegetable powder, such as asparagus, spinach, beet, or carrot
¾ cup flour (depending upon the amount of moisture in the flour, an additional ¼ cup flour may be needed)
⅛ teaspoon salt

In a bowl, beat the eggs until combined, add the dried vegetable powder of choice, and stir to combine. Let the mixture sit for 5 minutes.

Add the ¾ cup flour to the egg mixture, a little at a time, stirring with a fork until the flour and eggs are combined. Add the salt. The texture should be dense but elastic.

Dust the countertop and your hands with flour, and knead the dough, adding up to ¼ cup additional flour at the most. (You will know when you have added enough flour: The dough will not be able to incorporate any more.) Knead the dough for about 1 minute, or until it is fairly stiff but still elastic. Flatten the dough into a disk, then with a floured rolling pin, roll it out on the floured surface into a 14-inch square. With a sharp knife, cut the dough into quarters, then stack the pieces. Be sure to sprinkle the bottom layer with flour before arranging the next dough sheet on top. Roll the stack into a log.

With the knife, cut the log into ⅛- to ¼-inch strips, depending upon how thick-cut you want the noodles. With every third cut, dust the noodles with a little flour, separating them to prevent them from sticking together.

Cook the noodles fresh.

(To cook either fresh or dried noodles, bring a saucepan of water to a boil with a little vegetable oil. Add the noodles and cook them just until tender, several minutes. Drain immediately and top with your favorite sauce or just butter.)

Makes 2 cups noodles, enough for 4 servings

— —

Scalloped Potatoes

Blanched vegetables always rehydrate faster than unblanched ones, and here blanched potato slices, dipped in lemon juice and water, rehydrate best of all. In this wonderfully pleasing old-fashioned combination, use regular grated Cheddar cheese if you cannot find dried Cheddar powder. It's becoming increasingly available in supermarkets, however, thanks to the popularity of cheese-flavored popcorn!

2 tablespoons nonfat dry milk
2 tablespoons all-purpose flour

2 tablespoons cornstarch
1 teaspoon salt
½ teaspoon dried onion powder
⅛ teaspoon pepper
3 cups dried potato slices
3 tablespoons butter
2⅓ cups boiling water
⅔ cup milk
Dried Cheddar cheese powder for dusting

In a small bowl, combine the first 6 ingredients and set aside.

Grease a 2½-quart casserole and arrange the dried potatoes in the bottom. Sprinkle them with the dry milk-cornstarch mixture and dot the potatoes with the butter, cut into bits. Mix together the boiling water and the milk, and pour over the dried potatoes. Let sit for 15 minutes to rehydrate.

Preheat the oven to 400°F.

Cover the potatoes and bake them for 30 to 35 minutes. Dust with the Cheddar cheese powder just before serving.

Serves 4

~~

Fruited Hominy Grits

To some people, Southerners excepted, hominy grits—ground kernels of hulled corn—may be too bland. But when flavored with fruit powder and topped with butter and a sprinkling of sugar, they take on another dimension. Serve these fruited grits as a side dish with eggs and sausage or bacon for breakfast; or take the dried mixture in your backpack when outdoor adventuring.

Serve the variation, vegetable-flavored grits, with lunch or a light dinner.

2 cups water
½ teaspoon salt
½ cup instant grits
1 tablespoon dried fruit powder, such as strawberry, apricot, or peach
Butter as needed
Sugar as needed

In a saucepan, bring the water with the salt to a boil. Stir in the grits, cover, and cook over low heat, stirring often to prevent scorching, until the grits are tender, about 5 minutes.

Remove the pan from the heat and stir in the fruit powder.

To serve, divide the hot grits among bowls and top each serving with butter and sugar, as desired.

Serves 4 to 6

Vegetable Hominy Grits: Simply replace the fruit powder with the same amount of mushroom or green bell pepper powder. Top with grated melting cheese, such as shredded mozzarella.

⁓

Dried Fruit Relish

Chop the fruits in this marvelous relish into very small pieces— to render them really relishy. Figs, peaches, plums, prunes, and raisins can all be substituted for the fruits here. For the best flavor a total of six different fruits seems to do the trick. Serve this relish at Thanksgiving or Christmas holiday meals. It goes particularly well with game and pork dishes. Or you can tie a bow around the jar to present as a gift any time of the year.

½ cup dried cranberries
½ cup dried pineapple pieces (¼-inch cubes)
½ cup dried pear pieces (¼-inch cubes)
½ cup dried kiwifruit pieces (¼-inch cubes)
½ cup dried apricots (¼-inch cubes)
½ cup dried apple pieces (¼-inch cubes)
3 cups port wine

In a large bowl, combine all the dried fruits and stir to mix. Place the fruits in a 1-quart canning jar. Pour the port wine over the fruits, cover the jar with the lid, and place the jar in the refrigerator for at least 2 days. Each day, turn or shake the jar to make sure all the fruit is covered with the port.

Serve with meat dishes. The relish will keep for weeks in the refrigerator.

Makes 3 cups

~~~

Spinach Pesto

As anyone who makes pesto with homegrown fresh basil knows, there's no substitute for its magnificent flavor. Basil's growing season does end, but you can still make pesto—with dried ingredients. If you combine dried basil and spinach, rather than using all basil, the strong taste of which is often overwhelming, you end up with a sauce that's good in color and texture—and flavor. I also like to add this pesto to stir-fried vegetable dishes just before serving.

2 tablespoons dried basil
2 tablespoons water
½ teaspoon fresh lemon juice
½ cup olive oil
¼ cup (1 ounce) dried spinach leaf pieces, rehydrated in ¼ cup water for 5 minutes, *or* 1 cup fresh spinach leaves, well washed and stemmed
1 teaspoon chopped garlic
⅓ cup pine nuts or sunflower seeds
½ cup freshly grated Parmesan cheese

In a cup, combine the dried basil with the 2 tablespoons water and the lemon juice. Let sit for 10 minutes to rehydrate.

In a blender, combine the olive oil and the rehydrated spinach pieces, or the fresh spinach leaves, and blend to a puree. Add the garlic and the pine nuts or the sunflower seeds, and grind them until pureed. Transfer the sauce to a bowl and stir in the Parmesan cheese. Store, covered, in the refrigerator.

To use as a sauce on pasta: In a small saucepan, heat a little olive oil until warm. Add the pesto and warm it, stirring constantly, until heated through. Serve over hot cooked pasta, with additional Parmesan cheese and sunflower seeds for garnish.

Makes 1 cup

~~~

Rich Cream Sauce

To flavor this sauce or the variation, add a favorite dried herb—or a combination of herbs—or a touch of curry powder, or even another vegetable powder, such as 1 tablespoon dried spinach powder. Or use a combination of dried tomato, mushroom, and herb powders. For a new taste treat, try using fruit powder— apricot or plum. This sauce can be easily doubled or tripled, and it's wonderful when used as the base for cooked seafood and chicken. Serve over rice or Vegetable-Flavored Homemade Noodles (page 214).

¼ cup (½ stick) butter
½ teaspoon chopped garlic
1 cup whipping cream
½ cup sour cream
1 tablespoon dried mushroom powder
⅓ cup freshly grated Parmesan cheese

In a saucepan, melt the butter over low heat, add the garlic, and simmer it until golden, about 2 minutes. Add the whipping cream and the sour cream, stir in the mushroom powder, and simmer the mixture, stirring often, until the sauce thickens to the desired consistency, about 10 minutes.

Remove the pan from the heat and stir in the Parmesan cheese. Serve over hot cooked pasta.

Makes 1½ cups, or enough sauce for 4 servings

Easy Cream Sauce: You can make a version of the above sauce— albeit not as rich or flavorful—with just 2 ingredients: Simmer 1 tablespoon butter in ½ cup whipping cream and let the liquid come to a slow, rolling boil. Cook until the sauce reduces by half and thickens. A pinch of nutmeg adds a nice accent. Makes enough sauce for 2 servings of cooked noodles.

―〜―

Tomato Meat Sauce
(Dried Tomato and Tomato Powder Version)

This sauce combines dried tomato slices (crushed) and dried tomato powder (rehydrated to paste) for a great tomato taste. Remember that dried tomato slices are much easier to crush if they are frozen or at least chilled for 15 to 30 minutes. Break them up with your hands or put them in the blender. When broken into small pieces, the tomatoes rehydrate faster and the skins blend much better into the sauce. Double or triple this sauce to feed a crowd. The sauce also freezes very well.

1 cup frozen or chilled dried tomato slices (about 20)
2 tablespoons dried bell peppers
2 tablespoons dried onions
2 tablespoons dried mushroom pieces
1 tablespoon dried celery powder
1 teaspoon chopped garlic
1 teaspoon Worcestershire sauce
3½ cups water, divided
1 pound lean ground beef
½ teaspoon salt
½ teaspoon dried basil
½ teaspoon dried oregano
½ teaspoon dried fennel
½ cup dried tomato powder
½ teaspoon sugar
¼ teaspoon pepper
¼ cup chopped green olives

With your hands, crush the cold dried tomato slices. In a bowl, combine the crushed tomatoes with the next 6 ingredients. Pour in 3 cups of the water and let the mixture sit for 15 minutes to rehydrate.

In a skillet, brown the beef and drain off any excess fat. Add the salt, the basil, the oregano, and the fennel, and stir in the rehydrated tomato mixture, including the liquid. Simmer the sauce over low heat, stirring occasionally, for at least 30 minutes, adding more water, if necessary, if the sauce becomes too thick.

When the sauce has just about finished cooking, combine the tomato powder in the remaining ½ cup water, add the sugar and the pepper, and stir to combine. Let sit for 10 minutes.

Add the rehydrated tomato powder to the meat sauce and simmer the sauce slowly for at least 10 minutes. Just before serving, stir in the olives. Serve over hot cooked pasta, with grated Parmesan cheese as an accompaniment.

Makes 2 cups sauce, or enough for 4 servings

Chapter 14

Cakes, Pies, and Puddings

W̲omen of past generations, including our mothers, knew the value of putting food up, most often in canning jars, but also in dried forms. Winters were long; livelihoods were precarious; the well-being of a family depended, in large part, upon the foods that were stored for the coming months. How often in old cookbooks do we see combinations for dried fruit pies or compotes? Fruit had to last and there were several ways of doing that: One was to dry it.

As ingenious as many of those women were at preserving and drying foods, I wonder if they might not be surprised at how versatile dried foods are, particularly in dessert making. Did they ever imagine that one could make a cheesecake fragrant with the aroma of pears, including the crust? This elegant recipe appears on page 223. Similarly, wouldn't some of our forebears be amazed to discover that plum pudding needn't be filled with raisins, but with plums—dried ones? Or that carrot cake could be made with dried carrots and taste as tempting as the fresh carrot version, cream cheese frosting and all?

For many people, dessert is the favorite part of a meal. (For more informal snack-type sweets, see page 231.) Some of the desserts in this chapter are elegant, some are simple. What they share, besides being plain good, is that each is intriguing to make and uses a given dried food as an ingredient. Let these recipes please you, and just as important, tempt you into experimenting with making your own desserts with dried foods.

~~~

Carrot Cake with Cream Cheese Frosting

Is it possible to make this great all-time favorite American cake with dried shredded carrots? You bet it is! And the crumb remains exceptionally moist, just like the one in the fresh version that we all love. This is so good, in fact, that it served as our wedding cake. If you like, vary the flavors by substituting equal amounts of chopped dried pineapple and fig pieces for the walnuts and raisins. Of course, it's also very tasty served without frosting, with a simple dusting of confectioners' sugar on top.

1 cup dried shredded carrots
1 cup water
1 cup (2 sticks) butter, softened
1 cup granulated sugar
1 cup loosely packed brown sugar
4 eggs, beaten
2 cups all-purpose flour
2 teaspoons baking soda
1 teaspoon ground cinnamon
1 teaspoon salt
1 cup chopped walnuts
1 cup dried grapes (raisins)

For the frosting:

2 cups confectioners' sugar
½ pound cream cheese, softened
¼ cup (½ stick) butter, softened
1 teaspoon vanilla
Pinch of powdered orange peel

For the topping:

¼ cup chopped walnuts
1 tablespoon finely crushed dried shredded carrots
1 tablespoon dried shredded coconut

Preheat the oven to 350°F. Grease a 13 × 9-inch baking pan.

In a small bowl, combine the dried carrots with the water. Let sit for 5 minutes to rehydrate. Drain.

In a bowl, cream together the butter and the granulated and brown sugars until combined. Stir in the eggs and combine the mixture well.

In a large bowl, stir together the flour, the baking soda, the cinnamon, and the salt. Add the rehydrated carrots and stir to coat them with the dry ingredients. Stir in the walnuts and the raisins. Add the butter mixture and stir until the batter is thoroughly combined. Pour the batter into the prepared pan and let sit at room temperature for 10 minutes before baking.

Bake the cake for 35 minutes, or until a toothpick inserted in the center comes out clean. Let the cake cool on a rack before frosting.

While the cake is cooling, prepare the frosting: In a large bowl, with a mixer, combine all the frosting ingredients until smooth and fluffy.

Spread the frosting decoratively over the top of the cake and top with the walnuts, the shredded carrots, and the coconut. Cut into squares and serve.

Serves 24

Pear Amaretto Cheesecake

In this unique, glorious cake, the almond-scented pears perfume not only the graham cracker crust, but the filling as well. Thus it is when you use dried pear powder for flavoring: It is light enough to become evenly distributed throughout the cake. Two other very appealing combinations, using powders flavored with a full-bodied liqueur, are apricot mango cheesecake and cranberry apple cheesecake.

3 ounces dried pears, pulverized (you will need ½ cup dried powder)
½ cup Amaretto (almond-flavored liqueur)

For the crust:

1 cup graham cracker crumbs
1 tablespoon butter, melted
2 tablespoons pear-Amaretto mixture (from above)

For the filling:

Three ½-pound packages cream cheese, softened
5 eggs

For the topping:

2 cups sour cream
½ cup sugar
1 teaspoon vanilla

In a small bowl, combine the dried pear powder and the Amaretto. Let sit for 30 minutes to rehydrate.

Prepare the crust: In a bowl, combine the graham cracker crumbs, the butter, and 2 tablespoons of the pear-Amaretto mixture until crumbly in texture. Press the crust evenly over the bottom of a 9-inch springform pan. Set aside.

Preheat the oven to 325°F.

Prepare the cheesecake filling: In a bowl, blend the cream cheese with a mixer until it is soft. Add the eggs, 1 at a time, blending thoroughly before adding the next. Beat the mixture on medium speed until it is smooth and creamy. (The mixture should be as free of lumps as possible before the remaining pear mixture is added.) Add the rehydrated pear-Amaretto mixture and blend completely. Pour the batter into the graham cracker–lined springform pan.

Bake the cheesecake for 1 hour—the top of the cake should hold together. Remove the pan from the oven to a rack to cool.

Prepare the topping: In a bowl, combine all the topping ingredients completely.

Spread the topping evenly over the top of the cake, then return the cake to the oven to bake for 10 minutes. Remove the cake from the oven and let it cool on a rack before chilling in the refregerator. Remove the sides of the springform pan before serving.

Serves 6 to 10

Grandma's Coffee Cake

I teach an aqua-fitness class and one day, one of the coteachers, Sue, brought this simple, always-good-to-eat cake for brunch following our swim. This is an old-fashioned cake that can be varied with any number of different dried fruits. Not only did my grandmother Bell and grandmother True dry foods, but, it turns out, so did Sue's grandmother.

1 cup dried peach pieces (1-inch size)
1½ cups milk, divided
2 cups all-purpose flour
1½ cups sugar
½ cup (1 stick) butter, softened to room temperature
2 teaspoons baking powder
2 eggs
1 teaspoon vanilla

In a small bowl, combine the dried peaches in 1 cup of the milk. Let sit for 1 hour to rehydrate.

Preheat the oven to 350°F. Grease an 11 × 7 × 2-inch baking pan.

In a bowl, with a hand-held mixer, combine the flour, the sugar, and the butter until crumbly in texture; reserve 1 cup of the crumb mixture for the topping.

Add the baking powder to the remaining flour-sugar-butter mixture. Stir in the remaining ½ cup milk, the eggs, and the vanilla. And the rehydrated peaches and the rehydrating liquid, and combine the batter well. (It will be fairly thin in consistency.) Pour the batter into the prepared baking pan and sprinkle the reserved 1 cup crumb topping evenly over the batter.

Bake the coffee cake for 30 minutes.

Let the cake cool slightly and serve it directly from the pan, cut into 2-inch squares.

Serves 8 to 12

~~

Strawberry Angel Food Cake

The main component of fresh food is water, and when you remove the water, as you have seen throughout recipes in this book, you have many options as to how to use that dried food. Here, I began by pulverizing—actually grinding to a powder—dried strawberries. I've always loved the idea of using food to flavor food. I could have used that powder to sprinkle on plain yogurt or ice cream. Instead, I decided to semirehydrate it (re-constitute it only halfway back to its fresh state), and add it to packaged angel food cake mix. It worked better than I could have imagined. Mango or pineapple powder are also very good used in this fashion. Needless to say, this simple premise has dra-matically expanded my repertoire of cakes that I can put together in a moment's notice!

I have also discovered that larger-sized dried fruit pieces can be added to other cake mixes: rehydrated apples to spice cake mix; rehydrated raspberries or cherries or strawberries to devil's food cake mix. However, don't be tempted to add larger fruit pieces to the angel food cake mix: The powder works best.

2 tablespoons dried strawberry powder
1 tablespoon water
1 box angel food cake mix

In a small bowl, combine the strawberry powder and the wa-ter, stirring to combine.

Make the angel food cake according to the instructions on the box, adding the semirehydrated strawberry powder when you add the flour packet. Bake the cake according to the direc-tions on the box. Let the cake cool and cut it into slices for serving.

Serves 12

A Surprising Variation: My husband's interest in shiitake mush-rooms once impelled him to add dried shiitake powder to angel food cake mix. As unlikely as it sounds, the cake turned out to be wonderful. We spread it with butter, like bread. You'll be astonished at how sweet mushroom powder is.

———

Dried Apple Pie

Although the recipe calls for dried apples, this pie can be made with many other dried fruits—peaches, raspberries, cherries, and so on. Adjust the spices to enhance the specific fruit. Know, though, that the tarter the fruit, the more flavorful the filling. If the dried apples you use are particularly sweet, add lemon or orange or pineapple juice to the rehydration liquid for balance.

Remember, too, to vary the liquid when you make this pie with other dried fruit.

Pastry Dough (page 199) for a double-crust 10-inch pie
3 cups peeled dried apple slices
2 cups apple juice or water, warmed
½ cup sugar, plus additional for sprinkling on crust
2 tablespoons cornstarch
½ teaspoon ground cinnamon
Pinch of ground nutmeg
1 tablespoon butter
Milk for brushing top crust

In a saucepan, combine the dried apple slices and the warm juice or water. Let sit for 15 minutes to rehydrate.

Place the pan over medium heat and bring the liquid to a boil. Simmer the mixture for 5 minutes until the apples are soft but not mushy. Let cool.

Preheat the oven to 400°F.

While the apple mixture is cooling, line the bottom of a 10-inch pie plate with the pastry. In a small bowl, combine the sugar, the cornstarch, the cinnamon, and the nutmeg, and sprinkle half of the sugar mixture over the unbaked pie shell. Pour the apple mixture into the shell and sprinkle the filling with the remaining sugar mixture. Dot with the butter, cut into bits.

Roll out the dough for the top crust. Trim, then moisten the rim of the bottom crust. Arrange the top crust over the filling, trim, and seal the bottom and top edges together firmly. Flute the edges, if desired. With a sharp knife, cut slits in the top crust as steam vents. Brush the top crust with milk and sprinkle it with sugar.

Bake the pie for 10 minutes. Lower the heat to 350°F and bake the pie for 25 more minutes, or until bubbly and lightly browned on the top. Let the pie cool on a rack.

Serves 8

Mock Mincemeat Pie

I call this mock mincemeat pie because although there is not a trace of either meat or suet in it—both imperative components of a true mincemeat pie—the filling looks like mincemeat and tastes like it, too. This pie is good served cold. It keeps well, and is a wonderful way to use dried ingredients that did not meet your expectations—the leather was too brittle or the fruit too sour. Chopped nuts and dried cherries can also be added to the filling.

Pastry Dough (page 199) for an 8-inch single-crust pie
1 cup apple juice or orange juice
1 cup dried grapes (raisins)
1 cup berry leather, broken into pieces
¾ cup dried pineapple pieces
½ cup dried apple pieces
¼ cup chopped candied citrus rind (page 42)
1 teaspoon ground cinnamon
½ teaspoon ground cloves
½ teaspoon ground nutmeg
½ teaspoon ground ginger
3 eggs
1 cup firmly packed brown sugar
3 tablespoons butter, melted

Roll out the dough on a lightly floured surface and fit it into the pie plate. Trim and crimp the edge. Preheat the oven to 350°F.

In a large nonreactive bowl, combine the apple or orange juice with the next 5 ingredients. Let sit for 1 hour to rehydrate. Stir in all the ground spices.

In another bowl, beat the eggs until combined. Stir in the brown sugar and the melted butter. Pour the egg mixture over the spiced fruits and stir to combine well. Pour the filling into the pie shell and bake the pie for 1 hour. Let the pie cool on a rack before serving. If desired, serve with fresh whipped cream or softened ice cream.

Serves 6 to 8

~~~

Plum Pudding

I must say that I'm partial to this pudding: I love making it, sharing it, and giving it away as a gift at Christmastime. Unlike the English plum pudding, which has no plums (but plenty of raisins), this pudding is plum-filled. You will taste the difference. Don't forget to dry a good supply of plums when they come into season. Then you'll be all set to make this pudding for the holidays, when it is at its most timely best.

1 cup whiskey
1 cup dried plum pieces (1-inch size)
¾ cup orange juice
4 slices white bread, broken into pieces
1 cup firmly packed light brown sugar
2 eggs, beaten
2 cups dried grapes (raisins)
1 cup finely chopped pitted dried dates
½ cup chopped walnuts
1 cup all-purpose flour
2 teaspoons ground cinnamon
1 teaspoon ground cloves
1 teaspoon baking soda
½ teaspoon salt

In a bowl, combine the whiskey and the dried plum pieces, cover, and let soak overnight in the refrigerator. The next day, drain the plums, reserving the whiskey. Measure it and add enough of the orange juice to make 1 cup.

In a bowl, place the bread pieces. Pour the whiskey–orange juice mixture over them and stir to combine. Stir in the brown sugar and the eggs, and combine well.

In a large bowl, combine the rehydrated plums, the raisins, the dates, and the walnuts. In another bowl, combine the flour, the cinnamon, the cloves, the baking soda, and the salt. Add the dry ingredients to the fruit mixture and stir to combine. Add the softened bread crumb–egg mixture and combine. Pour the pudding into a well-greased 2-quart pudding mold—do not use a ring mold or a tube pan—and cover the mold with aluminum foil. Tie string around the edge of the mold to secure the foil and prevent water from seeping into the pudding.

Bring 1 inch of water to a boil in a deep kettle. Place the mold on a rack in the kettle and cover the kettle with a tight-fitting lid. Steam the pudding for 3½ hours, adding more boiling water when necessary to maintain the level of water in the kettle.

Let the pudding cool for at least 10 minutes before removing it from the mold. Securely wrapped, this pudding keeps in the refrigerator for months.

Serves 24

~~~

Tapioca Pudding with Dried Fruits

This recipe came to me from my husband's mother, Adeline, a great cook, whose own mother cooked for ten people at every meal. Then, as now, tapioca was a crowd pleaser, a sweet treat—a good dessert. In this milkless, eggless rendition, the dried fruits add nutrients—a consideration not to be overlooked when choosing a dessert to serve your family or friends.

5 cups water, divided
1 cup pearl tapioca
1½ cups dried apple pieces (1-inch size)
½ cup dried grapes (raisins)
¾ cup sugar
¾ teaspoon ground cinnamon
½ teaspoon salt
1 teaspoon fresh lemon juice

In a 9½-inch square ovenproof bowl, 2 inches deep, combine 2 cups of the water and the tapioca, and let soak, covered, overnight.
Preheat the oven to 350°F.
The next day, add the dried apple pieces, the raisins, the sugar, the cinnamon, and the salt, and stir to combine. Add 1 more cup of water to cover the ingredients and stir to combine. Bake the mixture, uncovered, for 15 minutes.
Remove the bowl from the oven and stir in 1 more cup of water. Bake the pudding, uncovered, for 15 minutes more.
Remove the bowl from the oven again and add the remaining 1 cup of water and the lemon juice. Stir to combine. Lower the heat to 325°F and bake the pudding, uncovered, until the tapioca becomes glossy, about 30 minutes. Serve the tapioca while it is still warm.

Serves 10 to 12

Chapter 15

Quick Breads, Cookies, and Snacks

*T*he recipes that follow are informal fun foods, snack-type treats. And each is made with a twist—a dried food or several dried foods. Zucchini bread, for example, is made from dried zucchini powder; banana bread, from dried banana slices; and corn bread from corn that I urge you to grind yourself in order to discover the exquisite flavor of home-dried, home-ground cornmeal. You no longer need fresh fruits or vegetables to make a specific recipe. With a food dehydrator, a little preplanning, and a surprisingly limited amount of shelf space for storing your home-dried ingredients, you can proceed to bake and cook with remarkably pleasing results.

Of the ten recipes in this section, campers and outdoor enthusiasts will undoubtedly relate quickest to the two gorps—one of which is made with five different dried vegetables and two dried fruits—a high-energy snack if there ever was one. Lastly, there is a granola recipe, which my family and friends have loved for years, as well as a combination for cookies made with that granola.

Banana Bread

How many times have you longed for a piece of home-baked banana bread when there are either no bananas in the house or the ones you do have are not soft enough for mashing? With dried banana slices on hand, a homebaked loaf is only about an hour or so away—a very reassuring thought in our household! Serve this for breakfast, spread with a little butter, or for dessert with fruit salad on a hot summer day. It also makes a very nice gift, and it freezes beautifully. If you think that only fresh bananas are suitable for making this favorite quick bread, this will change your mind.

1 cup dried banana slices
1 cup milk
2 cups all-purpose flour
1 teaspoon baking soda
½ teaspoon salt
½ cup (1 stick) butter, softened
2 eggs
½ cup firmly packed brown sugar
½ cup granulated sugar
1 teaspoon vanilla
1 cup chopped walnuts

In the container of a blender, combine the dried banana pieces and the milk. Let sit for 15 minutes to rehydrate. Blend the banana pieces until smooth, then let the mixture sit again for at least 10 minutes to allow the puree to thicken.

Preheat the oven to 325°F. Grease two 8 × 3½-inch loaf pans.

In a small bowl, stir together the flour, the baking soda, and the salt. In a large bowl, cream together the brown and the granulated sugars. Add the eggs and the vanilla, and combine the mixture well. Stir in the banana puree. Add the flour mixture and the chopped nuts, and combine thoroughly. Pour the batter into the prepared loaf pans, dividing it equally, and let sit at room temperature for at least 10 minutes before baking.

Bake the breads for 1 hour, or until a toothpick inserted in the centers comes out clean. Remove the loaves and let them cool on racks.

Makes 2 loaves

~~~

Corn Bread

Until you dry your own corn and grind it for meal, you have no idea how fragrant homemade cornmeal can be. It is a striking golden yellow color, and the meal actually smells like corn. Gone is the smell of a cardboard carton, the "aroma" of commercially prepared cornmeals.

This bread is especially good with a bean or root vegetable soup. Should you have any left over, reheat it in the microwave for best results.

1 cup dried corn
1½ cups all-purpose flour
½ cup sugar
1 tablespoon baking powder
1 teaspoon salt
2 eggs
1 cup evaporated milk
½ cup canola or sunflower oil

Preheat the oven to 350°F. Grease a 12 × 7-inch baking pan.

In a blender, grind the dried corn into cornmeal. You will need ¾ cup meal. In a bowl, combine the cornmeal with the flour, the sugar, the baking powder, and the salt.

In another bowl, combine the eggs, the milk, and the oil. Add the egg mixture to the cornmeal mixture, stirring only enough to mix. Pour the batter into the prepared pan and bake the bread for 30 minutes, or until a toothpick inserted in the center comes out clean.

Let cool slightly, then serve warm with butter and honey.

Makes 16 pieces

~~~

Zucchini Bread

This recipe demonstrates another way to use food that has been dried for cooking. Whereas in Banana Bread (page 231) I used dried banana slices, rehydrated them in milk, then blended them for the batter, here zucchini powder—dried zucchini pulverized in a blender—is rehydrated in water. In similar fashion, you could use dried apricot powder to make apricot bread.

Next time you have a late-summer bumper crop of zucchini, give some of it away then dry what remains and pulverize some of it. A zucchini two feet long and about eight inches wide, when dried and pulverized, can be stored in a pint jar!

¾ cup dried zucchini powder
1½ cups water
3 eggs
¾ cup canola or sunflower oil
2 cups sugar
1 teaspoon vanilla
1 teaspoon ground cinnamon
½ teaspoon ground ginger
½ teaspoon ground cloves
3 cups all-purpose flour
1 teaspoon baking powder
1 teaspoon baking soda
½ teaspoon salt
1 cup chopped black walnuts, if available, or pecans

Preheat the oven to 325°F. Grease two 7 × 3-inch loaf pans.

In a small bowl, stir together the dried zucchini powder and the 1½ cups water. Let sit for 15 minutes to rehydrate.

In a large bowl, beat the eggs, stir in the oil, the sugar, and the vanilla. Add the rehydrated zucchini mixture with the cinnamon, the ginger, and the cloves.

In another bowl, stir together the flour, the baking powder, the baking soda, and the salt. Add the dry ingredients to the egg mixture and combine the batter well. Stir in the nuts. Divide the batter evenly between the two prepared pans and let them sit at room temperature for at least 10 minutes.

Bake the breads for 1 hour, or until a toothpick inserted in the centers comes out clean. Remove the loaves from the pans and let them cool on wire racks.

Makes 2 loaves

~~

Fruit Muffins

With home-dried blueberries or raspberries on hand, you won't have to wait for berry season to make delicious muffins. To rehydrate the fruit, I like to use freshly squeezed orange juice, but apple juice, cranberry juice, grape juice, or even apricot nectar are all delicious. As for nuts, I am partial to chopped almonds, but let your preference prevail. These muffins, filled with grains that are good for you, make nice treats—good for picnic baskets or lunch boxes or to enjoy with a cup of tea any time.

¾ cup dried fruit pieces (½-inch size), such as blueberries, raspberries, cranberries, or pineapple
1 cup fruit juice of choice
1 cup all-purpose flour
¾ cup chopped nuts of choice
½ cup bran
½ cup old-fashioned rolled oats
½ cup wheat germ
2 teaspoons baking soda
Pinch of salt
1 cup milk
½ cup firmly packed brown sugar
⅓ cup liquid shortening
1 egg, beaten

In a bowl, combine the dried fruit and the fruit juice. Let sit for 30 minutes to rehydrate. Remove the softened fruit from the liquid with a slotted spoon and discard the soaking liquid.

Preheat the oven to 375°F. Grease a 12-cup muffin tin.

In a large bowl, combine the flour, the nuts, the bran, the rolled oats, the wheat germ, the baking soda, and the salt. Add the rehydrated fruit and stir to coat the pieces with the dry ingredients.

In another bowl, stir together the milk, the brown sugar, the liquid shortening, and the egg until the sugar is dissolved. Add the liquid ingredients to the dry ingredients, and stir only to combine. Do not overmix. (The batter should remain a little lumpy.) Spoon the batter into the prepared pan, filling each cup three-quarters full.

Bake the muffins for 20 to 25 minutes, or until a toothpick inserted in the center of one of the muffins comes out clean. Serve warm or at room temperature.

Makes 12 muffins

~~~

Cakey Granola Bars

These bars are more cakelike than cookie in texture. However, if you like granola as much as I do, you will be having them for breakfast. And don't forget to take them along when traveling: They make a healthy snack. Should you be feeling fancy, you can frost the cooled bars with Cream Cheese Frosting (page 222) or rehydrate a sheet of your favorite fruit leather and use that as a type of glazed frosting. Here, the bars are drizzled with honey, a simpler way of sweetening them.

¾ cup dried pear pieces (¼- to ½-inch size)
⅓ cup water
2 eggs
½ cup sugar
½ cup all-purpose flour
1 teaspoon baking powder
¼ teaspoon salt
1½ cups Granola with Dried Fruit (page 239)
½ cup chopped walnuts
¼ cup honey, heated until warm

In a small bowl, combine the dried pear pieces and the ⅓ cup water. Let sit for 15 minutes to rehydrate. Drain the pears and discard the water.

Preheat the oven to 350°F. Grease an 8-inch square baking pan.

In a medium bowl, beat the eggs lightly. Stir in the sugar. Add the flour, the baking powder, and the salt, and stir to combine. Add the granola and the walnuts, and combine the batter well. Stir in the rehydrated pears gently. Pour the batter into the prepared baking pan and let sit for 10 minutes.

Bake the cookie batter for 30 minutes, or until a toothpick inserted in the center comes out clean. Let cool on a rack, drizzle the top with the honey, and cut into 2-inch squares.

Makes 16 bars

Date Nut Bars

It may be almost impossible to find fresh dates in the market to home-dry. Know that a 1-pound package of pitted dried dates, available at virtually any supermarket, equals 3 cups when chopped into ½-inch pieces. Use a sharp, wet knife to chop them—they are very sticky.

3 cups dried date pieces (½-inch size)
1¼ cups water
⅓ cup sugar
2 cups firmly packed brown sugar
2 cups all-purpose flour
3 cups old-fashioned rolled oats
1 teaspoon baking soda
1 cup (2 sticks) butter, melted
½ cup finely chopped walnuts

In a saucepan, combine the date pieces, the water, and the sugar, and bring the water to a boil, stirring to dissolve the sugar. Cook the dates over medium heat, stirring frequently, until all the water evaporates, about 5 minutes. Let the date filling cool slightly while you make the dough.

Preheat the oven to 350°F. Grease a 17 × 11-inch jelly-roll pan.

In a bowl, combine the brown sugar, the flour, the rolled oats, and the baking soda. Add the melted butter and stir until it is incorporated. Divide the oatmeal dough into 2 equal pieces.

Press 1 of the pieces of oatmeal dough in an even layer on the bottom of the prepared pan. With a spatula, cover it evenly with the date filling. Sprinkle the remaining oatmeal dough and the walnuts over the filling.

Bake the cookies for 30 minutes. Let cool before cutting into 2½ × 1½-inch pieces.

Makes 32 bars

~~~

Aunt Grace's Apple Raisin Cookies

In collecting the recipes for this book, I was fortunate to have many people contribute their energy, thoughts, and time. One day, a special friend, Pam Eyden, brought her aunt Grace's cookies over to share. Aunt Grace's recipe puts to use both home-dried apples and grapes. (If you have neither, use commercially available dried apple chips and raisins—either dark or golden.) You can keep a jar of these cookies in your pantry for 3 or 4 days; after that, store them in the refrigerator.

1 cup dried apple pieces (¼- to ½-inch size)
1 cup dried grapes (raisins)
1 cup apple juice
1 teaspoon baking soda
1 cup (2 sticks) butter, softened
¾ cup firmly packed brown sugar
¾ cup granulated sugar
3 eggs
2 cups all-purpose flour
½ teaspoon ground cinnamon
½ teaspoon ground cloves
½ teaspoon ground nutmeg
½ teaspoon salt
2 cups old-fashioned rolled oats
1 cup chopped nuts, such as walnuts, pecans, or peanuts

In a bowl, place the dried apple pieces, the raisins, the apple juice, and the baking soda, and stir to combine. Let sit for at least 15 minutes to rehydrate.

Meanwhile, in a large bowl, cream the butter with the brown and granulated sugars until smooth. In a small bowl, beat together the eggs, then add them to the butter mixture, stirring well.

In another bowl, combine the flour, the spices, and the salt. Add the rehydrated fruit mixture, including the liquid, and stir to coat all the fruit pieces thoroughly. Stir in the rolled oats. Add the fruit-oat mixture to the butter-egg mixture and combine the dough thoroughly. Stir in the nuts. Let the dough stand, loosely covered at room temperature, for 15 minutes.

While the dough rests, preheat the oven to 350°F. Grease a cookie sheet.

Drop the dough by the tablespoon on the prepared cookie sheet, leaving 2 inches between to allow the cookies to expand. Bake the cookies for 12 to 15 minutes, or until they are firm to the touch and just starting to brown. Let cool on a rack.

Makes 6 dozen cookies

~~

Granola with Dried Fruit

Friends and family agree that this is a great recipe. Of course, feel free to vary it. There is one point, though, that I will not negotiate, and that is taking the time to stir the granola every 20 minutes or so while it bakes. Frequent stirring promotes even heating and toasting, prevents sticking and burning, and guarantees a granola free of big clumps.

Many of the ingredients called for here you will already have in your cupboard if you've been drying fruits as they come into season—the easiest and certainly the most economic way of doing it. I recommend purchasing the remaining ingredients at a reliable health-food store.

4 cups old-fashioned rolled oats
½ cup wheat germ
½ cup bran
½ cup sesame seeds
½ cup dried shredded coconut
½ cup sunflower seeds
½ cup cashew pieces
½ cup slivered almonds
⅓ cup canola or sunflower oil
⅓ cup honey
2 cups dried fruit pieces, such as apples, pears, grapes (raisins),
    cherries, cranberries, figs, or dates

Preheat the oven to 300°F.

In a 13 × 9-inch baking pan, combine the first 8 ingredients. In a cup, combine the oil and the honey, pour it over the dry ingredients, a little at a time, and with a fork stir it into the dry ingredients.

Bake the granola for 20 minutes. Remove the pan from the oven and stir the mixture thoroughly. Bake another 20 minutes, remove, and stir again. Repeat this baking and stirring process once more, for a total baking time of 1 hour. When done, the granola should be light golden in color.

Remove the pan from the oven and let the granola cool. Stir in the dried fruits of choice. Store granola in an airtight container at room temperature.

Makes 10 cups

~~~

Fruit Gorp

Once only a simple raisin-and-peanut combination, this high-energy snack now can also include dried apples, peaches, pears, apricots, papaya, or pineapple. To vary the nuts, don't forget filberts, which I advocate buying (and this includes all nuts) in bulk. And for something really sweet, you can always add chocolate, butterscotch, or carob chips, or M&Ms, or Reese's Pieces. While not light in calories, this is delicious as a "take-along" anywhere, including your backpack.

2 cups sunflower seeds
1 cup roasted soybeans (available at health-food stores)
1 cup chopped walnuts
1 cup raw cashews, toasted, if desired
1 cup chopped Brazil nuts
1 cup chopped pitted dried dates
1 cup dried banana slices
½ cup dried grapes (raisins)
½ cup dried shredded coconut

In a large bowl, combine all the ingredients. Store in an airtight container.

Makes 9 cups

~~~

Vegetable Gorp

I was given this recipe idea by a couple I met one day when giving a talk on food dehydrating for a health-food store in a suburb of Minneapolis. They came up with this recipe when they decided they wanted something healthful to snack on during work breaks. This fits the bill just fine and can be varied in any number of ways. Try adding nuts or seeds or more dried vegetables, such as dried broccoli or mushrooms or bell peppers. If you want to take it along on a backpacking or camping trip, it will keep for several weeks; for longer storage, keep it in the refrigerator or freezer to prevent the oil, in which some of the vegetables are fried, from turning rancid.

½ cup thin soy-dipped carrot slices (page 48)
½ cup soy-dipped zucchini chips (page 48)
½ cup thin fried carrot chips (page 48)
½ cup thin fried parsnip chips (page 48)
½ cup thin fried turnip chips (page 48)
½ cup dried apricot pieces
½ cup dried pear slices
½ cup dry-roasted, toasted, or raw peanuts
¼ cup dried tomato chips (page 49)
¼ cup large-flake dried coconut
1 tablespoon dried dill pickle pieces (page 50)

In a large bowl, combine all the ingredients. Transfer to a plastic bag and/or airtight container.

Makes 4½ cups

Chapter 16

Beverages and Syrups

$\mathcal{I}$'ve spent the better part of this book telling you how to remove water from foods, then how to return the liquid in varying amounts.

Sometimes when I put a drink together I start with pieces of a dried fruit; at other times, with a powder. At still other times, I use dried leather or even dried herbs. As you can see, your options are many, and so is the variety of beverages you can make. Enjoy, for example, Dried Fruit Cordial (page 244), made with brandy; or Apricot Cordial (page 245), made with white wine (reserve the fruit for a humdinger of a breakfast treat). Or make Mint Tea (page 249), using your own homegrown, home-dried herbs. Or serve your guests a Dried Fruit Punch (page 243)—it's nonalcoholic and perfectly lovely for sipping.

I've also included three special syrups: Strawberry (page 247), Apricot Leather (page 248), and Dried Cherry (page 248). Each adds flavor to pancakes or waffles, and can be used as a topping for pound cake or coffee cake. You might also want to combine any of these with a glass of chilled seltzer for a particularly cooling drink.

I hope that this handful of combinations shows you how versatile dried foods can be when you use your imagination to make delicious beverages and syrups with them.

Cranberry Apple Drink

If you do not want to buy commercial cranapple drink, this is the recipe for you. And you can control the amount of sugar in it. You will need dried cranberries, but you probably already have some on hand. For backpacking, pulverize all the dry ingredients first and take the blend along in a plastic bag. Boil water on the trail, add the mix to the boiling water, let cool, then enjoy.

1 cup boiling water
½ cup small dried cranberry pieces (¼-inch size or smaller)
¼ cup small dried apple pieces (¼-inch size or smaller)
1 cup cold water
½ cup sugar
⅛ teaspoon ground cinnamon

In a heatproof bowl, combine the 1 cup boiling water, the dried cranberry pieces, and the dried apple pieces. Let sit for 15 minutes to rehydrate.

Pour the rehydrated mixture into a blender and add all the remaining ingredients. Puree until smooth. Serve the drink over ice cubes in tall glasses.

Makes 2 drinks

Dried Fruit Punch

I'm going to serve this easy-to-make nonalcoholic punch at my next New Year's party. It's so good, and my friends who have made it say that the flavor compares to other healthful soft drinks.

If you're wondering why I use rhubarb powder here, it's because it grows profusely in the Midwest and is a plant that benefits from continual harvesting. Also, I really like it. To see its stalks poking through still frozen ground is one of the first sure signs that summer will come again after our notoriously long winters and late springs. If you don't have or don't care for rhubarb, you can substitute either dried cranberries or dried apricots.

2 quarts ginger ale, divided
⅓ cup dried rhubarb powder
One 12-ounce can frozen lemonade concentrate, thawed
¼ cup sugar
Ice cubes
Dried apple rings and/or dried strawberries to float on top

In a punch bowl, combine 1 cup of the ginger ale and the dried rhubarb powder, and stir to mix thoroughly. Add the lemonade concentrate, the sugar, and the remaining ginger ale, and stir until the sugar is dissolved and the punch is combined. Let sit for at least 15 minutes to rehydrate. Add ice cubes to chill. Float the dried apple rings or strawberries on the top.

Makes 10 cups

Dried Fruit Cordial

There are several advantages to flavoring cordials yourself. First, you can use your own fresh or dried fruit. Second, once a dried fruit has steeped—be aware that you will need 4 weeks for steeping—and the alcohol has been flavored, you can reserve the fruit and use it in cooking. (Fresh fruits generally do not lend themselves to this type of recycling because they do not hold together as well after being soaked.) Last, making your own cordials is fun and provides endless opportunities for inviting friends over for sipping.

2 cups dried fruit, such as blackberries, pears, cherries, straw-
    berries, raspberries, or plums
1½ cups sugar
1 cup dry white wine
1 cup brandy

Put the dried fruit of choice in a 1-quart canning jar. Add the remaining ingredients and stir to combine. Cover the canning jar securely with the lid and place it where you can see it. You will need to turn the jar over once a day for the next 4 weeks.

Strain the liqueur into a clean bottle, reserving the fruit. Serve the drink in cordial glasses over ice.

Makes 3 cups

~~~

Apricot Cordial

Here's a variation on the Dried Fruit Cordial (page 244) that you can enjoy after just 1 week. I like to have the wine-and-brandy–steeped apricots fried in batter for breakfast. First, pat the apricots gently to dry them, then dip them in a light pancake batter and fry them. You might want to just call it a day after that— and go back to bed. They are delicious.

8 large pitted dried apricots
2¼ cups dry white wine
1–1½ cups sugar
1 cup brandy
½ teaspoon ground cinnamon

In a saucepan, bring the apricots to a boil in the white wine. Add the sugar, the brandy, and the cinnamon. Stir to dissolve the sugar and remove the pan from the heat. Let cool. Pour the apricots and the liquid into a 1-quart canning jar and cover tightly.

Turn the jar over once a day for 1 week. Strain the liqueur into a clean bottle, reserving the fruit and using it as suggested above.

Makes 3 cups

~~~

Dried Fruit Smoothie

This popular drink has only three major ingredients, and all of them are good for you. On a hot day, a smoothie can be cooling and refreshing; on a cool day, nourishing and filling; and after a hard day, it's a high-energy pick-me-up. You can have a smoothie for breakfast along with a cup of Granola with Dried Fruit (page 239). If left to sit for a few minutes after blending, the smoothie thickens and turns almost maltlike.

1 cup milk
½ cup dried fruit pieces, such as peaches, pears, bananas, or
    pineapple (½-inch size)
1 cup yogurt, such as vanilla or plain
Sweetener, sugar, or honey
Ground cinnamon to taste

In the container of a blender, combine the milk and the dried
fruit of choice. Let sit for 5 minutes to rehydrate.

Blend the combination to chop the fruit into small pieces. Add
the yogurt and blend thoroughly until smooth. Add the sweetener and cinnamon to taste.

Divide the mixture between glasses.

Makes 2 drinks

Strawberry Smoothie: Use dried strawberries, then add strawberry yogurt to the blender for a nutritional and very flavorful
variation.

~~~

Strawberry Shake

This recipe can be enjoyed both outdoors—note the use of dried
milk—or at home, and it is also very good made with apricot or
raspberry powder, or a combination of powders, like strawberry
and banana. The recipe can be easily multiplied.

1 cup cold water
5 tablespoons instant dried milk
1 tablespoon dried strawberry powder
1 tablespoon sugar, or to taste

In a 12-ounce covered container, combine all the ingredients
and shake well. Let sit for 10 minutes to allow the flavors
to blend. Shake again and serve as is or over ice cubes, if
desired.

Makes 1 drink

Orange-Carrot Juice

This simple and nutritious drink is great for breakfast, with Cakey Granola Bars (page 236) or Grandma's Coffee Cake (page 224), chilled or served over ice. Remember a basic tenet about food leather here: The smaller the pieces, the faster the leather rehydrates.

1½ cups warm water
¾ cup orange-carrot leather pieces (1-inch size)

In a bowl, combine the 1½ cups warm water and the leather pieces. Let sit for 30 minutes, stirring with a fork. Or after 15 minutes of rehydration, transfer the mixture to a blender and blend until smooth, adding more water if necessary.

Makes 2 drinks

Orange-Carrot-Yogurt Drink: For a creamy variation, add dried yogurt when you rehydrate the leather. Use an equal amount of dried yogurt to water: For example, ¼ cup dried yogurt to ¼ cup water.

Strawberry Syrup

This basic syrup recipe lends itself to almost any dried fruit. Use the syrup on pancakes. At home, use it to candy fruits and vegetables (for procedures, see pages 40–41). Or add sliced fresh strawberries for a dried- and fresh-fruit combination. A pinch of ground nutmeg or cinnamon is nice, too.

½ cup water
½ cup dried strawberries
1 cup brown sugar

In a saucepan, combine the ½ cup water and the dried strawberries. Let sit for 10 minutes to rehydrate.
Place the pan over high heat and bring the mixture to a boil. Add the brown sugar, reduce the heat to low, and simmer the

mixture for 10 minutes. Let cool, during which time the syrup will thicken. Store in an airtight container in the refrigerator.

Makes 1 cup

〜〜

Apricot Leather Syrup

In the recipe for Strawberry Syrup (page 247), dried fruit is used to make syrup. Here, I use leather. When you're ready to use the leather, all you have to do is add water in varying amounts, depending on the fruit. To hasten rehydration, tear the leather into 1-inch pieces and use hot or warm water. By returning a specific amount of water to the dried food, you not only reduce cooking time but you alter or control the finished product. Add chopped nuts, if you want syrup with crunch.

1 cup water
1 cup apricot leather pieces (cut or torn into pieces)

In a saucepan, combine the water and the apricot leather pieces. Let sit for at least 10 minutes to rehydrate.

Place the pan over high heat and bring the mixture to a boil, stirring to break up the leather. Remove the pan from the heat, cover, and let sit for at least 10 minutes.

Adjust consistency by adding more water, a little at a time. By adding just a little water, you do not have to cook foods down to achieve the desired consistency—unless you added too much at the start!

Stir to combine. Use the syrup while still warm on pancakes, as a fruit topping, or as a simple dessert. Let cool. Store in a covered airtight container in the refrigerator.

Makes 1 cup

〜〜

Dried Cherry Syrup

This syrup is delicious on flapjacks. If there's some syrup left over, simply add more dried cherries to it and serve that as a fruit pudding. It's good over pound cake or simple yellow cake.

1 cup water, plus 2 tablespoons cold water
½ cup dried cherries
½ cup sugar
⅛ teaspoon dried lemon peel
1 tablespoon cornstarch
½ teaspoon vanilla

In a saucepan, combine the 1 cup water and the dried cherries. Let sit for 10 minutes to rehydrate.

Place the pan over high heat and bring the mixture to a boil. Reduce the heat to low, add the sugar and the lemon peel, and stir to dissolve the sugar. Simmer the cherries for 15 minutes until they are soft and tender, adding more liquid if necessary.

In a small dish, stir together the remaining 2 tablespoons cold water and the cornstarch until blended. Add the cornstarch mixture and the vanilla to the pan and simmer, stirring constantly, until the syrup is thickened. Serve while still warm over pancakes or camp breads.

Makes 1 cup

Mint Tea

I'm a tea drinker, and here's one of my all-time favorite teas. As herb growers know, the combinations you can create with herbs to make teas are virtually limitless. Once perennial herbs, such as mint, thyme, and sage, are firmly established where they grow, they produce large harvests. Consider making these blends: mint and thyme; raspberry leaf and mint; clover blossoms and raspberry. Figure on 1 tablespoon dried product per 1 cup boiling water. Lastly, don't let the tea boil; it becomes bitter or too strong. Only the water should boil.

2 cups water
1 teaspoon dried spearmint leaves
1 teaspoon dried peppermint leaves
¼ teaspoon dried orange peel
⅛ teaspoon ground cinnamon
Sugar, honey, or fruit powder as a sweetener

In a kettle, bring the water to a boil. Place the dried herbs, the peel, and the cinnamon in a tea ball and put it in a teapot. Pour the boiling water over the tea ball, cover the pot, and let steep for 5 to 10 minutes, depending upon how strong you like your tea. Remove the tea ball from the pot and serve the tea with the sweetener of choice.

Makes 2 cups

A Flower Petal Variation: In Seattle I once enjoyed a marvelous Earl Grey tea made with lavender petals. The tea was perfectly beautiful and its flavor was out of this world. You can add flower petals—like lavender or rose—to your own homemade herbal blends, or to store-bought teas. Either way, I think you'll agree the petals make for a very special cup of tea.

Chapter 17

Beauty and the Beast

O ver the course of the past twenty years I've become much more familiar with the ins and outs of my food dehydrator than my own car and certainly my computer! As alluded to in Chapter 7, one of the greatest pleasures of using a food dehydrator is the opportunity it provides to preserve not only my vegetable and herb gardens but my flower gardens as well. The snow may be falling and the ground may be completely snow-covered, but the flowers that I have dried will last far beyond even the start of my new garden. The enjoyment of dried flowers is personal, but I know of no one who does not welcome a dried flower wreath or arrangement. And who does not appreciate a gift of hand-made potpourri? Dried flowers bring back all the wonder of spring, the joy of summer, the melancholy of fall. They are about time and beauty and aroma. And they can be prepared remark-ably easily in many food dehydrators.

Among the flowers I particularly like to dry are rose petals, lavender blossoms, lilacs, clover, mums, dandelions, and nastur-tiums. In the early morning, I take walks through fields or along country roads in search of wildflowers. Sometimes I pick flowers for their color, at other times for their shape, and at still other times for how they would look with other blossoms. Let your own creativity be your guide.

HOW TO PICK FLOWERS FOR DRYING

It is important always to pick flowers for drying when they are at their peak, which is usually the first day they have opened completely. Like herbs, pick them early in the day, after the morning dew has evaporated.

Flower heads can be dried whole or the petals can be removed from the heads and dried separately. If you are thinking about drying roses, select ones with a strong aroma and good color. Avoid watering flowers before picking, and do not pick them after there has been a rain shower: Dirt may have splashed onto them. Finally, I do not advise drying any flowers that have been sprayed with insecticides.

When you have cut the flowers you want to dry, check each one over carefully for insects and remove unwanted leaves and stems. You may have to rinse the fresh flowers.

HOW TO DRY FLOWERS IN A FOOD DEHYDRATOR

As with drying herbs, there are two factors that contribute to optimizing the conditions for the successful drying of flowers: low temperature and very good air circulation. Ideally, your dehydrator should have a temperature control and a fan speed. With these controls, you are able to retain both color and fragrance at their peak.

Begin by trimming the flowers. Then scatter buds, whole flowers, or petals in a single layer on the drying tray. Take care not to overlap any petals, as the overlapped ones will discolor when dried. Place the tray in the dehydrator and dry at 100°–110°F for 2 to 4 hours, depending on the make of dehydrator, until the petals are corn-flake dry. Know that flowers when dried shrink to about half their original size. Be sure the flowers are completely dry before removing them from the drying tray, as they can become moldy if moisture remains.

Store dried flowers you intend to eat in airtight containers; and it goes without saying that you have done all the research necessary to know which ones are edible and which are not. Among the edible flowers, my favorites include nasturtiums, lilacs, roses, violets, and apple and plum blossoms.

What follows is a method for not only preserving flowers but also rendering them extraordinarily beautiful by frosting or candying them. I am sure you have seen candied flowers in gourmet food stores in tiny boxes for large sums of money. Now these fanciful treasures, so lovely as decorations on special cakes or desserts, are a step away with a food dehydrator.

Key Technique 13: To Frost Fresh Flowers for Drying
This basic technique can also be used to frost fresh herbs, such as mint leaves or borage flowers, for decoration on baked goods or use in arts-and-crafts projects. Among the flowers I like to frost are rose petals, nasturtium flowers, lilac blossoms, scented geraniums, violas, violets, pansy petals, and apple or plum blossoms.

1. Dip the flower (or herb) of choice in a bowl of water to rinse, then shake off excess water gently.
2. In a small bowl, beat the white of 1 egg.
3. Dip the flower into the egg white, covering it completely but not drenching it.
4. Sprinkle the dipped flower with superfine or confectioners' sugar.
5. Arrange the flower on a mesh sheet on a drying tray. Keep dipping and sugaring flowers, arranging them in a single layer on the drying tray. Place the drying tray in the dehydrator. Dry at 140°F for 2 to 6 hours, depending on the make of dehydrator, until the flowers are brittle and completely dried.
6. Store frosted flowers in airtight containers.

POTPOURRI

A potpourri is a mixture of dried flowers, the petals, heads, or leaves, that is blended and used as a scent or perfume. A classic combination is composed primarily of dried rose petals, but herbs, fruits, vegetables, seed pods, and wood chips can also be included. There are no absolute rules to making a potpourri. The experience should be fun, fragrant, and fanciful.

There are two types of potpourri: a dry combination, wherein all the ingredients are dried until brittle; and a moist one, whose ingredients are only partially dried and then treated with salt and a liquid fixative, such as brandy or vodka. A moist potpourri must be aged for at least a month before being displayed, whereas dry potpourri can be enjoyed immediately.

Every potpourri has four separate major components, which when combined create the beauty of the whole. Potpourri is truly the sum of its parts—and then some.

Main Scent: Understandably, dried flowers with a strong fragrance are most commonly used to provide the main scent of a potpourri, and these include roses, honeysuckle, magnolia, jasmine, and violets.

Fillers: I like to choose fillers by color, shape, and aroma, although in reality the possibilities are almost endless. Here are some suggestions:

- Dried flowers, such as mums, clover, asters, chamomile blossoms, baby's breath, lavender, lilacs, lily of the valley, and zinnias;
- Dried herbs, tree leaves, or rosebush leaves;
- Woodsy items, such as wood chips and bark, pine needles and cones, cedar chips (get these at the pet store and dye different colors), fir chips, sandalwood chips;
- Dried citrus rind;
- Spices, such as whole cloves, cinnamon sticks, whole nutmeg, coriander seeds, whole ginger, whole allspice. (Whole rather than ground spices are preferred because they can be mixed evenly into the potpourri blend, whereas ground spices will settle on the bottom.);
- Seeds, such as anise, fennel, caraway, and rose hips;
- Berries, such as dried blueberries and juniper berries;
- Grains, such as wheat berries;
- Canning salt to absorb moisture.

Essential Oil: Essential oil, similar to perfume, adds the lasting aroma to potpourri. It is available in many scents, among the most popular being rose, lavender, and citrus. Others include musk, cinnamon, lemon, honeysuckle, jasmine, lilac, carnation, rosemary, clove, coconut, and vanilla. Essential oil can be bought at perfume shops, herb shops, and health-food stores.

In general, 6 to 20 drops of essential oil are used per quart of dried material. That range is, admittedly, a sizable one; no definitive amount of oil can be suggested, however, because the measurement depends upon the ingredients you have selected for your potpourri.

Fixatives: The fixative is extremely important to the composition of a potpourri and should never be omitted. It contains substances that combine with the volatile essential oils in other botanicals in the potpourri to release their oils gradually. The most effective and popular fixative is orrisroot, the root of *Iris germanicus* (Florentine iris), which smells like violets. Powdered orrisroot is available in pharmacies and is never to be consumed. Gum arabic, another popular fixative, is often available in health-food stores. Other fixatives include ground coriander seeds, bay leaf, sweet woodruff, cloves, mint leaves, myrrh, musk, ambergris, frankincense, gum benzoin, oak moss, and cellulose (ground corn cobs).

Use 1 tablespoon fixative per 1 quart potpourri.

Key Technique 14: To Make Potpourri

Now that you know the main components of a potpourri you can plan ahead, which is basically what making a potpourri is about. You will need an assortment of dried flowers; choose your favorite essential oil, and settle on a fixative. Then amass a supply of fillers. With the components on hand, you are now ready to make your first potpourri.

Example: An Easy Potpourri

1. In a large airtight jar, combine dried lilacs, clover, mums, and roses. The amounts will vary depending upon your sense of color and the desired balance of the finished blend. In utilizing this technique, however, I suggest composing 1 quart of dried flowers.
2. In a small airtight jar, add 6 to 20 drops of essential oil to 1 tablespoon fixative. Cover and store for 24 to 36 hours. Never add the essential oil directly to the dried flower combination.
3. Add the oiled fixative to the dried flowers and toss.
4. Transfer the potpourri to a decorative jar, or simply tie a ribbon around the jar and give the potpourri to a good friend. It makes a special gift.

Note: Remember to keep potpourri away from children and pets. It is not to be consumed.

SOME FAVORITE DRIED FLOWER CREATIONS

~~~

Lavender Rose Petal Sachet

The Greeks made amulets by placing dried leaves, flowers, roots, and seeds in a linen bag tied with silk thread. These bags were worn under garments and were intended to make those who wore them agreeable and loved by all (or, at the very least, smell a little better!).

Along the same lines, sachets, small fabric pillows of different charming shapes, can be filled with two or three dried ingredients—mint, lavender, rosemary, rose petals, geranium, thyme, violets, and lilacs. The fabric used should be lightweight enough to let the fragrance emerge, but not so sheer that the contents fall through. Some people cut paper coffee filters into rectangular shapes, fill one half with potpourri, then sew the halves together at the top and tie with a ribbon.

When a sachet is made with southernwood, wormwood, and lavender, it not only perfumes woolens but keeps moths away.

1 cup dried lavender
1 cup dried rose petals
½ cup dried citrus peel

In a bowl, combine all the ingredients and fill small cloth pillows. Sew the ends of sachets closed. Use sachets to scent bureau drawers and linen or clothes closets.

~~~

Dried Flower and Herb Hair Rinse or Skin Freshener

Soak dried flowers, like lavender and rose petals, and dried herbs, such as sage, thyme, rosemary, sweet marjoram, or all varieties of mint, in water. Use as a hair rinse or as a skin freshener, or add to bath water. The flowers of the European linden tree are known to have soothing properties when added to bath water.

⌒⌒

Dried Flower and Herb Bath Bag

Place 1 tablespoon dried flowers or herbs, or a combination of both, in a small cotton or cheesecloth bag. Close the bag securely.

To use, draw a bath of hot water, add the bath bag, and let it steep for 5 to 10 minutes before you get into the bathtub.

Or place a bag of dried herbs in 1 quart of boiling water. Let steep, then add the herb infusion to the drawn bathful of water. Save the bath bag, empty it, dry it, and use it for filling with a new combination of dried flowers or herbs.

An Herbal Cosmetic

If herbs have been employed for centuries for medicinal purposes, they can also be turned into cosmetics aids. Here's how to make a simple scrub:

In a cloth bag, combine 1 tablespoon dried herbs with 2 tablespoons oatmeal. Close the bag and use it as a scrub cloth in the bath. Discard the contents when the whitish liquid from the oatmeal no longer appears in the water.

⌒⌒

Dried Flower and Herb Body Splash

In a saucepan, combine 1 cup dried flowers and herbs. Remove from the heat and add 1 cup 70% ethyl alcohol. The addition of alcohol enhances the scent. (You can also buy rose water at the pharmacy or drugstore and add herbs to scent it.) Let steep for 2 hours. Add 1 quart water, then bring to a boil. Cool and strain. Use as a body splash. Store in a covered container. *Do not drink!* (Ethyl alcohol is poisonous.)

Rose Hips

Rose hips are the seed pods of the rose; they are the natural fruit of the rosebush. The small berrylike pods form as the flower petals fall off; when they turn bright red, the pods are harvested. Remove the white heel/claw from each pod and cut the berry in half for drying. The seeds inside the pod can be removed and dried separately. Dried rose hips can be added to soups, gelatins, and sauces, and used in making teas.

OTHER WAYS TO ENJOY DRIED FLOWERS

- Use edible dried flowers, whole or only the petals, to decorate cookies, cakes, or muffins.
- Add edible dried flowers to fruit and vegetable salads as an intriguing garnish.
- Use dried nasturtium seeds in place of capers in your favorite recipes.
- Use as air fresheners: Place dried flowers and herbs in a wide, shallow bowl. Or toss dried herbs into a smoldering fire.

AN OLD-FASHIONED WAY OF DEHYDRATING

Burying objects in sand has to be one of the oldest techniques of dehydrating. Ancient as it is, it is very useful when it comes to drying flowers, as it lets you maintain a certain amount of control over the shape of the finished product. This is important if you are planning to use dried flowers in bouquets or arrangements or in framed art.

You will need very clean, very fine, and completely dry sand with no salt, debris, or dust in it.

Begin by placing a layer of sand in the bottom of a container, such as a shoe box. On the sand, place flower buds, seed pods, or petals arranged in the shape you ultimately desire. Do not overlap the flowers.

When the flowers are arranged the way you want them, very gradually allow sand to trickle through your fingers onto the items in the box. The trickle must be slow enough not to jostle the flowers, and all parts of the flower should be covered with sand. Let the container stand at room temperature, without being moved, for 3 to 5 weeks, at which time the flowers should be dry and brittle.

Carefully pour off the sand. Remove the dried flowers and, if desired, you can spray them with hair spray to make them stiffer and stronger.

A MORE MODERN VARIATION

Instead of using pure sand, combine 1 part Borax (available in the soap and detergent section of most supermarkets) with 3 parts cornmeal, breaking up any clumps with the back of a spoon. Use like sand, as directed above.

Another old-fashioned drying method is even simpler. Just put the flowers, leaves, or ferns that you want dried between layers of heavy newspaper or between the pages of several telephone books to press them dry. Every 3 or 4 days check to see how much drying is taking place.

THE "BEAST" EXPLAINED

What would you say if I were to tell you that there is yet another use for your food dehydrator—one, though, that has nothing to do with drying food, herbs, or flowers for human consumption? I am talking about making pet treats in your machine! Yes, pet treats. Given the importance of many a pet in the American home (my own included), this is yet another aspect of a food dehydrator that may come in very handy. Just ask your pets!

Friends of mine, Colleen and Dale Westerberg, own a kennel and pet training center in the Twin Cities. The pet-treat recipes that follow were actually tested out on their food-sensitive, quite "particular" dogs and cats. In addition, my daughter Sally gave the liver treats here to her standard poodle, Baby, and Baby loved them.

Making 100 percent natural treats for your pet is one way to eliminate preservatives, salt, and artificial colors from your pet's diet while at the same time providing an opportunity to add medicine or vitamin C, brewer's yeast, rice flour, whole grains, and proteins to the food. As for aesthetic considerations, if you add a little dried beet powder to the treats, they will be redder in color. And if you want to go the whole nine yards for Fido or Kitty, add some dried tofu powder for additional protein. Your pets will love it!

Denali Liver Treats

1 pound raw beef liver, cut into 1- to 2-inch cubes, or strips 3–4
  inches long by 1 inch wide
Garlic powder, if desired

Arrange the liver cubes or strips on mesh sheets or on mesh sheets placed on top of solid leather sheets in the drying trays. If desired, sprinkle with garlic powder. (Or marinate the liver for additional flavor.) Place the drying trays in the dehydrator and dry at 145°F or above for 6 to 8 hours.

Once dried, the liver can be pulverized and added to other foods, including Mo's K-9 cookies (below).

One pound liver dries to 3 ounces and makes ¾ cup dried liver powder. To make the powder, cut the dried liver into 1-inch pieces and pulverize it in the blender.

Mo's K-9 Cookies

¼ cup rye kernels
¼ cup plus 1 cup chicken broth
1¾ cups whole wheat flour
¾ cup dried liver powder
½ cup cornmeal (page 233)
½ cup rolled oats
2 tablespoons oil
1 teaspoon garlic salt

In a small bowl, combine the rye kernels and the ¼ cup chicken broth. Let sit for 15 minutes.

In a bowl, combine all the ingredients, including the soaked rye kernels. The mixture will look and feel like uncooked meat loaf.

Form the mixture into 1-inch balls, flatten them between your hands to ¼ inch thick, and place them on a mesh sheet on a drying tray. Place the drying tray in the dehydrator and dry at 150°F, for about 6 hours, or until hard like a biscuit. Halfway through the drying time, turn the biscuits over.

Store in an airtight container.

Makes about 2 dozen biscuits

～

Colleen's Dried Salmon Burgers

I drain the canned salmon over my dog's food bowl. It goes without saying that cats would appreciate the juice, too!

One 14¾-ounce can pink salmon, drained and picked over, with all bones and hard bits removed
1 teaspoon minced garlic
2 egg yolks
1 tablespoon whole wheat flour
1 tablespoon bran

In a bowl, stir all the ingredients together with a fork.

Form tablespoons of the mixture into burgers about ¼ inch thick. Place the burgers in a single layer on a mesh sheet on a drying tray. Place the drying tray in the dehydrator and dry at 150°F for about 6 to 8 hours, or until dried as firm as crackers.

Makes 2 dozen treats

~~

Shaker's Turkey Dollops

One 5-ounce can chunk turkey, drained over your pet's food
   bowl
2 tablespoons whole wheat flour
2 tablespoons bran
1 egg yolk
¼ teaspoon minced garlic

In a bowl, combine all the ingredients well with a fork.
Form tablespoons of the mixture into balls, then flatten each
to about ¼ inch thick. Place in a single layer on a mesh sheet on
a drying tray. Place the drying tray in the dehydrator and dry
for about 6 to 8 hours, or until hard.

Makes 2 dozen treats

~~

Shep's Cat Treats

Even barnyard cats, those raised on mice, will eat these treats!
Be sure to break these into pieces—that is how cats like them
best.

One 6⅛-ounce can tuna packed in water, drained over your cat's
   food bowl
1 tablespoon cornmeal (page 233)
½ teaspoon minced garlic
1 egg white
1 tablespoon grated Parmesan cheese, plus ¼ cup for dusting on
   top of biscuits

In a bowl, combine all the ingredients and mash together with
a fork.
By the tablespoon, form the mixture into balls. Using the bottom of a glass, press the balls to ¼ inch thick, dust the top of
each treat with some of the remaining Parmesan, and gently

press into the "dough" with the glass bottom. Place the flattened rounds in a single layer on a mesh sheet on a drying tray. Place the drying tray in the dehydrator and dry at 150°F for about 6 to 8 hours, or until the treats are hard.

Makes 2 dozen treats

Index

NOTE: Page numbers in **boldface** refer to recipes.

Accessory sheets, 14–15
Air-drying herbs and flowers, 106
Air flow, source of, 12–13
Air fresheners, 258
Air temperature, inside dehydrator, 25
All-American marinated beef jerky, **91–92**
Amaretto pear cheesecake, **223–224**
Angel food cake:
  shiitake, **226**
  strawberry, **225–226**
Antioxidant solutions, 33–34
Apple(s), 52
  cranberry drink, **243**
  dried, pie, **226–227**
  drying peeled dipped slices of, 47
  raisin cookies, Aunt Grace's, **238–239**
  uncooked, apple leather from, **125–126**
Apple leather:
  cherry, **123**
  easiest-of-all, **122**

from homemade applesauce, **125**
  minted, **125**
  raspberry, **123**
  from uncooked apples, **125–126**
Applesauce:
  homemade, apple leather from, **125**
  tomato leather made with, **132**
Appliances, for drying foods, 6–7, 9–17
Apricot(s), 52–53
  cordial, **245**
  leather, syrup, **248**
Artichokes, Jerusalem, 71–72
Asparagus, 63–64
  eggs with tofu and, **207**
  soufflé, **201–202**
Aunt Grace's apple raisin cookies, **238–239**

Baba ghanouj, **193**
Baby food, 177
Backpacker:
  fancy macaroni and cheese, **160–161**
  jerkied tomato rice, **159–160**
  jerky stew, **157–158**

Backpacker: (*continued*)
meatless spaghetti sauce,
162–163
rice balls wrapped in nori,
156–157
simple dried veggies and
brown rice, 206
spaghetti sauce, 161–162
trail pudding, 164
tuna à la king, 158–159
vegetarian tomato soup, 155–
156
yogurt rice pudding, 165–
166
see also Trail food
Bacon, drying, 91
Baking:
as key technique, 37
stick, 149–150
trail food, 148–150
Banana(s), 53
bread, 231–232
commercially dried, 33
peeling, slicing, and drying,
32
rainbow, 35
Barbecue-soy sauce dip, 48
Bars:
cakey granola, 236–237
date nut, 237
Bath bag, dried flower and
herb, 257
Beans, 64
dried, soup, 181–182
sloppy Joe chili, 204–205
Beef:
for jerky, 83
marinating, 86
Beef, ground:
backpacker spaghetti sauce,
161–163
drying, 95
meat loaf, 197–198
onion jerky, 94–96
sloppy Joe chili, 204–205
sloppy Joes, 203–204
spicy jerky, 96
taco jerky, 97
tomato meat sauce, 219–220

Beef jerky:
all-American marinated, 91–
92
basic, 87–88
beer-marinated, 92–93
Betsy and Jim Oman's
favorite, 93
elegantly marinated, 92
oven-dried, 88
Beer-marinated beef jerky, 92–
93
Beet(s), 64–65
borscht, 184–185
drying cooked sliced, 37
leather, 135
Beet greens, 71
Berries, 54
cold soup, 190–191
of herbs, 104
raspberry apple leather, 123
strawberry angel food cake,
225–226
strawberry shake, 246
strawberry smoothie, 246
strawberry syrup, 247–248
Betsy and Jim Oman's favorite
beef jerky, 93
Beverages, 242–247
apricot cordial, 245
cranberry apple drink, 243
dried fruit cordial, 244–245
dried fruit punch, 243–244
dried fruit smoothie, 245–
246
flower petal tea, 250
mint tea, 249–250
orange-carrot juice, 247
orange-carrot-yogurt drink,
247
strawberry shake, 246
strawberry smoothie, 246
tea from roots, 105
Blanching:
checking, 36–37
and drying cranberries, 36–37
as key technique, 35–36
microwave-, 36
steam-, 36
water-boil, 36

Blueberries, 54
Body splash, dried flower and
herb, 257
Borscht, **184–185**
Botulism, 20
Bouquet garni, **112–113**
Breads:
banana, **231–232**
corn, **233**
fruit muffins, **235–236**
quick, 231–236
stick, **149–150**
vegetable loaf, **194**
zucchini, **234–235**
Breakfast:
eggs with tofu and fresh
asparagus, **207**
fruit leather cookies, **131**
Brie, party, **192–193**
Broccoli, 65
and pineapple salad, **213–214**
soup, cream of, **187–188**
Broth, vegetable powder, **80–81**
Brown rice:
and dried veggies, simple,
206
and vegetable stir-fry, **205–
206**
Brussels sprouts, 65–66
Burgers, Colleen's dried
salmon, **261**
Butter, for trail food, 144
Butters, herb, **113**
Butterscotch pudding leather
cookies, **130–131**

Cabbage(s), 66
dried toasted, **50**
Cakes, 221–225
carrot, with cream cheese
frosting, **222–223**
coffee, Grandma's, **224–225**
pear Amaretto cheesecake,
223–224
shiitake angel food, **226**
strawberry angel food, **225–
226**
Cakey granola bars, **236–237**
Calories, in dried food, 20

Candied treats, 42–46
ginger, **44–45**
honeyed orange peel, **43**
lemon or orange peel, **42–43**
mock figs, **45–46**
watermelon rind, **43–44**
Candying:
in combined techniques, 47
cut-up fruits and vegetables,
40–41
as key technique, 38–40
Canned foods, 140–141
Carrot(s), 66–67
cake with cream cheese
frosting, **222–223**
corn chips, **138**
crisp chips, **48–49**
-orange juice, **247**
-orange juice to leather and
back, **123–124**
-orange-yogurt drink, **247**
Cat treats, Shep's, **262–263**
Cauliflower, 67
soup, cream of, **187–188**
Celery, 67–68
powder, **80**
Checking (blanching), 36–37
Cheese, 144
backpacker fancy macaroni
and, **160–161**
cottage, and fruit leather, **129**
cream, frosting, **222–223**
Cheesecake, pear Amaretto,
223–224
Cherry(-ies), 54–55
apple leather, **123**
dried, syrup, **248–249**
rhubarb leather, **127**
Chicken:
basic jerky, **89–90**
creamed smoked, fettuccine
with, **196–197**
for jerky, 83, 84–85
marinating, 86
vegetable soup, basic, **180–
181**
Chili, sloppy Joe, **204–205**
Chips:
corn, real, **137–138**

Chips: (*continued*)
  corn carrot, **138**
  crisp carrot, **48–49**
  dried pickled mushroom, **49–50**
  easy, 48–50
  mushroom leather, **135–137**
  rehydration of, **136–137**
  soy-dipped zucchini, **48**
  tomato, **49**
  tomato leather, 124, **134–135**
  vegetable, 48–50, 134–138
Chocolate pudding leather
  cookies, **129–130**
Chowder, fish, **182–183**
Citrus fruits, 55–56
Citrus peel, 55–56
Clear tomato leather, **133**
Coconut, 56
Coffee cake, Grandma's, **224–225**
Cold berry soup, **190–191**
Collard greens, 71
Colleen's dried salmon burgers, **261**
Combining techniques:
  slicing, cooking, and dipping, 46
  slicing, dipping, and drying, 48
  slicing, peeling, and candying, 47
  slicing, peeling, and dipping, 46–47
Contamination, 27
Convection ovens, 6–7
Cookies, 231, 236–239
  Aunt Grace's apple raisin, **238–239**
  butterscotch pudding leather, **130–131**
  cakey granola bars, **236–237**
  chocolate pudding leather, **129–130**
  date nut bars, **237**
  fruit leather breakfast, 131
  Mo's K-9, **260–261**
Cooking:
  in combined techniques, 46

dried corn, rehydrating and, **173–174**
  and drying sliced beets, **37**
  for jerky, 85
  as key technique, 37
  microwave-cooking dried foods, 178
  with rehydrated foods, 174–176
  for rehydration, 171
  trail food, 154–155
Cordials:
  apricot, **245**
  dried fruit, **244–245**
Corn, 68–69
  bread, **233**
  carrot chips, **138**
  chips, real, **137–138**
  creamed, **173–174**
  dried, rehydrating and cooking, **173–174**
Cornstarch, tomato leather made with, **132–133**
Cosmetic, herbal, 257
Cottage cheese and fruit leather, **129**
Cranberry(-ies), 56
  apple drink, **243**
  blanched (checked), drying, **36–37**
Cream cheese frosting, carrot cake with, **222–223**
Creamed corn, **173–174**
Creamed smoked chicken, fettuccine with, **196–197**
Cream of broccoli soup, **187–188**
Cream of cauliflower soup, **187–188**
Cream of tomato soup, **185–186**
Cream sauce:
  easy, **219**
  rich, **218–219**
Creamy mushroom soup, **186–187**
Crisping dried food, 26
Cucumbers, 70
Cutouts, fruit leather, 124

Date(s), 56–57
  nut bars, **237**
Dehydrators, *see* Food
  dehydrators
Denali liver treats, **260**
Dipping:
  in combined techniques, 46–
    48
  and drying cooked potato
    slices, **46**
  and drying peeled apple
    slices, **47**
  and drying sliced pear, **35**
  and drying zucchini chips,
    48
  and flavor, 34
  as key technique, 33–34
Dips:
  baba ghanouj, **193**
  barbecue-soy sauce, **48**
  French dressing, **48**
Dressings:
  dried tomato vinaigrette, **211**
  French, dip, **48**
  my favorite vinaigrette, **212**
Dried food:
  appearance of, 19
  crisping, 26
  safety of, 20–21, 25, 26, 27
  storage of, 27–29
  tests of, 25, 26
  weight of, 21
Drinks, 242–247
  apricot cordial, **245**
  cranberry apple, **243**
  dried fruit cordial, **244–245**
  dried fruit punch, **243–244**
  dried fruit smoothie, **245–246**
  flower petal tea, **250**
  mint tea, **249–250**
  orange-carrot juice, **247**
  orange-carrot-yogurt, **247**
  strawberry shake, **246**
  strawberry smoothie, **246**
  tea from roots, **105**
Drying trays, 13–14

Eggplant, 70
  baba ghanouj, **193**

Eggs, 143
  asparagus soufflé, **201–202**
  with tofu and fresh
    asparagus, **207**
Electric food dehydrators, 10–
  17
  accessory sheets for, 14–15
  air flow in, 12–13
  components of, 11
  drying trays for, 13–14
  and heat source, 11–12
  questions about, 15–16
  repairs to, 17
Elegantly marinated beef jerky,
  92
Endive, 71
Equipment:
  for drying food, 22
  for leathers, 118–119
Essential oil, 254–255

Fats, in trail food, 143–144
Fettuccine with creamed
    smoked chicken, **196–197**
Figs, 57
  mock, **45–46**
Fillers, for potpourri, 254
Fines herbes, **112**
Fish:
  backpacker tuna à la king,
    158–159
  chowder, **182–183**
  Colleen's dried salmon
    burgers, **261–262**
  drying, 82–85, 98
  for jerky, 84, 85
  jerky, snacks, **90**
  marinating, 86
  old-fashioned salt-marinated
    dried, **98–99**
  rehydration of, 173
  temperature for, 51, 85
  Tom's red wine–marinated
    dried, **101**
  Tom's spice-marinated dried,
    99–101
Fixatives, for potpourri, 255
Flavor, and dipping, 34
Flavors, mingling of, 25

Flower petal tea, **250**
Flowers:
  for drying, 107–108
  in food dehydrator, 252–253
  frosting for drying, 253
  picking for drying, 252
  temperature for, 51, 85
Flowers, air-drying, 106
Flowers, dried, 251–263
  and herb bath bag, 257
  and herb body splash, 257
  and herb hair rinse or skin freshener, 256–257
  lavender rose petal sachet, 256
  in potpourri, 253–255
  rehydration of, 173
  rose hips, 258
  scrub, 257
  storage of, 108
  ways to enjoy, 258
Flower vinegar, **114**
Food dehydration, see Food drying
Food dehydrators, 9–17
  accessory sheets for, 14–15
  air flow in, 12–13
  air temperature inside, 25
  components of, 11
  drying flowers in, 252–253
  drying herbs in, 102–103
  drying trays for, 13–14
  electric, 10–17
  as heat source, 11–12
  location of, 16
  nonpassive units, 13
  passive units, 12
  questions about, 15–16
  repairs to, 17
Food drying:
  appliances for, 6–7, 9–17
  basic facts about, 18–29
  benefits of, 19
  equipment for, 22
  history of, 3–8
  modern method of, 259
  in modern times, 5–6
  and nutrition, 20

  old-fashioned method of, 258–259
  preparation for, 30–51
  time needed for, 23–25
Foods:
  for drying, 22
  for jerky, 83–84
  for leathers, 118
Forest Resource Center (FRC), 73
Freeze driers, 7
Freezer:
  and contamination, 27
  and crisping, 26
  and spoilage, 25–26
  for storage, 28
French dressing dip, **48**
Frosting, cream cheese, carrot cake with, **222–223**
Frosting fresh flowers for drying, 253
Frozen food, 141–142
Fruit, dried:
  cordial, **244–245**
  and fresh fruit salad, **209–210**
  gorp, **240**
  granola with, **239–240**
  Jell-O mold, **210**
  muffins, **235–236**
  powders and sugars, 59, 176
  punch, **243–244**
  rehydration of, 172
  relish, **217**
  smoothie, **245–246**
  soup, **189–190**
  stick bread, **149**
  tapioca pudding with, **230**
Fruited hominy grits, **216–217**
Fruit leather(s), 120–127
  apple, easiest-of-all, **122**
  apple, from homemade applesauce, **125**
  apple, from uncooked apples, **125–126**
  apricot, syrup, **248**
  basic, **126**
  breakfast cookies, **131**
  cherry apple, **123**
  cherry rhubarb, **127**

cottage cheese and, **129**
cutouts, 124
to juice and back, **123–124**
key technique, 120–121
minted apple, **125**
orange-carrot, **123–124**
pectin content of, 119, 120
raspberry apple, **123**
rhubarb, **126–127**
sugar content of, 119–120
yogurt, **123**
Fruits, 52–63
citrus, 55–56
rehydration of, 172
temperature for, 51, 85
see also specific fruits

Game, for jerky, 84
Garbanzo mushroom salad,
212–213
Gelatin, unflavored, tomato
leather chips made with,
134–135
Ginger, candied, **44–45**
Glacéing (candying), 38–40
Gluten, wheat, 145–146
Gorp:
fruit, **240**
vegetable, **241**
Grains, 147–148
Grandma's coffee cake, **224–225**
Granola bars, cakey, **236–237**
Granola with dried fruit, **239–
240**
Grapes, 57
Greens, 71
as trail food, 165
Grits, hominy, 69
fruited, **216–217**
vegetable, **217**
Ground beef:
backpacker spaghetti sauce,
161–163
drying, **95**
meat loaf, **197–198**
onion jerky, **94–96**
sloppy Joe chili, **204–205**
sloppy Joes, **203–204**
spicy jerky, **96**

taco jerky, **97**
tomato meat sauce, **219–220**

Hair rinse, dried flower and
herb, 256–257
Ham, root soup with, **183–184**
Heat, source of, 11–12
Herbal cosmetic, 257
Herbes, fines, 111
Herb-flavored oil, **113**
Herbs:
air-drying, 106
butters, **113**
cleaning, 105
drying, 102–116
for drying, 107–108
drying, as key technique, 106
drying fresh parsley sprigs,
105–106
drying in food dehydrator,
102–103
favorite blend of, 110
mustard, **116**
parts, 103–105
pleasure of, 110
recipes, **111–116**
rehydration of, 173
sugars, **115**
temperature for, 51, 85
vinegar, **114**
Herbs, dried:
bouquet garni, **112**
and flower bath bag, 257
and flower body splash, 257
and flower hair rinse or skin
freshener, 256–257
rehydration of, 174
scrub, 257
storage of, 108
uses of, 109
High-energy trail foods, 145–
147
High-fiber trail foods, 152
History of food drying, 3–8
Hominy, 69
Hominy grits:
fruited, **216–217**
vegetable, **217**
Honeyed orange peel, **43**

Horseradish, 105
Humidity, and drying time, 24

Indian meal moth, 27
Insects, contamination from, 27

Jars, for storage, 28
Jell-O mold, dried fruit, **210**
Jerkied stick bread, **150**
Jerkied tomato rice,
    backpacker, **159–160**
Jerky, 82–98
    all-American marinated beef,
      91–92
    basic beef, **87–88**
    basic chicken, **89–90**
    basic turkey, **88–89**
    beer-marinated beef, **92–93**
    Betsy and Jim Oman's
      favorite beef, **93**
    defined, 82
    elegantly marinated beef, **92**
    fish snacks, **90**
    foods for, 83–84
    key technique, 85, 87
    marination for, 84, 85, 86
    onion ground beef, **94–96**
    oven-dried beef, **88**
    pemmican, **97–98**
    preparation and
      pretreatments, 84–87
    soy-marinated turkey, **93–94**
    spicy ground beef, **96**
    stew, backpacker, **157–158**
    taco ground beef, **97**
    teriyaki-marinated turkey, **94**
    as trail food, 152
Jerusalem artichokes, 71–72
Juice:
    to leather and back, **123–124**
    orange-carrot, **247**

K-9 cookies, Mo's, **260–261**
Kale, 71
Key techniques, 30
    1, slicing, 30–31
    2, peeling, 32
    3, pretreatment by dipping,
      33–34

    4, pretreatment by blanching,
      35–36
    5, cooking or baking, 37
    6, seeding, 37
    7, candying, 38–40
    8, pulverizing dried
      vegetables, 80
    9, making jerky, 87
    10, drying herbs, 106
    11, making fruit or vegetable
      leather, 120–121
    12, rehydrating and cooking
      dried corn, 173–174
    13, frosting fresh flowers for
      drying, 253
    14, making potpourri, 255
Kiwifruit, 58
Kohlrabi, 72

Lavender rose petal sachet, 256
Leathers, 117–138
    apple, easiest-of-all, **122**
    apple, from homemade
      applesauce, **125**
    apple, from uncooked apples,
      125–126
    apricot, syrup, **248**
    basic fruit, **126**
    beet, **135**
    butterscotch pudding
      cookies, **130–131**
    cherry apple, **123**
    cherry rhubarb, **127**
    chips, rehydration of, **136–
      137**
    chocolate pudding cookies,
      129–130
    cottage cheese and fruit, **129**
    cutouts, 124
    equipment for, 118–119
    foods for, 118
    fruit, 120–127
    fruit, breakfast cookies, **131**
    to juice and back, **123–124**
    key technique, 120–121
    minted apple, **125**
    mushroom chips, **135–137**
    orange-carrot, **123–124**
    pectin content of, 119, 120

pumpkin, **128–129**
puree for, 119, 121
raspberry apple, **123**
rehydration of, 173
rhubarb, **126–127**
in sandwiches, 124
as snacks, 124
spaghetti sauce, **123**
stickiness of, 122
sugar content of, 119–120
tomato, **132–135**
tomato chips, 124
tomato sauce from, **163–164**
uses for, 124
yogurt, **123**
Leather sheets, solid, 14–15
Leaves, of herbs, 103–104, 107–108
Leftover food, 142
baby food, 177
Lemon peel, candied, **42–43**
Lemons, 55
Limes, 55
Liquid, for rehydration, 169–170, 171
Liver treats, Denali, **260**
Luncheon meats, for jerky, 84

Macaroni and cheese,
backpacker, **160–161**
Main courses, 195–207
asparagus soufflé, **201–202**
brown rice and vegetable
stir-fry, **205–206**
eggs with tofu and fresh
asparagus, **207**
fettuccine with creamed
smoked chicken, **196–197**
meat loaf, **197–198**
shiitake wild rice casserole,
200
simple dried veggies and
brown rice, **206**
sloppy Joe chili, **204–205**
sloppy Joes, **203–204**
tomato vegetable quiche,
202–203
turkey and vegetable pie,
198–199

Mangoes, 58, 60
Margarine, for trail food, 144
Marination, for jerky, 84, 85, 86
Meatless spaghetti sauce,
backpacker, **162–163**
Meat loaf, **197–198**
Meats:
drying, 82–85
for jerky, 83–84, 85
marinating, 86
rehydration of, 173
temperatures of, 21, 51, 85
see also specific meats
Melons, 60
Menus, trail, 150–152
Mesh sheets, 14, 15
Microwave-blanching, 36
Microwave ovens, 7, 29
cooking dried foods in, 178
for rehydration, 172
Milk, 143–144
Mincemeat pie, mock, **227–228**
Minted apple leather, **125**
Mint tea, **249–250**
Miso:
drying, 192
as trail food, 152
Mock figs, **45–46**
Mock mincemeat pie, **227–228**
Mold, 20
Mo's K-9 cookies, **260–261**
Muffins, fruit, **235–236**
Mushroom(s), 72
chips, dried pickled, **49–50**
creamy soup, **186–187**
garbanzo salad, **212–213**
leather chips, **135–137**
shiitake, 73
shiitake angel food cake, **226**
shiitake wild rice casserole,
200
Mustard, herb, **116**
My favorite vinaigrette, **212**

Nasturtium seeds, 258
Nectarines, 60
Nonpassive units, 13
Noodles, vegetable-flavored
homemade, **214–215**

Nori, backpacker rice balls
wrapped in, **156–157**
Nut(s):
date bars, **237**
as trail food, 152
Nutrition, dehydration and,
20

Oil:
essential, 254–255
herb-flavored, **113**
for trail food, 144
Okra, 74
Old-fashioned salt-marinated
dried fish, **98–99**
Onion(s), 74
dried toasted, **50**
ground beef jerky, **94–96**
Orange(s):
-carrot juice, **247**
-carrot juice to leather and
back, **123–124**
-carrot-yogurt drink, 247
Valencia, 55
Orange peel:
candied, **42–43**
honeyed, **43**
Oven-dried beef jerky, **88**
Ovens:
convection, 6–7
microwave, 7, 29
Oxidation, 33

Packaged foods, with trail
food, 152
Packing, for trail, 152–154
Papayas, 60–61
Parsley, drying, **106**
Parsnips, 74–75
root soup with ham, **183–
184**
Party Brie, **192–193**
Passive units, 12
Pasta:
fettuccine with creamed
smoked chicken, **196–197**
salad with dried tomatoes,
210–211
sloppy Joe chili, **204–205**

vegetable-flavored
homemade noodles, **214–
215**
Pasteurization, 27
Peaches, 61
Pear(s), 61
Amaretto cheesecake, **223–
224**
dipped sliced, drying, **35**
Peas, 75
Pectin:
increasing, 120
and leathers, 119, 120
tomato leather made with,
133
Peeling:
in combined techniques, 46–
47
dipping, and drying apple
slices, **47**
as key technique, 32
slicing, and coring
pineapples, **47**
slicing, and drying banana,
32
Pemmican, **97–98**
Peppers, 75–76
Pesto, spinach, **218**
Pet treats, 259–263
Colleen's dried salmon
burgers, **261**
Denali liver, **260**
Mo's K-9 cookies, **260–261**
Shaker's turkey dollops, **262**
Shep's cat treats, **262–263**
Picking flowers for drying, 252
Pickled mushroom chips, dried,
49–50
Pickles, dried, **50**
Pies, 221, 226–228
dried apple, **226–227**
mock mincemeat, **227–228**
turkey and vegetable, **198–
199**
Pineapple(s), 61–62
and broccoli salad, **213–214**
slicing, coring, and peeling,
47
Plastic bags, for storage, 28

Plum(s), 62
  pudding, **228–230**
Potassium, replacement of, 152
Potato(es), 76
  drying cooked dipped slices
    of, **46**
  homemade flakes, **189**
  root soup with ham, **183–184**
  scalloped, **215–216**
  soup, **188–189**
  sweet, 78
Potpourri, 253–255
  essential oil, 254–255
  fillers, 254
  fixatives, 255
  main scent, 254
Poultry:
  basic chicken jerky, **89–90**
  basic chicken vegetable soup,
    180–181
  basic turkey jerky, **88–89**
  fettuccine with creamed
    smoked chicken, **196–197**
  for jerky, 83, 84–85
  marinating, 86
  Shaker's turkey dollops, **262**
  soy-marinated turkey jerky,
    93–94
  teriyaki-marinated turkey
    jerky, **94**
  turkey and vegetable pie,
    198–199
Powders:
  dried celery, **80**
  fruit, 59
  tomato meat sauce from,
    219–220
  tomato sauce from, **163**
  vegetable, 80
  vegetable broth, **80–81**
  see also Pulverization
Preservation of food, 18, 98
Pretreatment, 23
  by blanching, 35–36
  by dipping, 33–34
  for jerky, 84–86
Protein, in trail food, 143–144
Puddings, 221, 228–230
  backpacker trail, **164**

backpacker yogurt rice, **165–
  166**
butterscotch, leather cookies,
  130–131
chocolate, leather cookies,
  129–130
plum, **228–230**
tapioca with dried fruit,
  230
Pulverization, 176
  for baby food, 177
  as key technique, 80
  see also Powders
Pumpkin(s), 76–77
  leather, **128–129**
Punch, dried fruit, **243–244**
Puree, for leathers, 119, 121

Quiche, tomato vegetable, **202–
  203**
Quick breads, 231–236

Radishes, 77
Rainbow bananas, **35**
Raisin apple cookies, Aunt
  Grace's, **238–239**
Raspberries, 54
Raspberry apple leather, **123**
Red wine–marinated dried fish,
  Tom's, **100**
Rehydration, 169–175
  and cooking, 171, 174–176
  of dried fruits, 172
  of dried herbs and flowers,
    173
  of dried meats and fish, 173
  of dried vegetables, 172–173
  of food leathers, 173
  as key technique, 173–174
  of leather chips, **136–137**
  liquid needed for, 169–170,
    171
  methods of, 171–172
  and salt, 173
  and storage, 177
  and sugar, 173
  time needed for, 170
  of trail food, 153–154
Relish, dried fruit, **217**

Rhubarb, 62–63
  cherry leather, 127
  leather, 126–127
Rice, 147–148
  backpacker jerkied tomato,
    159–160
  brown, and dried veggies,
    simple, 206
  brown, and vegetable stir-fry,
    205–206
  wild, shiitake casserole, 200
  yogurt pudding, backpacker,
    165–166
Rice balls wrapped in nori,
    backpacker, 156–157
Roma tomatoes, seeding, 37
Root(s):
  of herbs, 104–105, 107–108
  soup with ham, 183–184
  tea from, 105
Rose hips, 258
Rose petal lavender sachet, 256
Rutabagas, 77

Sachet, lavender rose petal, 256
Safety, of dried food, 20–21, 25,
    26, 27
Salads, 208–214
  broccoli and pineapple, 213–
    214
  dried fruit Jell-O mold, 210
  fresh and dried fruit, 209–
    210
  garnish for, 258
  mushroom garbanzo, 212–
    213
  pasta, with dried tomatoes,
    210–211
Salmon, dried, Colleen's
    burgers, 261
Salt:
  marinade, 86
  -marinated dried fish, old-
    fashioned, 98–99
  as preservative, 98
  and rehydration, 173
  replacement of, 152
Sandwiches, vegetable leathers
    in, 124

Sauces, 208, 218–220
  backpacker meatless
    spaghetti, 162–163
  backpacker spaghetti, 161–
    162
  backpacker tomato, 163–
    164
  cream, easy, 219
  cream, rich, 218–219
  spaghetti, leather, 123
  spinach pesto, 218
  tomato meat, 219–220
Scalloped potatoes, 215–216
Scent, potpourri, 254
Scrub, herbal, 257
Seeding:
  as key technique, 37
  Roma tomatoes, 37
Seeds:
  of herbs, 104, 107–108
  as trail food, 152
Sesame eggplant dip (baba
    ghanouj), 193
Shake, strawberry, 246
Shaker's turkey dollops, 262
Sheets:
  accessory, 14–15
  mesh, 14, 15
  solid leather, 14–15
Shellfish:
  dried, 100
  for jerky, 84, 85
Shep's cat treats, 262–263
Shiitake, 73
  angel food cake, 226
  wild rice casserole, 200
Side dishes, 208–209, 214–217
  dried fruit relish, 217
  fruited hominy grits, 216–
    217
  scalloped potatoes, 215–216
  vegetable-flavored
    homemade noodles, 214–
    215
  vegetable hominy grits, 217
Size and surface area, and
    drying time, 24
Skin freshener, dried flower
    and herb, 256–257

Slicing:
  in combined techniques, 46–48
  coring, and peeling pineapples, 47
  drying, and dipping pears, 35
  as key technique, 30–31
  peeling, and drying banana, 32
  tomato, 31–32
Sloppy Joe chili, 204–205
Sloppy Joes, 203–204
Smoothies:
  dried fruit, 245–246
  strawberry, 246
Snacks, 231, 239–241
  fish jerky, 90
  fruit gorp, 240
  granola with dried fruit, 239–240
  leathers as, 124
  for pets, see Pet treats
  vegetable gorp, 241
Sodium bisulfite, 34
Soufflé, asparagus, 201–202
Soups, 179–192
  backpacker jerky stew, 157–158
  backpacker vegetarian tomato, 155–156
  basic chicken vegetable, 180–181
  borscht, 184–185
  cold berry, 190–191
  cream of broccoli, 187–188
  cream of cauliflower, 187–188
  cream of tomato, 185–186
  creamy mushroom, 186–187
  dried bean, 181–182
  dried fruit, 189–190
  fish chowder, 182–183
  potato, 188–189
  root, with ham, 183–184
  tofu, 191–192
  vegetable powder broth, 80–81
Soy-dipped zucchini chips, 48

Soy-marinated turkey jerky, 93–94
Soy sauce barbecue dip, 48
Spaghetti sauce:
  backpacker, 161–162
  backpacker meatless, 162–163
  leather, 123
Spice-marinated dried fish, Tom's, 99–100
Spicy ground beef jerky, 96
Spinach, 71
  pesto, 218
Spoilage, 20–21
  and freezing, 25–26
  and storage, 27
  and temperature, 21
Sprouts, as trail food, 165
Squash, 78
Standing, for rehydration, 171–172
Starters, 179–180, 192–194
  baba ghanouj, 193
  party Brie, 192–193
  vegetable loaf, 194
Steam-blanching, 36
Steaming, for rehydration, 171
Stew, backpacker jerky, 157–158
Stick bread, 149–150
  fruit, 149
  jerkied, 150
  vegetable, 149
Stickiness, of leathers, 122
Stir-fry, brown rice and vegetable, 205–206
Storage:
  of dried foods, 26–29
  of dried herbs and flowers, 108
  in freezer, 28
  of rehydrated foods, 178
  time for, 27, 29
  and vitamin A, 27
Strawberry(-ies), 54
  angel food cake, 225–226
  shake, 246
  smoothie, 246
  syrup, 247–248

Sugar content, 24
and leathers, 119–120
Sugars:
fruit, 59
herb, **115**
and rehydration, 173
Sugar syrup, 39
Sulfuring, 23
Sun-dried tomatoes, **38**
Surface area, and drying time,
24
Sweet potatoes, 78
Swiss chard, 71
Syrups, 242, 247–250
apricot leather, **248**
dried cherry, **248–249**
strawberry, **247–248**
sugar, 39

Taco ground beef jerky, **97**
Tangerines, 55
Tapioca pudding with dried
fruit, **230**
Tea:
flower petal, **250**
mint, **249–250**
from roots, **105**
Temperature:
of air inside dehydrator, 25
and heat source, 11–12
reminders, 51, 85
and safety, 21
Teriyaki-marinated turkey
jerky, **94**
Tests, of dried food, 25, 26
Three-ingredient tomato leather
(made with pectin), **133**
Time:
for drying food, 23–25
for rehydration, 170
for storage, 29
Tofu, 146–147
eggs with fresh asparagus
and, **207**
soup, 191–192
Tomato(es), 79
backpacker jerkied rice, **159–
160**
chips, **49**

dried, pasta salad with, **210–
211**
dried, vinaigrette, **211**
drying without skins, 32
Roma, seeding, **37**
slicing and drying, **31–32**
soup, backpacker vegetarian,
155–156
soup, cream of, **185–186**
sun-dried, **38**
tomato meat sauce from,
219–220
tomato sauce from, **164**
vegetable quiche, **202–203**
Tomato leather(s), 132–135
chips, 124
chips, fancy (made with
unflavored gelatin), **134–
135**
clear, **133**
easy (made with applesauce),
132
(made with cornstarch), **132–
133**
three-ingredient (made with
pectin), **133**
tomato sauce from, **163–164**
Tomato paste, seasoning, **163–
164**
Tomato sauce:
backpacker options for, 163
from dried tomato leather,
163–164
from dried tomato pieces,
164
from dried tomato powder,
163, 219–220
meat, **219–220**
seasoning, **163**
Tom's red wine–marinated
dried fish, **101**
Tom's spice-marinated dried
fish, **99–101**
Touch test, 26
Trail food, 139–166
baking, 148–150
canned, 140–141
cooking, 154–155
fats in, 143–144

frozen, 141–142
grains, 147–148
greens, 165
high-energy, 145–147
high-fiber, 152
ideas, 152
jerky, 152
leftovers, 142
miso, 152
nuts, 152
packing, 152–154
planning meals of, 150–152
and potassium replacement,
    152
protein in, 143–144
recipes, **155–165**
rehydration of, 153–154
rice, 147–148
and salt replacement, 152
seeds, 152
sprouts, 165
supply of, 140
tomato sauce, 163–164
yogurt, dried, 152
see also Backpacker
Trail pudding, backpacker, **164**
Trays, drying, 13–14
Treats, for pets, *see* Pet treats
Tuna à la king, backpacker,
    158–159
Turkey:
    basic jerky, **88–89**
    for jerky, 83, 84–85
    marinating, 86
    Shaker's dollops, **262**
    soy-marinated jerky, **93–94**
    teriyaki-marinated jerky, **94**
    and vegetable pie, **198–199**
Turnips, 79
    root soup with ham, **183–184**

Unflavored gelatin, tomato
    leather chips made with,.
    134–135

Vacuum packing, 28
Valencia oranges, 55
Vegetable chips, **48–50**
    carrot, **48–49**

corn carrot, **138**
dried pickled mushroom, 49–
    50
fancy tomato leather, **134–135**
and leathers, **134–138**
mushroom leather, **135–137**
real corn, **137–138**
rehydration of, **136–137**
soy-dipped zucchini, **48**
tomato, **49**
Vegetable leather(s):
    beet, **135**
    and chips, **134–138**
    to juice and back, **123–124**
    key technique, 120–121
    mushroom chips, **135–137**
    orange-carrot, **123–124**
    pumpkin, **128–129**
    in sandwiches, 124
    tomato, **132–135**
    tomato chips, **124**
    tomato sauce from, **163–164**
Vegetable(s), 63–80
    backpacker vegetarian
        tomato soup, **155–156**
    basic chicken soup, **180–181**
    borscht, **184–185**
    and brown rice stir-fry, 205–
        206
    dried toasted snack, **50**
    drying cooked sliced beets,
        37
    -flavored homemade noodles,
        214–215
    gorp, **241**
    hominy grits, **217**
    loaf, **194**
    powder broth, **80–81**
    powders, 80, 176
    rehydration of, 172–173
    simple dried veggies and
        brown rice, **206**
    stick bread, **149**
    temperature for, 51, 85
    tomato quiche, **202–203**
    and turkey pie, **198–199**
    see also specific vegetables
Vegetarian tomato soup,
    backpacker, **155–156**

Vinaigrettes:
 dried tomato, **211**
 my favorite, **212**
Vinegar:
 flower, **114**
 herb, **114**
Vitamin A:
 in nutrition, 20
 and storage, 27
Vitamin C:
 in antioxidant solution, 34
 in nutrition, 20

Water, hot, for rehydration,
 171
Water-boil blanching, 35–36
Water content, dehydration
 and, 24

Watermelon, 63
 rind, candied, **43–44**
Weight, of dried food, 21
Wheat gluten, 145–146
Wild rice shiitake casserole, **200**
Wine-marinated dried fish,
 Tom's red, **101**

Yogurt:
 backpacker rice pudding,
 165–166
 dried, as trail food, 152
 leathers, **123**
 -orange-carrot drink, **247**

Zucchini, 79
 bread, **234–235**
 chips, soy-dipped, **48**